POLITICAL PRESSURE and the ARCHIVAL RECORD

EDITED BY *Margaret Procter, Michael Cook, Caroline Williams*

D1564259

Chicago

The Society of American Archivists
527 S. Wells Street, 5ᵗʰ Floor
Chicago, IL 60607 USA
312 / 922-0140   Fax 312 / 347-1452
www.archivists.org

©2005 by the Society of American Archivists.
All Rights Reserved.

Printed in the United States of America

Library of Congress Cataloging-in-Publication Data
Political pressure and the archival record / edited by Margaret Procter,
Michael Cook, Caroline Williams.
     p. cm.
 "This book contains a selection of papers presented at an international
conference, 'Political Pressure and the Archival Record,' held in Liverpool,
U.K., in July 2003"—Pref.
 Includes bibliographical references and index.
 ISBN 1-931666-15-6 (alk. paper)
 1. Archives—Political aspects—Congresses. I. Procter, Margaret, 1959–
II. Cook, Michael, 1931– III. Williams, Caroline (Caroline M.)

CD923.P65 2006
027—dc22

                                        2005036554

Graphic design by Matt Dufek, dufekdesign@yahoo.com.
Fonts: Adobe Caslon (text and footnotes); Clarendon (title pages and
A-heads); Bickham (authors' names); Linoletter (B-heads).

Table *of* Contents

ETHICAL DILEMMAS IN THE PUBLIC SERVICE

GOVERNMENTS UNDER PRESSURE?
THREATS AND RESPONSES

AT WAR: RECORDS AND
INTERNATIONAL CONFLICT

MODELLING THE FUTURE

PREFACE

This book contains a selection of papers presented at an international conference, "Political Pressure and the Archival Record," held in Liverpool, U.K., in July 2003. Although explicitly focused on the implications for records and recordkeepers, the real substance of the conference derived from the exploration of the effects of "political pressure" beyond any narrow subject boundaries.

Records and recordkeeping are features of practically all human activity, and no human activity operates outside the framework of a political system. Consequently no activity is "safe" from politics and hence, potentially, from perceptible political pressure. The papers here come from a breadth of disciplines (history, archives, the law, social and anthropological sciences) and from a wide-ranging geographical area (Australasia, Asia, Europe, Africa and North America). Their content spans some 200 years.

In common with all conference proceedings, there is some evidence here to support the assertion that "a week is a long time in politics." The reader will allow for the fact that circumstances and attitudes may have shifted in the two years between the origination of the papers and their publication. But the underlying issues remain constant, and the editors hope that the volume will encourage further studies that explore and develop understanding in this area of political and ethical activity.

MARGARET PROCTER
MICHAEL COOK
CAROLINE WILLIAMS

Liverpool, U.K., 2005

INTRODUCTION

Margaret Procter

What is "political pressure"? We would all claim to know it when we see it, but the force of any single definition will vary in relation to where we, politically aware individuals of varying degrees, are geographically located, and to the kinds of ideological baggage we may, (un)consciously, be carrying. Is it any easier to define the phrase "archival record"? Fortunately, while every archivist and recordkeeper has his or her own definition and own understanding, here, within the framework in which these papers were written and delivered, the similarities far outweigh any substantive differences.

This volume is made up of papers given at the conference, "Political Pressure and the Archival Record," organised by the Liverpool University Centre for Archive Studies held in Liverpool in July 2003. In the call for papers, there *was* an attempt to define political pressure:

> All governments keep records on their people. These records are essential to the quality of governance and are the long-term guarantee of the personal and property rights of the citizens. Eventually such documentary evidence becomes the raw material of research covering many fields: history, geography, politics, population studies, human rights, to name just a few.
> It is clear that the character of the regime that controls the recording function deeply affects the nature of the record, and its level of penetration into the lives of citizens. Inevitably political needs shape, directly or indirectly, the professional lives and practices of the archivists and record-keepers who work within the sphere of the political regime. We have noted that special conditions arise at different times and places. Some regimes appear to have a particular need for enhanced records management, and for the creation of records that penetrate strongly into the personal and business lives of their populations. There are also cases where records have been destroyed as a matter of policy.

This definition of political pressure concentrates on the effect on the citizen of all types of administration, benign democracy or repressive dictatorship, which have the power to affect individual lives. It also refers to the effect that any given administration has on the professional lives of archivists and recordkeepers. The extent to which it is possible to separate one's professional and personal lives is touched on in some of these papers and requires further examination in its own right. These effects are continuing, pervasive, and often routine; we may not consider them as pressure at all.[1] It is sudden, deliberate, and blatant pressure that focuses our attention: invasion, war, terrorist actions, single acts of destruction. Records provide evidence of political pressure, yet can also be used to exert it, one tool among many for political activity. Records and the political process are inextricably interwoven; this made it difficult to identify discrete topics that might be addressed by delegates, but as a start contributors were invited to consider

- the use of records as a tool of government
- the destruction of records as a political act
- the effects of corruption or ideology on the record
- secrecy and accountability
- the nature and use of records resulting from repressive policies.

In retrospect, these themes appear to belong primarily to the "sudden, deliberate, and blatant" school of political pressure. One notable outcome of the conference was the delegates' sensitisation to the less obvious, or unintentional ways, in which political pressure might be exerted both on the creation of the record, and on archivists' ability to manage and exploit it thereafter. The current situation in the United Kingdom epitomises this type of low-level pressure perfectly. The Labour administration's "Modernising Government" and "Modernising Public Services" initiatives have had a far-reaching impact on

---

1   It has been noted that the routines of recordkeeping can continue under the most extreme circumstances. The recordkeeping abilities of the Nazi regime are well documented; the efficiency of that recordkeeping has, ironically, subsequently helped to provide restitution for their victims. (See for example Edwin Black, *IBM and the Holocaust: The Strategic Alliance Between Nazi Germany and America's Most Powerful Corporation* (New York: Crown Publishers, 2001) for the use of technology in Nazi information management.) But the record may also be consistently falsified to meet the regime's expectations: See for example Boris V. Anan'ich, "The Historian and the Source: Problems of Reliability and Ethics," *Comma* 2002: 3-4, 61-68, within the context of Stalinist show trials, and the 1825 Decembrist uprising. Similarly James O'Toole describes how Spanish invaders legitimised their land seizures by ensuring that a notary was on hand to record the "transaction." See "Cortes's Notary: The Symbolic Power of Records," *Archival Science* 2002: 1-2, 45-61.

both records managers and archivists (not a factor, one imagines, which featured in any risk assessment exercise for those initiatives).

Electronic records management (specifically *not* document management) is a requirement from 2004 for all central government departments to facilitate the modernisation agenda; selection of archives from these ERM systems is a current requirement under the Public Records Act, thus archivists must learn the skills—and vocabulary—of digital preservation, and the systems must be resourced to meet legislative requirements. Thus it appears that changes to professional behaviour or professional attributes are being caused by an apparently external political programme. However, it must also be the case that the archivist routinely makes decisions of a political nature and with a long-term political impact. The process of selecting records, a keystone of professional activity, will shape the record as it appears to the future (the record of government in the case of the National Archives), and the insuperable dilemmas this presents have underpinned the appraisal policies of many national archives in recent years.[2]

We can continue this theme. A "modern" government is an "open" government, one which makes information available, which works actively to make information accessible. The United Kingdom's Freedom of Information Act 2000 explicitly provides for a code of practice on records management as the only way in which such access can be effective. The concept of "records management" has therefore been introduced for the first time to the majority of the many thousands of bodies which fall within the scope of the Act.[3] Access to archives (those records selected for permanent preservation) is, equally, part of the open government agenda, desirable not just from the evidential point of view but from a cultural one, as both a national and as an individual desideratum. The Council of Europe's Recommendation on Access to Archives—to be implemented within the national legislative environment—explicitly equates access to archives with democratic credentials:

---

2   Many of the issues raised in this paragraph are addressed by Sarah Tyacke in "Archives in a Wider World: The Culture and Politics of Archives," *Archivaria* 52 (Fall 2001): 1–25.

3   Lord Chancellor's Department. *Code of Practice on the Management of Records under Freedom of Information* 2002, http://www.dca.gov.uk/foi/codemanrec.htm (accessed 5 July 2004).

> [A] country does not become fully democratic until each of its inhabitants has the possibility of knowing in an objective manner the elements of their history.[4]

In the United Kingdom specifically, the marriage of open government, the access agenda, and the "social inclusion" agenda has resulted in the huge increase in digitisation and Web-based projects. Public funding is certainly there to carry out these projects—as long as certain conditions are fulfilled. By what criteria and on whose terms are records selected for digitisation? The skewing of professional priorities to take advantage of available funding is pragmatic and understandable; there are clear benefits—but there may also be disadvantages when the priorities identified by ARM practitioners do not chime with those of their political paymasters. Routine, necessary work with no obvious quick wins loses out. General underfunding of services, or budget cuts, may have a political impact too—by only paying for non-specialist staff, or by cutting down on opening hours, a public authority is reducing access to records and information when it should be encouraging it.[5]

The relationship between archivist and politics lay at the heart of many of the papers, which unsurprisingly did not, of course, fall neatly into the themes envisaged. While we have chosen to present them in this volume under certain headings, the issues under discussion really defy orderly arrangement; these headings represent some of the main themes that came out of the conference and provoked debate.

- The historical legacy
- Access and the public interest
- Ethical dilemmas in the public service
- Governments under pressure? Threats and responses
- At war: Records and international conflict
- Modelling the future

---

4   Council of Europe. Recommendation No. R (2000) 13 of the Committee of Ministers on a European policy on access to archives, http://cm.coe.int/ta/rec/2000/2000r13.htm (accessed 2 March 2004).

5   And see also Kwanten, chapter 8, in this volume.

The Historical Legacy

It can of course be argued that any transactions recorded in the past may have consequences in the present. The genealogist who discovers through marriage registers that his grandfather was a bigamist or through adoption records that his natural mother abandoned him; the householders who discover that their property extends for 10 metres beyond the fence erected by their neighbours in 1980; however routine or minor the matter recorded, it continues to have an impact. As sources for research, the academic interpretation and exploitation of archives has the potential to change perceptions of the past and therefore of society's understanding of the present. *Re*interpretation of records from different perspectives can enhance (as well as confuse) understanding; the discovery of records which a previous historian has overlooked (or ignored) can provoke radical reinterpretation. The gaps in the archival record are as important as what survives—but it may be in the interest of the state not to have those gaps plugged. The loss and destruction of records in the Asia-Pacific region at the end of the Japanese occupation there in 1945 means that the history of the period remains unclear, allowing nationalistic interpretations to predominate. Japanese reluctance to accept responsibility for World War II war crimes was typified by the scandal 50 years later of a new history textbook which failed to acknowledge the scale or indeed the existence of such crimes. Nationalist historians took advantage of the fact that very few records were available for the wartime period and therefore it was difficult for evidence to be gathered which could refute their presentation of events.[6] Masahito Ando's painstaking work in Japanese, Chinese, and U.K. archives has tried to bring to light the fate of these "lost" records in order to inform the present.

The need of individuals to access such records to provide the evidence needed to seek reparation for wartime abuse and deprivation is a well-documented phenomenon[7] and can be a major role for the con-

---

6   Masahito Ando, "Recovering Memory, Sharing Memory," in *Essays in Honour of Michael Cook,* ed. Margaret Procter and Caroline Williams (Liverpool: Liverpool University Centre for Archive Studies, 2003), 15.

7   See *Comma* 2004:2 which is devoted to the proceedings of the International Conference of the Round Table on Archives (CITRA) held in Cape Town in 2003 on the theme of Archives and Human Rights.

temporary archivist;[8] but individuals may also need access to these records because this is the only place in which their history has been recorded. This is a particular issue in societies which were predominantly oral and whose traditional way of life has been disrupted, typically by a colonial administration. Is it possible to extract a valid past from these records for those who were not participants in its creation (an argument which could be applied to the governed at most times in the past)[9] and particularly where the orality of the indigenous population made any participation invisible in any case? Jeannette Bastian's article asks whether it is indeed possible to find "whispers" of the past in such records, those which record 250 years of Danish colonial rule in the Virgin Islands.

In any such context, the need to access oral tradition in tandem with the written record is vital, but funding for such projects typically depends on the goodwill of the current government; post-colonial regimes are as likely as any other not to wish—for whatever reason—to go down this route.[10] The former colonial powers themselves are not immune from territorial or identity dislocation associated with regime change or major political upheaval. Former Bundesarchiv President Friedrich Kahlenberg discusses the impact that the uneasy political relationship between the German *Länder* (states) and the federal government has had on German archives during the twentieth century. After the fall of the Berlin Wall in November 1989, the centralised archival system in former East Germany not only regained its regional, *Land*-based organisation, but those services quickly began to help re-establish regional identities, masked since the end of World War II by

---

8 See for example Klaus Oldenhage, "Prosecution and Resistance, Compensation and Reconciliation—Two Repressive Systems in a Country. The Case of German Archives," *Comma* 2004:2, 75–80.

9 And hence the current popularity of appraisal policies which attempt to map the citizens' relationship with the state—a difficult process, as well as the state's own activities—a relatively easy process.

10 One might also reflect here on the relationship between former colonial nations and the records, created by the former colonial power, which in some cases may represent a large proportion of the written records relating to their country before independence. For many decades after independence in 1947, the Indian and Pakistan governments demanded the restitution of records of the India Office. This issue does not only affect the developing world: the U.S. Library of Congress ran a microfilming programme as early as 1939 in the Public Record Office (and elsewhere) which concluded in 1945; the Australian government began a similar project in 1945; and the Canadian National Archives had use of a room within the PRO up to 1959. See John D. Cantwell, *The Public Record Office 1838-1958* (London: HMSO, 1991), *passim*.

the Communist regime, through programmes which supported and promoted research into regional history. The archival record embodied the continuity of a suppressed regional identity and thus helped to reconstitute and confirm the identity of whole communities.

Past commercial imperatives may also have political consequences. Though "freedom of information" has a contemporary ring, there have been, at least in some respects, well-established rights of access to public records in attempts to prevent fraud, corruption and other legal abuses. The public registration of land ownership forms one of these categories,[11] and Dwayne Cox charts the progress of attitudes towards access to registers of deeds in late nineteenth- and early twentieth-century America. Although driven by commercial interests, case law began to shape the idea that citizenship *per se* was the basis on which to allow access to public records. The extent to which practice in private or commercial organisations has had an impact on the general culture of access throughout a society may be an area which deserves further investigation. Perhaps globalisation may have a positive role to play here?[12] Would it be desirable for the more consciously information-aware societies to advocate a culture of access to those areas of the world where access to information is not the norm? Corporate shareholder pressure is certainly political in the widest sense of the word.

Access and the Public Interest

In his conference paper, Verne Harris draws attention to the extensive literature relating to the relationship between the exercise of political power and the control of information. In particular he cites Noam Chomsky, "whose searing critiques of democracy, in the United States especially, demonstrate how elites depend on sophisticated informa-

---

11 Developments in English land law from the twelfth century onwards were largely driven by landowners and their lawyers trying to find loopholes in the presumption in favour of access.

12 With whatever motives, democratic governments clearly feel that they have a duty to intervene, to some degree, on behalf of individual citizens caught out by poor corporate governance; the introduction of the 2002 U.S. Sarbanes-Oxley legislation is a response to corporate debacles in the United States and will affect all foreign companies quoted on the New York stock exchange.

tion systems, media control, surveillance, privileged research and development, dense documentation of process, censorship, propaganda and so on to maintain their positions."[13] Access to—and consequently ability to manipulate—information confers power as the regular debates over newspaper and media ownership—Berlusconi in Italy and Murdoch practically everywhere else—continue to demonstrate. States which "allow" access to official information are applauded as possessing the desired democratic credentials. Harris again, here quoting French philosopher Jacques Derrida, says

> [E]ffective democratisation can always be measured by this essential criterion: the participation in and the access to the archive, its constitution, and its interpretation.[14]

The received view generally concurs with the philosophical one (though the sequence of cause and effect would reward investigation). The Council of Europe Recommendations on Access to Official Documents declares that access to official information

> allows the public to have an adequate view of, and to form a critical opinion on, the state of the society in which they live and on the authorities that govern them, whilst encouraging informed participation by the public in matters of common interest.[15]

It also, incidentally, makes clear that good recordkeeping is a prerequisite to any scheme of effective access. Thus governments are instructed to

- manage their documents efficiently so that they are easily accessible;
- apply clear and established rules for the preservation and destruction of their documents;
- as far as possible, make available information on the matters or activities for which they are responsible, for example by drawing up lists or registers of the documents they hold. [16]

---

13 Harris, chapter 11 in this volume, 173.

14 Harris, 174.

15 Council of Europe. 2002. Recommendation Rec (2002) R 13 of the Committee of Ministers on access to official documents, http://cm.coe.int/stat/E/Public/2002/adopted_texts/recommendations/2002r2.htm (accessed 2 March 2004).

16 In developing Freedom of Information legislation in the United Kingdom, a strong relationship between the Public Record Office and the executive resulted in the requirement for Code of Practice on Records Management being part of the Act itself (section 46). The Lord Chancellor's Code of Practice on the Management of Records under Freedom of Information can be viewed at http://www.lcd.gov.uk/foi/codemanrec.htm (accessed 25 June 2005).

We are not charting the comparative development of freedom of information legislation between nations here.[17] Indeed the introduction of such legislation is more likely to result from single interest group pressure rather than from a government's desire to enhance its democratic credentials (though governments have certainly seized on the introduction of legislation as added proof of their legitimacy). A change in attitudes on access to official documentation more often happens over a period of time. In the United Kingdom, for example, the process which led to the 2000 Freedom of Information Act (an act which was fully implemented in terms of access in January 2005) probably began with the reduction of the "50-year rule" to a "30-year rule" in 1967 (helped by the influence of academic historians), through the legislation governing access to personal information in medical, social services, and similar records in the 1970s and 1980s,[18] and the Open Government Code of the 1990s.

Specific incidents as well as gradual developments may either crystallise or provoke sudden changes in existing official attitudes to access. In post-World War II Europe it was the return as well as the original seizure of records that caused problems for archivists and governments. Astrid Eckert examines the way in which the West German government exerted pressure over access to such returned records. What started out as an attempt at openness resulted only in a tightening of access provision. The federal government suspected Eastern bloc researchers of wanting to access such material in order to discredit West German politicians previously involved in the Nazi regime. In the United Kingdom, Maureen Spencer analyses the access effects of the tragedy of the HMS Thetis (1942) where over 50 civilian passengers died in British waters. In wartime there may have been genuine national interest reasons for preventing access to documents, but the case set a precedent for the following quarter-century being used subsequently to uphold Crown Privilege over the interests of individuals even where cases were low level and totally uncontroversial. An event where there may have been an argument for non-disclosure of evidence (in wartime) established the everyday routine of non-disclosure.

---

17 For a good comparative introduction, see for example, Andrew McDonald and G. Terrill, *Open Government* (Basingstoke and London: Macmillan, 1998).

18 A substantial amount of information legislation was passed by the Thatcher government, although it has been noted that Mrs. Thatcher was far more willing to promote access to

Yet there can be no doubt that in many cases availability of records and access to them can be a double-edged sword. One of the most notorious examples of this is the events surrounding the release of Stasi case files: former GDR archivists who mediated access to such files witnessed the discovery of a vast network of informants in former East Germany, where, in some cases, family members were informing on each other over long periods of time. Such disclosures would have traumatic consequences for individuals.[19] How can the *public* interest be reconciled with individual interests at all times? The case of the Tuskegee Syphilis Study, in which syphilis in African-American men was allowed to go untreated for over four decades in order to chart its effects, is particularly complicated in this respect. Since this was clearly a public scandal (the trials only ended in 1972), there is an obvious need for access to the records. The closure of individual patient information until 2030 has been hotly contested, particularly as the names of 625 patients in the study have already been published, and many individuals are already dead.

Tywanna Whorley argues that the episode was so shocking that rights of access should be privileged over rights to privacy. The issues here, around government responsibility, medical ethics, race, and accountability, are many and complicated.[20] Can we really say that individual rights to privacy of information prevail in all cases over a general "right to know"?[21] A different set of questions arise, when organisations of private or semi-private (or indeterminate) nature contribute to or shape the political life of a country. Should these be classed as "private" records when they deal with actions which shape government policy and consequently affect individual citizens?

other people's information than to that of her own government. See D. Wilkenson, "Open Government: the Development of Policy in the United Kingdom in the 1990s," McDonald and Terrill, *Open Government,* chapter 1.

19 For an account of how these issues were addressed, see John Miller, "Setting Accounts with a Secret Police: the German Law on the Stasi Records," *Europe Asia Studies* 50:2 (1998), 305–330.

20 Also discussed by Whorley, "The Tuskegee Syphilis Study and the Politics of Memory" in Richard J. Cox and David A. Wallace, *Archives and the Public Good* (Westport, Conn.: Quorum Books, 2002), 165–175.

21 Debate over the introduction of identity cards in the United Kingdom crystallise some of these issues. The European view is more relaxed over the identity card question; it is seen primarily as a convenient way of proving identity without resorting to a multiplicity of documentation.

Godfried Kwanten examines how issues surrounding the records of
political parties have been resolved in Belgium,[22] but the similarly
ambiguous position of the papers of individual ministers, where
archives directly relating to state functions and activities are held as
personal papers, is a global and long-standing phenomenon.[23]

Ethical Dilemmas in the Public Service

Access to public sector archives is frequently regulated—and therefore,
in theory at least, made more straightforward—by legislation defining
access, closure and exemption conditions. Worldwide, the majority of
archivists, even outside the public sector where such a duty is a prerequisite, have a responsibility to provide some form of access to the
archives.[24] Those who manage an organisation's current records may
sometimes have a more difficult path to tread. Often trained in the
same way as colleagues working primarily in the "historical" sphere,
they have a direct responsibility to an employer whose mission is
unlikely to include making records routinely and publicly available.
Research into the moral questions and ethical dilemmas inherent in
recordkeeping is increasing, and contributors to these conference proceedings have been among the leaders in bringing the ethical dimension of the recordkeeper's work to the attention of the profession.

Undoubtedly, the general public still remains oblivious to the fact
that recordkeeping—whether of current records for a corporation or
of historical archives for public use—has such an ethical dimension;
yet that this is indeed the case is evident from any reading of newspapers over a given period or from routine audit activity in any organisational context.[25] Rick Barry provides a catalogue of such incidents
concluding that they "are not rare phenomena, but occur in all coun-

---

22 See chapter 8.
23 For example, English state papers of the sixteenth, seventeenth, and early eighteenth centuries are routinely accessible only within family archive collections. The situation might be
compared in some respects with access provision to records held in American presidential
libraries.
24 For example, Code of Ethics, www.ica.org; International Council on Archives.
25 Cox and Wallace list the records-related issues appearing in U.S. news media between
February and March 2001, pp. 5–7; U.K. National Audit Office reports make illuminating
reading in this respect—system weaknesses are invariably linked with records systems failures. See www.nao.gov.uk.

tries and sectors," yet he implicates practitioners in these failures; by their reluctance to implement sound recordkeeping policies and procedures, he suggests, they are "complicit partners of the violators."[26] This is a serious indictment, but the necessity of providing an ethical dimension within the education of future professionals was one of the conference's conclusions.[27]

The Heiner affair, an Australian *cause célèbre*, already features in the curricula of most training courses: a long-running saga of political interference in recordkeeping procedures, allied with, in some commentators' opinion, an unprofessional reluctance to "become involved." Chris Hurley, who was removed from his post as Keeper of the Public Records of Victoria following his exposure of repeated instances of unauthorized disposal of records, has written at length on the Heiner affair (or "Shreddergate" as it has also been called).[28] His paper urges archivists to take their responsibilities as "agents of accountability" seriously, suggesting that we must engage with, rather than take at face value, the political environment (and the legislation which it shapes) rather than merely assume that because we adhere to legislation, what we do is morally acceptable.

In taking responsibility in this way, archivists will find it difficult to separate themselves from the wider political environment in which they (along with the rest of society) exist. Verne Harris takes this approach one step further. His paper explicitly addresses the relationship between the archivist and politics, emphasising that such a relationship may be far stronger than practitioners within a democratic state would acknowledge. With his background of working for the National Archives of South Africa under the apartheid regime, he argues that "the archive is politics—not that it is political—but that it is politics."[29] His main thesis—that the archivist cannot divorce him/herself from the politics of the society in which she/he operates— is based, not just on his own experience of apartheid, but also on the

---

26 Chapter 9. Much relevant material is also available on Barry's website, www.mybestdocs.com.

27 Karen Benedict, *Ethics and the Archival Profession: Introduction and Case Studies* (Chicago: Society of American Archivists, 2003), provides some 40 short examples of situations that might be faced by practitioners, the ethical issues raised, and some solutions.

28 See the Caldeson Consultancy site, http://www.caldeson.com; Cox and Wallace, "Records and the Public Interest: The 'Heiner Affair' in Queensland," 293–318.

29 Chapter 11.

same concept of access to archives as an indicator of democracy as that enshrined in the European Council's access recommendations. That such access is an indicator of democracy was evidenced by the post-apartheid government's readiness to reorganise and empower the National Archives;[30] yet, according to Harris, after 1998 a "re-bureau-cratisation" process took place during which access to records has been far more tightly restricted than the National Archives Act intended.[31]

Governments Under Pressure? Threats and Responses

The inclination, whether real or perceived, of governments to control access to or use of their own information is aggravated when states are faced with some form of real or perceived external pressure. As we have noted, there is an explicit and overarching relationship between democracy and access. The short-term political situation may alter, whether subtly or very obviously, the extent to which governments chose to exercise such control over information access. In wartime, for example, it might be expected—and accepted—that governments act in the national interest to protect national information. In the West, and specifically in the United States, the idea of war has been rede-fined by the notion of the "war on terror" as a continuing struggle against global terrorist organisations in the aftermath of 9/11.

A swift (knee-jerk?) response to the events, the Patriot Act became law on 26 October 2001. It affects a wide range of other legis-lation, allowing *inter alia* "law enforcement agencies freedom to search and seize information, for and about 'potential' terrorists."[32] Clearly, such information may be available within any kind of organisation;

---

30 A similar process took place in post-revolutionary France where one of the first acts of the new government in 1790 was to declare the archives "archives nationales"; a centralised depository was legislated for in 1794.

31 One of Harris's examples was the lack (at the time of writing) of an access policy for the records of the South African Truth and Reconciliation Committee. For a more recent account see Graham Dominy, "'We Must Remember Our Past so that We Do Not Repeat It': Archiving and Accessing the Records of South Africa's Truth and Reconciliation Commission," *Comma* 2005:2.

32 Jackie Esposito, "'Any Tangible Thing': The U.S.A. Patriot Act and Its Impact on Higher Education," chapter 12.

Jackie Esposito's paper discusses the impact of the Patriot Act on u.s. universities and in particular on access procedures to student records. Given that several of the 11 September bombers entered the United States on student visas, the ethics of responding to what many might construe as political demands for access are hugely complicated.

Tom Connors suggests that the Patriot Act was merely a piece in the jigsaw puzzle of successive attempts over recent years to impose an "information lockdown" on government information. Processes such as removing information from government websites, easing restrictions on collecting information about individuals, and even providing disinformation, are undertaken in a bid to prevent terrorist activity. Like Harris, Connors urges the involvement of the archival profession in responding to these developments, at the very least by keeping the issues within the public domain through discussion and writing. The phenomenon is of course an international one; in the southern hemisphere Rachel Lilburn notes the upsurge of a similar spate of anti-terrorist legislation in New Zealand. Existing difficulties (despite enabling legislation) with accessing—or even transferring into the National Archives the records of security services—have been exacerbated by the current political situation there.

The ultimate effects on recordkeeping practice and on the involvement of records professionals of post-9/11 events are impossible to gauge at present. Given the evidence here, it is difficult to believe that there will not be long-term changes in the way in which archivists view their responsibilities towards society. Rather than just paying lip service to the notion of information access as a democratic marker, we may have to become proactive in defence of that ideal.

Perhaps one way forward is to work to ensure that good record-keeping becomes embedded in organisational management so that we can provide an effective response to information needs in a time of crisis without shifting the goalposts in terms of democratic accountability. Making a positive effort to establish a benchmark for "normal" service (for example, in the way that the United Kingdom and Scottish Freedom of Information (FOI) Acts do by providing for records management Codes of Practice) will help counter or at least focus attention on any extraordinary and possibly unreasonable demands. Chris Williams and Clive Emsley, who have investigated records of u.k.

provincial police forces, suggest that FOI is likely to have a positive effect on these bodies in terms of records management and archival access. Currently unregulated, their records systems and access practices compare badly with those of U.K. intelligence services, for example.

At War: Records and International Conflict

Warfare as commonly defined is the most extreme form of political pressure. As we have already seen, warfare encourages governments to begin to "protect" access to and use of their own records and other information resources, although such actions may have little direct impact outside their own borders. Once an army is an invading or an occupying force, however, the situation has clearly changed. Records are captured to provide both military intelligence in the first instance and the means to govern as an occupying force in the second. Beyond this, there are many instances throughout history of records being seized and removed from the country in which they were created. These may be the records of current administrations, but they might also be records taken from archive repositories which would be considered as cultural artefacts; formal conventions dealing with the seizure of records in wartime have developed over the past century.[33] Trudy Peterson draws attention to other, late twentieth-century reasons for the seizure of records. Human rights organisations may request, for example, that Iraqi government records be protected so that evidence of crimes of the previous regime is available and war crimes cases can be more effectively prosecuted.[34] This use of records (which of course was prefigured in the use of records in prosecuting Nazi war criminals and officials post-World War II)[35] is developing at the beginning of

---

33 "Reference Dossier on Archival Claims" compiled by the ICA Committee on Legal Matters brings together international legal and UNESCO texts, a statement of professional principles, and a note on captured archives in Russia. *CITRA Proceedings 1993–1995*, 209–268.

34 She is writing in the context of the second Gulf War. Iraqi government records seized by the Kurds (1991) in the aftermath of the first Gulf War were later transferred to the United States. See Bruce P. Montgomery, "The Iraqi Secret Police Files: A Documentary Record of the Anfal Genocide," *Archivaria* 52, 69–99.

35 See, for example, Kahlenberg, chapter 4.

the twenty-first century in tandem with the development of the procedures of the International Criminal Tribunals (ICT).[36]

The outright destruction of records by occupying forces can ultimately result in the loss of both personal and national (or ethnic) identities (as in the case of the Asia-Pacific nations discussed by Ando). The conflicts during the 1990s in the former Yugoslavia provided the impetus for the international archival community to become involved in the re-examination of the issues surrounding attacks on and destruction of cultural property: a second protocol to the 1954 Hague Convention for the Protection of Cultural Property in the event of armed conflict was adopted in 1999.[37] Whether protocols can prevent destruction on the ground and in the heat of battle is a moot point. More susceptible to, at least in theory, rational and measured resolution are problems surrounding *replevin,* the legal issue of the restitution of seized records, and a problem which archivists, certainly those working in a national repository, may well meet in their professional lives. During the twentieth century, the u.s. National Archives has held, for example, records belonging to Germany, Poland, Russia, Italy, Japan, North Korea, and Grenada.[38] Replevin is a complicated affair; the resolution of outstanding cases is naturally affected as much by the current political climate existing between nations, as by the historical event of conflict or any juridical conventions.[39]

External conflict may also have oblique or direct consequences on a nation's internal recordkeeping practices. In 1995, a Dutch peacekeeping force failed to prevent the massacre of 7,500 boys and men in Srebrenica, a so-called "safe enclave" it was protecting in Bosnia. The investigation into the circumstances surrounding this tragedy was hindered by inadequate records management procedures in the Dutch

---

36 In particular in the ICT Rwanda. See Tom Adami, "Archives and International Prosecutions—Genocide, Justice and Innovative Archival Practice," *Comma* 2004:2, 83–88.

37 Discussed by Mackenzie, chapter 16.

38 The majority now copied and returned. See Peterson, chapter 17 in this volume. For a discussion of the practicalities of such restitution, see Geraldine N. Phillips, "Duplication before Restitution. Costs and Benefits—the U.S. Experience," *CITRA Proceedings 1993–1995,* 167–171.

39 See "Reference Dossier on Archival Claims." For a review of some of the issues, see *CITRA Proceedings 1993–1995;* Hervé Bastien, "About Archival Claims," 63–68; and Leopold Auer, "Restitution of Removed Records Following War," 173–178. For an account of French records held in Russia, see Gerard Ermisse, "France and Archival Claims," *Comma* 2003:3–4, 159–166; and Jochen Kutzner, "The Return of Namibian Archives," *Janus* 1998:2, 24–26.

military. While records management is hardly a priority of front-line troops (and they destroyed all their records before leaving Srebrenica), its neglect by government offices at home created serious problems for investigators. It is not suggested that any criminal activity took place to avoid culpability; nevertheless, the incident highlighted once again the relationship between accountable government and good record-keeping. Indeed, Dutch Prime Minister Wim Kok and his government resigned a week after the final report on the event was published.[40]

Modelling the Future

The complexities of the relationship between a state and the records it creates was a theme that ran through the conference, bound up inextricably with the issues of democratic accountability and the state's role in defining how its records are managed and used. Technology has already changed the way in governments interact with their citizens. The drive towards e-government for all citizen-state transactions has already had a dramatic impact in many areas. The speed at which this has taken place is perhaps not appreciated by the majority of archives practitioners: the web has become the primary way for governments to communicate; transactions are routinely conducted on-line, and electronic voting has been adopted throughout the world.[41] Having emphasised the importance of the recordkeeper in supporting and promoting democratic principles, we now face the challenge of acquiring new skills to deal with these issues within the e-environment.[42] New ways of conducting democratic elections, new ways of conducting transactions which are evidence of the state-citizen relationship, and new ways of providing information for citizens nevertheless still require us to keep track of "the record" within a dynamic environment. More pragmatically, it requires formal recordkeeping systems to be in place—a recurring theme—so that these virtual objects retain their

---

40 These events are examined by Agnes E. M. Jonker, "Srebrenica: A Balkan Tragedy and the Making of a Dutch Affair," chapter 18.

41 Most notably in India, where nearly 380 million people voted this way in the 2004 general election.

42 See Sarah Tyacke in "E-government and Archives," *Archives in the UK and the Government Agenda*, ed. Caroline Williams (Liverpool: Liverpool University Centre for Archive Studies), 2002.

"recordness": authenticity, integrity and reliability. Moreover, the requirement for future archival access must also be tackled now. The stability and democratic credentials of any government are no guarantee of the archival survival of its digital records in the twenty-first century. In the two papers included here which discuss these issues, Claire Johnson considers some consequences of the application of e-democracy in Scotland, and Malcolm Todd highlights the broader issues surrounding the organisation and survival of the record.[43]

. . . And How to Get There

Although this volume has been arranged to reflect the major themes which emerged from the conference, it is clear that any attempt at arrangement is to some extent contrived. The issues invariably overlap, with individual papers picking up on aspects covered in greater depth elsewhere. Inevitably there were areas not discussed in any depth or omitted completely; examples which have been examined elsewhere include the use of records by repressive regimes; the aftermath of the collapse of those regimes, in the context of the former USSR[44] or of South America;[45] colonial recordkeeping and its legacy; and responses to oral recordkeeping cultures.[46] More immediately, events in Iraq during 2003 to 2004 have provided a microcosm of the interrelationships between state pressure, individual rights, and records and record-

---

43 Chapter 19, Claire Johnson, "The Relevance of Archival Practice within 'e-Democracy'"; chapter 20, Malcolm Todd, "'Brave New World'? Electronic Records Management—Who Will Be in a Position to Influence the Archival Record in the Future?", below.

44 See Hennadii Boriak, "Users and Their Demands in a Country in Transition: Ukraine," *Comma* 2003:2–3, 111–116; and *Comma* 2002:3–4, a special issue on "Archives and Archival Issues of Russia," in particular William G. Rosenberg, "Archiving Russia's Revolutions: Access, Scarcity and Loss in the Democratic Experience," 29–39; Bosir V. Anan'ich, "The Historian and the Source: Problems of Reliability and Ethics," 61–68; Jeffrey Burds, "Ethnicity, Memory and Violence: Reflections of the Special Problems in Soviet and East Europeans Archives," 69–82; Serhy Yekelchyk, "The Archives of Stalin's Time: Political Use, Symbolic Value, and the Missing Resolutions," 83–92.

45 See Ana Maria Cecchini de Dallo, "La demanda de las víctimas de un antiguo régimen represivo," *Comma* 2003:2–3, 81–89; Antonio González Quintana, "Archives of the Security Services of Former Repressive Regimes: Report Prepared for UNESCO on Behalf of the ICA," *Janus* 1998:2, 7–25.

46 *Comma* 2003:1 is devoted entirely to articles on "Archives and Indigenous Peoples" which touch on many of these related issues.

keeping and are worthy of a conference in themselves. Issues of seizure and destruction of records, of files "found" in Baghdad to incriminate a British MP, the evidence of Iraqi prisoner abuse (and faked evidence of the same), the "Dodgy Dossier" incident, and the Hutton enquiry into the death of a U.K. government scientist, all involve or centre on the management, use, and exploitation of records.[47]

Delegates were unanimous in agreeing that the subjects raised were ones which should be brought to the attention of the wider professional community, and that such attention needed to be sustained. A list of actions to achieve this was an unexpected conference outcome; these are summarised here and are intended to encourage readers of these proceedings to consider how they might—as individuals, as members of professional associations, as educators, and as employees of private and state institutions—take steps to sustain awareness of the inextricable link between the archive and politics. Actions include

- publication and wide dissemination of conference proceedings;
- further meetings to take the subject forward—planning to be done by a small virtual working party;
- taking back what had been learned to national associations and workplaces;
- ensuring that codes of practice and ethics should be made a component of archival training courses;
- establishment of an international register of events involving ethical and professional problems, to be available as a professional resource;
- compilation of codes of ethics and of professional practice, to supplement what is already available from the ICA and national associations;

---

47 www.unesco.org/webworld/ica_sio/docs/news_irak.rtf (accessed 5 July 2004); David Blair, "How I Found the Papers in a Looted Foreign Ministry Office," *Daily Telegraph*, 22 April 2003; the papers were later exposed as fakes. *The Guardian*, 19 May 2004, "Arrests over Photo Hoax at Mirror," 1–2, quoting general secretary of the National Union of Journalists; *Leader*, 15 May 2004, 25; the "Dodgy Dossier" was the name given to the evidence collated by the U.K. government in support of the war (and in particular about weapons of mass destruction alleged to be in Iraq), the Hutton Enquiry investigated the circumstances surrounding the suicide of a government scientist who had supplied information to the BBC; see http://www.the-hutton-inquiry.org.uk/ (accessed 11 July 2004).

- information on the political demands made of archivists to be made available to the European Union (EU), so that it could be relayed to colleagues in the newly joining countries (it was agreed that the appropriate bodies should be contacted on this, including the meetings of directors of national archives in the EU, and the relevant directorate of the European Commission);
- a media release explaining the content and significance of the conference;
- provision to be made for a meeting of interested colleagues at the ICA Congress in Vienna in August 2004; and
- the possibility of establishing a listserv on the subject of political records and political pressures on archivists, records managers, and others working in relevant fields.

The Historical
Legacy

I

THE ASIAN-PACIFIC WAR AND THE FATE OF ARCHIVES

Masahito Ando

Introduction

Historical analyses of the destruction, plunder, and displacement of records and archives during the Second World War and its aftermath have made remarkable progress in recent years. Patricia Grimsted's *Trophies of War and Empire* published in 2001 is certainly a monumental work in the field.[1]

Compared with Europe, fruits of study on this issue in the Asia and Pacific regions are scarce. Was there no destruction of records in these areas? No plunder and displacement of archives? Certainly there was. As many documentary and oral sources suggest, it is undeniable that an enormous amount of archival material including local public records and historical manuscripts was either looted or destroyed during the Second World War period in Asia too, especially in the former

---

1 Patricia Grimsted, *Trophies of War and Empire: the Archival Heritage of Ukraine, World War II, and the International Politics of Restitution,* Harvard Papers in Ukrainian Studies (Cambridge: Harvard University Press, 2001).

Japanese colonies and occupied territories. However, because, at the end of the war, the Japanese authorities destroyed almost all important records relating to wartime administration, both in inland and overseas territories, studies on the wartime history of Asian and Pacific archives have faced a serious difficulty in making any progress.

The lack of wartime records has caused continuous friction between Japan and other Asian and Pacific countries. Besides the recent Japanese history textbook issue, several examples can be shown. Among these are a number of lawsuits concerning compensation for wartime damage. An appreciable number of Asian and Pacific individuals (along with European and American people) who had been taken away forcibly as laborers or "comfort women" (sex slaves) for Japanese soldiers have entered actions against the Japanese government and Japanese companies in order to demand a formal apology and compensation. Most accusers, however, confront difficulties in tracing relevant records and quite often have lost cases because the documentary evidence was insufficient.

This situation makes it clear that it is an important part of the responsibility of Japanese archivists and historians to undertake urgent and intensive studies on the history of records and archives lost or displaced during the war period and, in doing so, to contribute to recovering and sharing memory among Asian and Pacific peoples. The present paper is a supplement to a previous essay,[2] and is intended to introduce more facts about wartime evacuation, plunder, requisition, and destruction of records and archives in the Japanese occupied territories, focusing on (but not limited to) Hong Kong and Malaya.

China

FROM THE FOUNDATION OF MANCHUKUO TO THE SINO-JAPANESE WAR

Japan, which had already absorbed Korea in 1910 as a bridgehead for aggression in the continent, occupied the whole of northeast China in

---

2 Masahito Ando, "Recovering Memory, Sharing Memory: Archives Lost and Displaced in the Asian-Pacific War and the Responsibility of Japanese Archivists," in *Essays in Honour of Michael Cook,* ed. Margaret Procter and Caroline Williams (Liverpool: Liverpool University Centre for Archive Studies, 2003), 14–28.

1931 after the "Manchurian Incident" and created a puppet state, Manchukuo, in 1932. In order to establish a colonial administration for Manchukuo, the Investigation Department of the South Manchurian Railway, a giant state company of Japan, and some other agencies, carried out a large-scale investigation into every aspect of the territory. In the process of investigation, a massive quantity of books and manuscripts was collected either by purchase or by seizure and accumulated in the South Manchurian Railway Library and the Feng-tian National Library of Manchukuo, among other places. As far as archival records were concerned, a special agency called *Kyu-ki Seiri sho* (Archives Administration Office) was set up within the Feng-tian National Library by the Ministry of State Affairs Order No.37 entitled "Centralized Management of Archives" on 28 May 1937.[3] By this order, more than 2,300,000 files of archival records were removed from about 380 central and local government agencies all over northeast China under the Manchukuo regime and sent to Feng-tian (now Shenyang) through the network of the South Manchurian Railway.[4] *Kyu-ki Seiri sho* became, in the eyes of Chinese people, one of the worst aspects of organizational plunder by the Japanese invaders.[5]

After the outbreak of the Sino-Japanese War in July 1937, the Japanese forces expanded the occupied territories into most urban areas of China, including Shanghai and Nanjing. In December 1937, the Special Service Division of the Japanese Army at Shanghai set up requisition committees for books and documents and for scientific materials in the occupied area, in cooperation with the Shanghai Branch of the South Manchurian Railway, *To-a Do-bun Shoin* College, and the Shanghai Institute of Natural Science. The Requisition

---

3 *Kyu-ki* is a Japanese term out of use which originally meant just "old records," but was defined in the Order as "archival records before the foundation of Manchukuo."

4 Mitsunaga Iyayoshi, "Tohoku Chiho (Kyu-Manshu) Toshokan no Kaikoshi (A retrospective history of libraries in Northeast China (former Manchuria))"; "Kyu-ki mondo (A dialogue on archives)"; "Kuni yaburete toshokan sonsu: Kokuritsu Shinyo Toshokan zenshi (The nation is in ruins, yet its libraries remain as they were: a preceding history of National Shenyang Library)," all in *Iyayoshi Mitsunaga Chosaku-shu (Collected Works of Mitsunaga Iyayoshi)*, vol. 2 (Tokyo: Nichigai Associates, 1981) (Japanese); Mitsunaga Iyayoshi, "Kyu Kokuritsu Hoten Toshokan no toan shimatsu-ki (The fact of the matter about the archives of the former Feng-tian National Library)," in Mittsunaga Iyayoshi, *Toho no sho (Book of the Orient)* (Tokyo: Makumosanbo Publishing Company, 1977) (Japanese).

5 See for example, *Xueheng Zhou, Zhong Guo Dang An Shi Ye Shi (History of Archival Enterprise in China)* (Beijing: Renmin University Press, 1994), 470 (Chinese). As regards *Kyu-ki Seiri sho*, see also, Masahito Ando, "Recovering Memory."

Committee for Books and Documents in the Occupied Area soon became the largest Japanese agency in occupied China specializing in such requisitioning. It is said, for example, that the committee took over about 800,000 books from libraries, universities, and government agencies in the Nanjing area in only one month, March–April 1938. It is also reported that the committee collected not only books but a quantity of archival records, excluding those which were to be seized by the army for military use.[6] However, the detail of the committee's activities concerning archives is so far unknown.

THE ASIAN-PACIFIC WAR PERIOD AND HONG KONG UNDER THE JAPANESE OCCUPATION

On 8 December 1941, Japan went to war with Britain and the United States. Regarding the situation of records and archives in the area during the Asian-Pacific War period, let us take the case of Hong Kong. Hong Kong surrendered on 25 December 1941, and the Japanese 23rd Army immediately set up a military government. It was replaced in January 1942 by the Government-General of occupied Hong Kong. Because of the importance of Hong Kong as a strategic point, it was placed under the direct control of the Imperial Headquarters. Previous studies have revealed some cases in which books and records were looted by the Japanese during the occupation. In my previous essay, too, I briefly mentioned the plunder of records of the Hong Kong Prize Court by the Japanese military police.[7]

A report by the British military administration of Hong Kong issued in April 1946, eight months after the Japanese surrender, describes the situation of certain administrative records as follows.

> The records of the Land Office were retrieved almost intact after the re-occupation and were returned to the Courts of Justice together with the records of property transactions effected under the Japanese occupation.
>
> All records of the Marriage Registry were destroyed.

---

6 Keiji Okamura, *Nokosareta Zosho: Mantetsu Toshokan, Kaigai Nihon Toshokan no Rekishi (Left books: The History of South Manchurian Railway Library and Other Overseas Japanese Libraries)* (Kyoto: A-Un Publishing Company, 1994) (Japanese).

7 Masahito Ando, "Recovering Memory."

Substantially all the records of the Registrar of Companies were destroyed, or otherwise disposed of, by the enemy. [8]

The varying fate of the records shown here seems to be more or less a reflection of the administrative policy and methods during the Japanese occupation.

Regarding the land and house administration, the Japanese Government-General of occupied Hong Kong decided not to make a rapid change in the British system and allowed local leaseholders to retain their ownership of houses, provided that their right of ownership was certified by the House Registry Office of the Government-General.[9] For the purpose of verification, the House Registry Office made heavy use of the land registers produced by the former (colonial) Land Office.

According to archival sources kept by the Hong Kong Record Office, the Land Office records including land registers had been evacuated from the office on 8 December 1941, immediately after the outbreak of war, and transferred to the Supreme Court building. During the Japanese occupation, these records were discovered and removed by the Real Estate Administration Section of the Japanese Army on 10 August 1942 and transferred to the Government-General's Real Estate Investigation Office, apparently for use by the House Registry Office which had just begun the certification work for local leaseholders on 1 August 1942. On 20 June 1943, the land records were removed again, probably because the certification work had by and large been finished. They were then stored at the Yaumati Government School and remained almost intact until the re-occupation of Hong Kong by the British.[10]

The Japanese authorities adopted a different policy in regard to control of the population. The Government-General of occupied Hong Kong tried from the beginning of the occupation to evacuate as many inhabitants as possible from Hong Kong in order to secure food supplies and to maintain public peace. In July 1942 the Government-General introduced a new administration system under which Hong

---

8   "Report of British Military Administration in Hong Kong, 1945 Aug.-1946. Apr." W0203/6076, Public Record Office, United Kingdom.

9   "Kaoku Toroku-sho Kiroku (Records of the House Registry Office)," Honkon Senryo-chi Sotoku-bu, Kaoku Toroku-sho (House Registry Office, Government-General of Occupied Hong Kong), HKRS 138-19-26, Public Record Office, Hong Kong.

10 "New Territories Land Records" HKRS 170-2-15, Public Record Office, Hong Kong.

Kong was divided into 28 small wards called *Ku* in Japanese. One of the main functions of each ward was to carry out an investigation into houses and inhabitants and to prepare new family registers. These were apparently to be used as fundamental data sources for accelerating the evacuation of population. As a result, it was reported that about 970,000 people, which was more than 60% of the total population, had been removed from Hong Kong, either compulsorily or semi-compulsorily by September 1943.[11]

The loss of all records of the marriage registry, as reported by the British military administration, was presumably a consequence of the Japanese system of population control. The newly prepared family registers must have invalidated such records as marriage registers, which had been used until the commencement of the occupation, and finally led to intentional or accidental destruction.

Southeast Asia, With Particular Reference to Malaya

INVESTIGATION AND REQUISITION ACTIVITIES BY THE JAPANESE FORCES IN SOUTHEAST ASIA

The Japanese invasion and occupation of Southeast Asia aimed to gain rich natural resources in the area, such as oil, ore, and rubber. This aim was reflected in the investigation and requisition activities by the Japanese forces.

Immediately after the fall of Singapore in February 1942, the military government of the Japanese 25th Army requisitioned the Raffles Museum at Singapore, probably aiming at its rich collection of research materials on the natural resources, culture, and industry of Malaya and other Southern areas.[12] Renamed the *Shonan* Museum under the Japanese regime, the Raffles Museum soon became a centre for requisitioning cultural and scientific institutions in all of the

---

11 Kwan Lai Hung, *Nihon Senryo-ka no Honkon (Hong Kong under the Japanese Occupation),* translated into Japanese by Michio Hayashi and Hideo Kobayashi (Tokyo: Ochanomizu Publishing Company, 1995) (Japanese); Hideo Kobayashi and Yoshio Shibata, *Nihon Gunsei-ka no Honkon (Hong Kong under the Japanese Military Administration)* (Tokyo: Shakai Hyoron Sha Publishing Company, 1996) (Japanese).

12 Yuji Otabe, *Tokugawa Yoshichika no 15-nen senso (Fifty Years War of Tokugawa Yoshichika)* (Tokyo: Aoki Publishing Company, 1988) (Japanese).

Japanese occupied territories in Southeast Asia. According to *Requisition of Cultural Institutions in Southern Area,* written by Professor Hidezo Tanakadate, who took part in the activities as an advisor to the Southern Army, around 70 cultural and scientific institutions in Malaya, Singapore, Borneo, Java, and Sumatra are reported to have been requisitioned by special teams of Japanese scientists during the first year of the occupation.[13] Reflecting Japanese occupation policy, most of them were institutions of natural science, such as geological institutes, survey offices, meteorological observatories, and agricultural experimental stations.

Investigation activities were then taken over and expanded by the military government Investigation Sections which were set up at the end of 1942 in each occupied area. Leading Japanese research institutes joined in the undertaking and sent members of their staff. The Institute of East Asian Economics at Tokyo University of Commerce, the Mitsubishi Research Institute of Economics, and the East Asia Research Institute sent staff to the Southern Army, the 14th Army (Philippines), and to the 16th Army (Java), respectively. Both the military governments of the 15th Army (Burma) and of the 25th Army (Malaya) were supported by the Research Department of the South Manchurian Railway Company.[14]

The military government Investigation Sections carried out a comprehensive scientific research programme, covering almost all fields ranging from ethnic customs, agriculture, fisheries, economics, and finance to traffic, communication, mining, and industry, though priority was clearly given to subjects relating to natural resources. Details of the activities done by these sections have not yet been revealed, but it is presumed, from the guidelines for investigation prepared by the sections, that every kind of source material, including books and historical archives, was collected, often under compulsion, from a variety of government agencies, libraries, universities, and scientific institutions all over the occupied territories.[15]

---

13 Hidezo Tanakadate, *Nanpo Bunka-shisetsu no Sesshu (Requisition of Cultural Institutions in Southern Area)* (Tokyo: Jidaisha Publishing Company, 1944) (Japanese).

14 Sumio Fukami, "Tonan-Ajia ni okeru Nihon Gunsei no chosa (Investigation by the Japanese Military Administration in Southeast Asia)," *Nanpo Bunka (Southern Area Culture),* No. 15, 1988 (Japanese).

15 "Marei Gun(sei) Chosa (Yo) ko soan (Draft Guideline of Investigation for the Military Administration of Malaya)," 1941. No. 20463, South Manchurian Railway Archives, Changchun, China (Japanese).

On the other hand, almost nothing has been clarified so far as to how the Japanese treated local administrative records in the occupied area in Southeast Asia. As a first step, I previously introduced[16] certain historical sources that were considered useful as clues for this topic. Here I add further examples of historical sources, with particular reference to Malaya.

EVACUATION OF RECORDS AND ARCHIVES IN MALAYA

(1) Evacuation of the Malayan Survey Records to Australia.

On 8 December 1941, Japanese troops landed in the northern part of the Malayan peninsula and advanced south, their momentum gathering at each step. In the confusion of emergency evacuation of the British and other government people, it is thought that public records in the northern states of British Malaya were mostly left behind and fell into Japanese hands. A reminiscence by R.H. Steed who was then stationed at Taiping, the state capital of Perak, as the Acting State Engineer describes the situation as follows.

> At 4 a.m. (19 December 1941), I received a message from the Acting British Resident to effect our evacuation to Ipoh as soon as possible. I drove my car round to Thatcher's quarters, where also were found Messrs Waddell, Jewkes, Boardman and Mallard. We set off for the PWD [Public Works Department] office and collected all the confidential papers and maps, placing them in my car. We could not burn or destroy anything from the office since fires were forbidden, so the office was left more or less intact. I had approached the Acting British Resident on 18th and suggested setting fire to the office building, as it was obvious that an evacuation was imminent, but he would not give approval, in fact, nothing was to be destroyed until the evacuation order was given which in this case proved too late. I consider it was a great mistake as the same block of buildings contained the Survey Office, in which there would be many records of value to the enemy.[17]

---

16 Masahito Ando, "Recovering Memory."

17 "A report by R.H. Steed, Senior Executive Engineer, Malayan Public Works Department, from Outbreak of War with Japan," MSS.Ind.Ocn.s.57, Rhodes House Library, University of Oxford.

As far as the survey office records mentioned here are concerned, however, the Malayan Survey Department had managed to start an emergency evacuation programme immediately after the outbreak of war. At least a part of the branch records, such as the original field books, plans, and maps of military importance, including those of the Taiping office is believed to have been sent to Kuala Lumpur before the Japanese advance. The Malayan Survey Department then carried out an evacuation of all maps and records of importance from Kuala Lumpur— first to Singapore by train at the end of 1941 and in January 1942 and then to Java by sea in February 1942 immediately before the fall of Singapore; they finally reached Australia in March 1942. The survey records thus evacuated to Australia are reported to amount to 8 tons in 71 wooden boxes, including fairsheets, glass negatives, standard sheets, and so forth. As well as this, some records were sent to India. Those of military importance left behind, such as printed military maps, had been almost destroyed before being taken over by the Japanese.[18] Table 1 summarizes a report prepared in 1943 by C. Noble, former senior surveyor of the Malayan Survey Department, which shows in outline form how the essential records of the Malayan Survey Department were disposed of when the Japanese invaded Malaya.[19]

(2) Evacuation of the Federated Malay States and Selangor Government Records.

According to archival sources, during the Japanese occupation a large part of the important Federated Malay States and Selangor Government records under British rule, which had been in the federal capital of Kuala Lumpur, were also evacuated to Singapore before the fall of Kuala Lumpur.[20] These included, for example, the records of Federal Secretariat, such as service registers and correspondence files, the records of the office of the Public Officers' Guarantee Fund and

---

18 "The Evacuation of Malayan Survey Department Military Maps and Mapping Material from Singapore to Australia, Feb. 1942, Report by C. Noble, Malayan Survey Service, covering the period 9 December 1941 to 28 February 1942." BMA/DEPT/3/16(12), National Archives of Malaysia; Mss.Ind.Ocn.s.199, Rhodes House Library, Oxford; co865/72(15), PRO, U.K.

19 "Preliminary Notes on the Reconstruction of the Survey Department, Malaya," by C. Noble, Senior Surveyor, Malayan Survey Service, at present Flight Lieutenant, Royal Australian Air Force. 26.10.1943. CO865/62, Public Record Office, U.K.

20 Sel. Kan (Selangor Syuseityo Kanbo) 106/02, National Archives of Malaysia.

Widows and Orphans' Pensions Fund, and also Federal Treasury and State Treasury records.

In 1942, the Japanese governor of Selangor at Kuala Lumpur sent a team of officers twice to Singapore, then renamed *Syonan*, to recover official records of the former regime which had been removed from Kuala Lumpur, considering their continuing importance as administrative tools for the Japanese military government. During the first visit to Singapore in October 1942, the team surveyed the old Treasury Building where all the official records evacuated from Kuala Lumpur were stored, and learned that the building had been cleared in order to house the Syonan Military Police about a month before, when "the records, account books, stationery, typewriters, etc., were sold to a Chinese for $300/— who removed them in 30 or 40 lorries to various places for storage or disposal." The team tried to trace the Chinese to whom records had been sold, without success.[21]

RECORDS AND ARCHIVES IN MALAYA UNDER THE JAPANESE OCCUPATION

(1) Policy of the Japanese Military Government Concerning Records and Archives.

The fundamental policy of the Imperial Japanese Government in occupying Southeast Asia is stated in the *General Plan of Administration of the Occupied Territories in the Southern Area*, prepared on 10 November 1941. It stresses the importance of utilizing the "remaining government organs of the former regime" and of respecting the "existing organizations and ethnic customs."[22] The Japanese 25th Army, in charge of the military government for Malaya and Singapore, on the whole following this policy, made as much use as possible of existing organizations inherited from the British regime, especially those of local administration. Thus, it can naturally be assumed that the official records of the former local governments were not always neglected by the Japanese, but often maintained and even systematically utilized as one of the necessary tools of the military administration.

---

21 Sel.Kan (Selangor Syuseityo Kanbo) 106/02, National Archives of Malaysia.

22 Institute of Defence, The Defence Agency of Japan, ed., *Nanpo no Gunsei (Military Administration in Southern Area)* (Tokyo: Cho-un Shinbunsha, 1985).

Because of the lack of records of the Japanese military government in Malaya, it is difficult to clarify how the Japanese treated local records, including those of former government agencies. There exist, however, some indirect sources such as the following interrogation report of Japanese officials after the end of the war, which refer to the treatment of records during the Japanese occupation.[23]

TRANSLATION REPORT NO.66: ANSWER TO 34 CORPS
QUESTIONNAIRE PART II, QUESTION NO. 57

57(a) (1) Reports, records and building plans received from the P.W.D. in SINGAPORE were returned to the SINGAPORE Municipal Government when part of the Military Administration moved to KUALA KANGSAR, PERAK State in Feb. 44. (omitted)

57(b) Survey Office records:
Records are kept at the SELANGOR State, Survey Office.

57(d) Any documents left in the courts and prisons at the time of the inception of the Military Judicial Administration were kept in the Military Administration Courts, the Public Procurator's Office and the various prisons.

57(e) (omitted)
The Japanese Army submits the following report concerning the management and disposal of the British Government's records, documents, tools, machines, etc.

57(e) Equipment in medical laboratories:
Malay Institute for Medical Research:
1. All records and documents are kept in the Institute for Medical Research (KUALA LUMPUR)
2. Number of tools and machines (omitted)
3. Buildings (omitted)

57(e) (ref. Telecommunication)
1. On the Japanese occupation of MALAYA, the military utilized to the utmost all records and documents with the intention of managing firms on the same lines. All these records and documents, however, have been burnt by the Japanese, in the course of the past three and a half years.

---

23 "Translation of interrogation of Japanese government officials in connection with the Japanese Govt. Administration of Malaya for the period 1942–1945." Sel.CA250/45(66), National Archives of Malaysia.

To sum up, no evidence has been found so far that the Japanese military administration of Malaya took any active and effective measure to protect records of the former regime from destruction and dispersal, in spite of their basic policy to utilize those records for their own. Under the circumstances, most of the records and archives were ultimately destined to be lost, intentionally or accidentally, like the records of the Federated Malay States and Selangor government, as well as the telecommunication records mentioned above.

(2) Influence of the Japanese Occupation on the Preservation of Records and Archives.

The most useful sources of information found so far on the influence of the Japanese occupation on archives are within the records of investigations undertaken by the British military administration (BMA) of Malaya immediately after the war.

After the Japanese surrender on 15 August 1945, the BMA Malaya carried out a series of investigations into the influence of the Japanese occupation on various matters in order to facilitate the reconstruction of British Malaya. Those included, for example, an investigation into the damage to cultural properties undertaken by the Monuments, Fine Arts and Archives Section (MFAA) of the BMA, an investigation of problems concerning the land system and land records, as well as an investigation of marriage, birth, and death records. Here, the latter two cases are introduced briefly.

(a) The Investigation into Land Records.

On 8 December 1945, the Land, Mines and Survey Department of the BMA distributed among all states and districts a questionnaire concerning problems of land arising out of the Japanese occupation. It contained a question on land records, namely, "Are all your land records intact? If not, please give full details of loss or destruction of any such records."[24] Some districts answered this question very briefly that all land records were intact, but a detailed answer such as the one below,

---

24 S.S.Treng./384/45(1), National Archives of Malaysia.

an extract from the answer of Kuala Selangor District, State of Selangor, seems to have been more common.

> Many of the land records are not intact. They were burnt when the district office building was set on fire prior to the Japanese occupation by the British civil authorities just before they evacuated. The Land Office strong room was fortunately not affected by the fire, but with the exception of the Mukim registers, all other files of documents, books, minutes papers, and so forth in the strong room were removed by unknown Chinese who forcibly broke it open. The removed documents were later seen being used as wrappers.
>
> The following records were burnt along with the district office building and also removed from the strong room during January 1942.
>
> > (a) Files of transfers, charges, discharges of charges, caveats, transmissions, miscellaneous documents, leases, powers of attorney, declarations, declarations of trust, assignments and applications for state land.
> > (b) Registers of T.O.Ls.,[25] distribution suits, etc.
> > (c) Rent rolls, drainage rolls and water rate assessment rolls.
> > (d) All minutes and papers pertaining to land.
> > (e) All varieties of printed forms.
>
> The following records which were in the strong room were intact and have been made use of during the Japanese occupation.
>
> > (a) Mukim registers.
> > (b) Index of titles and rolls of approved applications.
>
> A new set of books for the collection of land revenue was compiled for use during the Japanese occupation and these too were partly destroyed by the Japanese and partly by some Chinese. The destruction of the records by the Chinese was uncontrollable. The following records exist at present in the Land Office.
>
> > (a) Mukim registers, index of titles, roll of approved applications.
> > (b) Temporary occupation licence registers.[26]

As shown in this answer, direct causes of the loss of land records were various, though the principal responsibility must be placed on the Japanese.

---

25 T.O.L. stands for Tenant of Lots, presumably.
26 BMA436/45(19A), National Archives of Malaysia.

(b) The Investigation into Marriage, Birth and Death Records.

In April 1942, the Japanese military administration of Malaya introduced a new family registration system, modeled on similar systems traditional in Japan. In October 1943, they introduced another system called *Tonari Gumi* or neighbourhood association; this too was created after the organization of the same name in wartime Japan.[27] Both systems, intending to establish strict control of the Malayan population, must have brought about change or even destroyed the previous registry systems under the British regime, as they did in Hong Kong. This subject has not been studied deeply, but the investigation done by the BMA in September 1945 can be a starting point to study how marriage, birth, and death records of the British period were treated during the Japanese occupation. Table 2 is based on reports submitted by each state answering the instruction from the BMA Headquarters of 5 September 1945.[28] In the table, "Region" means a geographical division of the Malayan peninsula and of Singapore which the BMA introduced for administrative purposes. Some birth and death records are omitted for space reasons.

What we can see from this table is the diversity of the fate of marriage records during the Japanese occupation. There are only a few districts in which all marriage records were reported to be intact and kept up-to-date even during the occupation, while many others reported that records had been destroyed by the Japanese during the war period. It is not easy therefore to discover from this table a general overview of Japanese occupation policy and methods concerning the treatment of records and archives inherited from the former regime. It is important to dig up more detailed sources relating to each case shown here and to undertake further studies both from a historical and from an archival point of view.

---

27 Paul H. Kratoska, *The Japanese Occupation of Malaya: A Social and Economic History* (St. Leonards, Australia: Allen & Unwin, 1988), 79.

28 "Legal: Births, Marriages and Deaths—register for." BMA/DEPT/17/22, National Archives of Malaysia.

Conclusion

Tracing the fate of archives in wartime reveals how war damages people's memory, both because it causes accidental losses and because there are deliberate destructions. Tracing the fate of archives in wartime is at one and the same time a first step toward recovering and sharing memory among people across the boundaries of the states and nations concerned.

Repeated friction between Japan and other Asian countries concerning responsibility and compensation for wartime damage brings to light the serious loss of common historical memory between the two parties. This friction has always been caused by some Japanese politicians and scholars who are inclined to deny or distort the facts of Japan's war crimes. They often take advantage of the lack of wartime records or even find reasons in the nonexistence of records. Thus, it seems that tracing the fate of archives in wartime is fighting against the distortion of history.

Last but not least, studies of this kind are better undertaken with international collaboration. The comparative study of archival history in wartime Europe and Asia should be one of the most useful and important topics. Further opportunities for international exchange of studies are expected.

TABLE 1.

Effect of the Japanese Invasion on the Malayan Survey Records

Branch/Types of Records	Disposition of records
TRIGONOMETRICAL BRANCH	
(Kuala Lumpur) original field books sketches plans computations and compiled data	(1) TRIGONOMETRICAL DATA Photographed copies were safely dispersed, one with the Survey of India (Dehra Dun) and another in Australia. (2) FIELD BOOKS, PLANS, COMPUTATIONS Left in the strong Room of the Survey Office in Java Street.
TOPOGRAPHICAL BRANCH	
(Kuala Lumpur) original field books field sheets tracing and computations	(1) FIELD BOOKS Left in the Revenue Survey Office, Kuala Lumpur, because of minor importance. (2) ASSEMBLIES AND FAIR DRAWINGS Sent to Melbourne safely.
REVENUE SURVEY BRANCH	
(Each State) original field books certified plans lot registers computations standard sheets lithographs and compilations	KEDAH A few field books and plans were brought to Kuala Lumpur. The bulk remained in the Survey Office strong room in Kulim together with standard sheets because the evacuation was so hasty. They must have been lost unless the strong room contents were retained intact by the Japanese. PERAK Most of the records in the Taiping office were transferred to Batu Gajah and then Kuala Lumpur. The position is much the same as in Kedah. PENANG Position obscure. All records believed left in the strong room of the Survey Office. PANANG, KELANTAN AND TRENGGANU All records left behind. SELANGOR AND NEGRI SEMBILAN All field books and lot registers remained in the Revenue Survey Office strong room Kuala Lumpur. All plans and standard sheets were transferred to Singapore and left in the Survey Office strong room in the Fullerton Building. MALACCA Position obscure, but standard sheets believed to be in the Singapore Office. JOHORE Standard sheets are now in Melbourne. SINGAPORE All records were left in the Survey Office strong room.

(continued)

TABLE 1 CONTINUED

MAP PRODUCTION BRANCH	

(Kuala Lumpur)
  original drawings (fairsheets)
  assemblies
  proofs
  glass negatives and zinc plates
	(1) BLACK PULLS OF ALL MAPS
	   Sent to the Survey of India for safe custody from August 1940 onward before the Japanese invasion.
	(2) ORIGINAL DRAWINGS OF MALAYAN MAPS AND MAPS OF ADJOINING TERRITORIES
	   All removed to Singapore, and most were later transferred to Melbourne.
	(3) GLASS NEGATIVES
	   Brought as many as possible to Australia.
	(4) ZINC PLATES
	   Packed in railway trucks for transfer to Singapore but destroyed by bombing.
	(5) IMPORTANT MINUTE PAPER
	   Transferred to Singapore.
	(6) PRINTED MILITARY MAP, PRINTING GLASS NEGATIVES, ETC.
	   All burnt or broken before the Head Office was finally abandoned.

TABLE 2.

State of Marriage Records in Malaya of *1945*, after the War

REGION STATE	Marriage Records		
District / Department	HINDU	CHRISTIAN	MOSLEM
REGION 1			
Perlis, Kedah, and Kroh	Complete and intact as regards Alor Star.	Complete up to October 1941. No registration during Japanese regime.	Alor Star available. Registers kept at the District Shara'iah Courts at Langkwai, Yen, Kuala Muda, Kulim, and Bandar Bharu are intact. Some of the registers kept at the Shara'iah Courts at Jitra, Baling were lost during the war.
REGION 2			
Penang, Province Wellesley	Lost.	Records kept in Singapore.	Not intact before and during Japanese occupation.

(continued)

TABLE 2 CONTINUED

REGION 3			
Perak		No registers before December 1941 are available.	
Batang Padang District	All relevant books are intact.		All records intact and up-to-date.
Kuala Kangsar District	Register of Marriages and counterfoil receipt books are kept with the local Registrar. Registrar's Note Book and files of past Marriages Declaration book had been looted.		All records intact up to Japanese occupation and were kept up-to-date during occupation.
Krian District	Register of Marriages and the Marriage Certificate books are both intact.		All records intact and kept up-to-date but some old records are moth eaten.
Larut, Matang, and Selama District	Note Books, Declaration for Registration for Marriages, Register of Marriages (from 1925) and Certificate books (from 1927) are available.		All records are intact up to Japanese occupation and records kept up-to-date during occupation.
Dindings District	Register of Marriages, Extracts from Register of Marriages, Declaration for Registration of Marriage, and Register's Note Book are available. No records were kept during the Japanese occupation.		Records were destroyed by fire when the Panghulu's Court and Kathi's Office were burnt down by Japanese during the Japanese surrender.

(continued)

TABLE 2 CONTINUED

Upper Perak District	3 counterfoil books of extracts from the Register of Marriages are available but no register is available.		All records intact up to the Japanese occupation and were kept up-to-date during occupation.
Kinta District	Registers available.	Ipoh Subdistrict There are 4 Registers. All the records were intact up to Japanese occupation but in May 1945 the Kathi's Office was burgled and all records were lost. Batu Gajah Subdistrict Records in the Kathi's Court were destroyed by the Japanese when their troops occupied the building. Records of Marriage were kept up-to-date during the Japanese occupation. Kampar Subdistrict All records are intact and were brought up-to-date during the occupation. Parit Subdistrict Four books of Marriage Certificates and two books of Divorce Certificates were lost at the time of the Japanese occupation. Records were intact up to time of the Japanese occupation and were kept up-to-date during Japanese occupation.	
Lower Perak District	2 complete sets of the Register of Registration of Marriages are in possession.	None	All records intact up to and including the Japanese occupation, and recording of marriages is proceeding according to regulations.
Office of the Superior Court, Ipoh		No Registers prior to December 1941 are available as the Magistrate's Court Building was destroyed by fire.	

(continued)

TABLE 2 CONTINUED

Office of the Secretary to President		No Registers prior to December 1941 are available as they were destroyed by the Japanese forces when they occupied Taiping.	
REGION 4			
Selangor		Complete until April 1938.	
Klang District	Registers are intact.		Registers 1931–1943 available
Kuala Langat District	Registers are intact.		No books available.
Kuala Selangor District	Registers are intact. 18 books of Certificates of Marriage and 6 books of Certificates of Divorce issued during the Japanese occupation are available.		
Kathi, Kuala Lumpur	1 Receipt Book, 1 Marriage Certificate book, 2 Certificate of Divorce books, 1 Certificate of Marriage book, 1 Register of Divorce, 1 Register of Marriage, 1 Cash book.		
Ulu Langat District	All necessary forms of Hindu marriages are available	All Registers and Records of Christian Marriages since 20 April 1938 are complete. Registers previous to 20 April 1938 were in the custody of the Selangor Secretariat. Registers of Marriage under the Marriage Registration Enactment since 11 July 1912 are available.	Register of Divorce, Certificate of Divorce, Registers of Cases, and Cash Book are available.

(continued)

TABLE 2 CONTINUED

Ulu Selangor District	1 Register of Marriages.		1 Register of Marriages and 1 Register of Divorces (Japanese issue); 1 Register of Marriages and 1 Register of Divorces (British issue).
REGION 5			
Negri Sembilan	Records intact in Labour Office, Seremban, Port Dickson, Tampin, and Kuala Pilahbut, but not Jelebu. Not available; believed lost. Port Dickson District, Tampin, Kuala Pilah, except Jelebu, available.		
Malacca	(No information available)		
REGION 6			
Johore	All registers are intact with exception of a few outlying districts.		
REGION 7			
Kelantan	Partly available. All records with exception of the Marriage Notice Book were lost during the hostilities. During the Japanese occupation, no Christian marriages were registered. Registration under the Moslem Marriage & Divorce Enactment 1938 was continued during the Japanese occupation, and registers are intact and available.		
REGION 8			
Trengganu	A record of marriage is kept by the Chief Kazi. Records complete for last 15 years.		
REGION 9			
Pahang	Tamerloh and Kuantan District records lost. Nearly complete. Kuantan District records intact.		
REGION 10			
Singapore All records prior to 15 February 1942 are intact and available.			

2

WHISPERS IN THE ARCHIVES: FINDING THE VOICES OF THE COLONIZED IN THE RECORDS OF THE COLONIZER

Jeannette Allis Bastian

Introduction

In 1963, the British-Trinidadian author and Nobel prize-winner, V.S. Naipaul, in his early seminal work *The Middle Passage,* despairingly (and famously) lamented the dilemma of Caribbean history:

> How can the history of this West Indian futility be written? What tone shall the historian adopt? Shall he be as academic as Sir Alan Burns, protesting from time to time at some brutality, and setting West Indian brutality in the context of European brutality? Shall he, like Salvador de Madariaga, weigh one set of brutalities against another, and conclude that one has not been described in all its foulness and that this is unfair to Spain? Shall he, like the West Indian historians, who can only now begin to face their history, be icily detached and tell the story of the slave trade as if it were just another aspect of mercantilism? The history of the islands can never be satisfactorily told. Brutality is not the only difficulty. History is built around achievement and creation; and nothing was created in the West Indies.[1]

Portions of this essay were first published in *Owning Memory: How a Caribbean Community Lost Its Archives and Found Its History* (Westport, Conn.: Libraries Unlimited, 2003).

1 V. S. Naipaul, *The Middle Passage; Impressions of Five Societies—British, French and Dutch— in the West Indies and South America* (New York: Macmillan, 1963), 29.

At the time of writing Naipaul incurred the wrath of Caribbean academics who saw his despair as a negative reflection on the nationalistic hopes and aspirations of emerging Caribbean society. Since the 1960s, however, other Caribbean writers and historians have echoed Naipaul's hopelessness and resignation over the seeming "historylessness" of Caribbean peoples, people displaced from their native homelands to toil in colonies of European expansionism.

Another Nobelist, St. Lucian poet Derek Walcott, wryly observes that

> [W]hat is archival in the Caribbean, as the Caribbean writer knows, is what got lost in the annals of sugar cane burned every harvest like the library of Alexandria, what disappeared in spray in the wake of the slaves. A huge amnesia rather than a history.[2]

Haitian historian Michel-Rolph Trouillot, reflecting on the colonial history of Haiti, notes the silences in the creation of the sources (archives) themselves, the things left out, not deliberately but because at the time they seemed peripheral and not important to the central historical narrative that was taking place. He writes,

> [S]ilences are inherent in the creation of sources, the first moment of historical production. Unequal control over historical production obtains also in the second moment of historical production, the making of archives and documents.

As an example of the silences in the creation of sources, Trouillot refers to plantation records of births in which slave births were not recorded until it was seen that the child survived. He points out that the "silence" did not occur through negligence, nor through the wish to conceal anything, but rather "both births and deaths were actively silenced in the records for a combination of practical reasons inherent in the reporting itself."[3] Both writers see not a memory loss, but a historical hole where the history of the "other" never existed. Not a history forgotten, but one that was never recorded, therefore not remembered.

---

2   Derek Walcott, "A Frowsty Fragrance," *New York Review of Books*, June 15, 2000, 61.
3   Michel-Rolph Trouillot, *Silencing the Past: Power and the Production of History* (Boston: Beacon Press, 1995), 51.

These three writers are responding to the political and economic exploitation of the chain of islands formerly known as the Caribees, or the West Indies, explored by Columbus in the fifteenth century, "conquered" and claimed by various European powers in the seventeeth and eighteenth centuries. To make these colonies financially viable for plantation agriculture, a vast humanity was forcibly taken there from Africa and made to work as slaves. The descendants of these enslaved Africans form the majority population of the Caribbean today. This is the population that Naipaul, Walcott, and Trouillot see as "historyless," a people torn from their cultures, their language, and their humanity to toil on these islands within the alien constructs of colonial society.

This paper addresses one such island cluster and one such group of peoples in the Danish West Indies, today known as the u.s. Virgin Islands. The Danish West Indies, comprising the three major islands of St. Thomas, St. Croix, and St. John, were colonized by Denmark beginning in 1666 primarily for their economic potential as sugar plantations. While St. Thomas, due to its wide natural harbor and its geographical position at the top of the island chain, became a thriving commercial port; the plantations were only marginally successful despite the importation of thousands of Africans, primarily from the Guinea coast, as slave laborers. Following emancipation in 1848, the economy of the islands fell into decline, and in 1917, the Danish West Indies was purchased from Denmark by the United States and renamed the u.s. Virgin Islands. At the time of the 1917 transfer, the inhabitants, primarily of African descent, numbered approximately 25,000. Today, although the population of over 100,000 also includes a substantial percentage of second and third generation migrants from other Caribbean islands, Virgin Islanders remain the core majority.

Throughout the 250-year colonization of the islands, the Danish colonial bureaucracy kept meticulous records and when the Danes left the islands, they took most of these records with them and deposited them in the Danish National Archives in Copenhagen. Following the sale, the records created in the islands during the early part of the twentieth century, as well as those abandoned or overlooked by Denmark, were claimed by the National Archives of the United States. Except for property records and some court records, the only records found in the Virgin Islands today are contemporary ones dating from the mid-twentieth century. And so the marginalization of the Black population of the Danish West Indies, within colonial society and within its record-keeping, was continued by the removal of these records to the archives of the colonizing countries themselves. The Virgin Islands was left with no way to access its history, albeit a colonial one.

Is the amnesia described by Walcott so complete and absolute that the holes in the histories of whole communities of people are unrecoverable? Do the records created by the bureaucratic institutions of colonialism have any value to the colonized? Are there alternate ways in which these records can be interrogated to reveal the lives, the cultures, the feelings of those appropriated within them? How do the descendants of the enslaved, the descendents of that transported mass of silenced humanity, find the voices of their past, not the past as documented by the former planters, merchants, and colonial officials, but the past as experienced by their ancestors who created no official records themselves, but enter the record obliquely, as transactions perhaps, or as property.

In 1999 and 2000, I conducted a series of interviews with Virgin Islanders that sought to discover how they felt about this loss of their archives and whether they felt that this loss impacted the ability of the community to construct its memory. A major question was whether they saw these colonial records as part of their history at all, whether they felt this was a history that was worth reclaiming. During my interviews, it became clear not only that records did and could form one of the interweaving threads which, together with oral tradition, informed and expanded the sense of history and community memory in the u.s. Virgin Islands, but that the collective memory of a community draws from many sources. Although archives play a supporting though vital role particularly in the grounding of that memory, for post-colonial communities such as the Virgin Islands, archives seem to pose special problems that revolve around the contradictions inherent in the voicelessness of the majority segment of a society. With no input into the record-creating process, how can these communities reclaim their history? How can the voices of those who were silent be recovered? How can communities that were the victims of records, use these records to build reliable and positive constructs of their past?

Such communities may appear on the face of it not to be what we customarily think of as recordkeeping communities at all but only extreme examples of societies in which a small segment of the population produced records that controlled the lives of a disenfranchised majority. On the contrary, however, these communities share similarities with many of the silent segments of larger, more metropolitan societies who through class, caste, or some other man-made division seem voiceless and largely unknown but who nonetheless yearn for an identity and a history that they long to find. Archives can provide the keys to that quest if the searcher recognizes that records have both a text and a subtext, that records are both evidence and action, and that behind the record lies the trace.

Witnesses in Spite of Themselves

Both my interviews and my reading suggested ways in which records might be interrogated to reveal those silenced voices. In a 1980's longitudinal sociological study of the people of St. John, Danish anthropologist Karen Fog Olwig used Danish West Indian colonial records to try to understand this post-emancipation peasant society that left no written records of its own. Olwig theorized that archival records combined with other source materials, such as oral interviews with current inhabitants of St. John who still had memories of the Danish period, could produce reliable data on the local culture. She illustrated this by using census records, land registers, and administrative reports combined with interviews with St. Johnians to demonstrate the consolidation of land ownership and agriculture by an industrious peasantry following the 1848 emancipation. She showed that this legacy of landholding as a strong cultural value in St. John persists today. In this way, Olwig proved a viewpoint completely contrary to the hitherto accepted belief by Danish administrators that the people of St. John were a shiftless and unproductive peasant population.[4]

This method of historical analysis, first articulated by historian Marc Bloch in the 1930s, proposes two types of historical evidence,

4   Karen Fog Olwig, "'Witnesses in Spite of Themselves': Reconstructing Afro-Caribbean Culture in the Danish West Indian Archives," *The Scandinavian Economic History Review*, 32/2 (1984), 61-76.

"narrative sources" whose intention is to consciously inform readers, and "'the evidence of witnesses in spite of themselves,' sources never intended to be part of the historical record." Examples of such sources include administrative records, inscriptions, and material objects. Bloch suggests that when these sources are brought together and cross-examined against each other, they "contain implicit information about the society that produced them."[5] In this methodology, "primary sources are essentially 'results' or 'traces' or 'relics' or 'tracks' of histori-cal activity."[6] Olwig, attempting to understand the development of the culture of St. John over its 300-year history, sees this method of analy-sis as a way of countering existing historical narratives in which

> most of the descriptions of the slaves were written by planters, colo-nial officials, and visitors from Europe. These accounts are dis-torted by a misunderstanding of and negative attitudes toward people of African descent.[7]

She warns, however, that the records themselves may not contain explicit accounts of the lives of slaves or their families, and that the historian must know the questions to bring to the historical sources. She concludes that if the records themselves can be regarded as "unin-tentional witnesses of Afro-Caribbean life as it is reflected in encoun-ters between the colonial administration existing within a plantation society, the documents can yield a great deal of evidence."[8]

This view of how traces within the Danish West Indian archives can be used as a way of accessing the total society is also shared by con-temporary Virgin Islanders. During my interviews, Virgin Islands researchers and educators, when asked about the value of the Danish West Indian colonial records, identified that value in terms of finding the voices of their forebears within the subtext of official records. Virgin Islanders wanted to see and understand their history and their

---

5   Karen Fog Olwig, *Cultural Adaptation and Resistance on St. John* (Gainesville: University of Florida Press, 1987), 8.

6   Susan Grigg, "Archival Practice and the Foundations of Historical Method," *Journal of American History* (June 1991), 231.

7   Olwig, *Cultural Adaptation*, 8.

8   Olwig, *Cultural Adaptation*, 11.

society through the eyes and voices of their own people.[9] The archives offered one path to discovering those voices and constructing that view. A linguist from St. John discusses his concern with finding the authentic voices of the people in "settings that are informal, that are natural, that are vernacular." He offers an example of finding those voices in the court testimony of a Danish police court record.

> What does [the] lawyer say, how does [the] witness respond. To me that's getting pretty close to the voice that I want. And there are a lot of times you can see, not just when you hear a voice but you can hear the ticking of an intellect making sure he doesn't get entrapped by a slick lawyer, lawyers were slick then too. . . . that to me is interesting data . . . I see it as archival.

To this educator and linguist whose research has concentrated on tracing languages and reconstructing Dutch Creole as a path towards understanding his own culture, this type of access is the primary value of the records; "that's the only point that I'm interested in. . . . I want to get my ears as close as possible to that whisper of a people that were oppressed and have something to say."[10]

A historic preservationist on St. Thomas who has been actively working with the Danish National Archives to make their records more accessible to Virgin Islanders points out that chance remarks or observations in the colonial records often contain clues to the background and origin of the slave population.

> [T]here may be something that person said that may speak of African retention, or a White man's documentation of walking through a slave village and even if he had mispronounced the word, it might be close enough to give you a link to an ethnic group in West Africa.

---

9   Twenty-three people including community leaders, government officials, educators, historians, and four archivists were interviewed by the author between 1998 and 1999. Of these persons, 17 lived in the Virgin Islands and 11 were Virgin Islands natives or Virgin Islanders. All had engaged in historical or cultural research about the Virgin Islands at some time during their careers. Several had written doctoral dissertations, books, and articles, and a number were currently actively engaged in historical research. All twenty-three interview subjects had ties to the Virgin Islands. Two of the non-Virgin Islanders resident in the United States had lived in the Virgin Islands for several years and had strong Virgin Islands connections. Both archivists in Denmark worked with the Danish West Indian records at the Danish National Archives and personally knew many of the researchers from the Virgin Islands. Both had visited the Virgin Islands several times. Of the other two archivists, one was a Virgin Islander resident in the United States and one was an independent consultant resident in the Virgin Islands.

10   Gilbert A. Sprauve, interview by author, tape recording, St. Thomas, U.S. Virgin Islands, December 18, 1998.

He suggests that the danger both of translations and of the transcriptions of testimony is that a recorder may have left out things because he did not recognize them or think of them as important—and these maybe exactly those things that have cultural significance. He emphasizes that although the colonial records were produced by a Danish administration, for Virgin Islanders, "This history is linked to us, it's our history! It would not have been created if it were not for us!" This point of view is shared by many Virgin Islanders who, while acknowledging a legitimate Danish claim to the records, also feel that their claim is equally as strong. The historic preservationist explains why and why this ownership is so important when he says,

> the attitude has always been it is Danish, these are Danish archives, the Danish West Indies, and for some reason . . . we're not included in that picture, and we surely are, and whether it's through the records, the economic or financial records of a company who profited from sugar or slavery, or mercantile business, it's our story and we should have access to it, when we need to have access to it to even write our story or even just to understand, to have a complete picture . . . otherwise anyone could tell you anything they want.[11]

A similar point about the ownership of history is made by another St. Thomian, a political science educator and politician with strong pan-African interests, who notes that primary source material is vital for Virgin Islanders who essentially only have access to secondary sources written many years after the fact because the writing of history is so dependent on who is reading, interpreting, and selecting the records. He emphasizes that the interpretation of the records is at least as important as the records themselves as he says,

> We need more history from the point of view of the African slaves rather than the planters, it's too planter-focused and less plantation-worker focused. It depends on who's reading the records and the records selected. How will we know?[12]

---

11 Myron Jackson, interview by author, tape recording, St. Thomas, U.S. Virgin Islands, March 8, 1999.
12 Malik Sekou, interview by author, tape recording, St. Thomas, U.S. Virgin Islands, December 30, 1998.

From the viewpoint of Virgin Islanders, the administrative records of the colonized contain at least two potential paths to the "silent" history of the colonized. The first occurs within the nature of the records and the recordkeeping systems themselves and the information they impart both through their administrative functions and their content.[13] The second, more unconscious and accidental, relies on discovering the words or actions of the colonized, the "whispers" within the records, either through transcription of proceedings or testimony or through observations by the record creator. And while this latter path is of necessity mediated by a third party, it can yield valuable clues to the nature and character of a people and a society.

The effect of using administrative records as tools to reconstruct the "hidden" society of the Danish West Indies is well demonstrated in a 1989 essay written by Jamaican historian Neville Hall who used records to describe the life and career of a nineteenth-century St. Croix freedman, Apollo Miller. Miller first comes to Hall's attention through an 1831 registry listing of free coloured adult males that includes occupations. He is intrigued by Miller's listing as restaurateur, the only such one on the list. Hall explains,

> Apollo Miller was thus an unusual freedman if only by virtue of the fact that in 1831 he earned his livelihood in an area void of other freedmen but himself . . . with the exception of Apollo Miller the sale of spirituous liquor by retail was a white preserve.[14]

Drawing on his deep understanding of the nature and purpose of colonial records created in the Danish West Indies in the early nineteenth century, Hall uses the few records that actually mention Miller to trace the bare bones of Miller's life and gives flesh to these bones through well-reasoned speculation about his character and activities against the backdrop of a slave society. Miller's entrepreneurial activities not only as a restaurateur but also as a promoter of cockfights, purveyor of ice cream, and eventually innkeeper mark him out as unusual; however, although according to Hall, Miller was probably literate,

---

13 From an archival standpoint, an example of Schellenberg's "evidential value."
14 Neville A.T. Hall, "Apollo Miller, Freeman: His Life and Times," *Journal of Caribbean History* 23 (1989), 196.

aside from newspaper notices advertising various activities, he personally left no records. Through registries, property records, and ordinances, Hall weaves the recorded remnants of Miller's life into the fabric of pre-emancipation colonial life on St. Croix.

In this way Hall gives a voice as well as a form to a segment of the colonial society that had been voiceless and invisible, at the same time presenting a view of St. Croix society from the bottom up. Hall's choice of Apollo Miller as a subject rests not only on the fact that Miller was an unusual person and an example of determination and creativity overcoming adversity, but was undoubtedly influenced by the fact that Miller's many activities and interactions within the society increased the possibilities that there would be records about him to discover. At the same time, by selecting Miller's name from a list, Hall implies that there may be many such stories. By examining the subtext of the records, Hall brings a whole population to life. Certainly this interpretive use of records reinforces the concept of the meaningful record-creating presence of the Black population in developing the societal values of the Virgin Islands.

In similar fashion, recent doctoral research uses census records, tax rolls, and wills to trace the histories of two generations of six "free-colored" families living in St. Croix up to the time of Emancipation. None of these families left their own personal records, but the purpose of the study "was to formulate and recreate their every day living without the advantage of autobiographies, diaries, or personal firsthand writings by the subjects being investigated."[15] Here again, records become "witnesses" to a silent society, a community that is the subject of the records rather than their maker but one that is no less involved in their creation. From the viewpoint of the Virgin Islands, colonial records are intertwined with the growth and development of the Black society, and regardless of whose hand penned the records or the original administrative purpose for which they were created, "the records are," in the words of one Virgin Islander, "about us."

The recognition of other voices within the records has offered ways for researchers to trace the origins of and reconstruct the Creole

---

15 Elizabeth Rezende, "Cultural Identity of the Free Colored in Christiansted, St. Croix, Danish West Indies 1800–1848" (PhD diss., Union Institute, 1997), 4.

language used by the transplanted African society on St. Thomas and St. John. Researchers have found official records to be valuable sources for language study through both the transcriptions of words and the descriptions of their subjects and their subjects' origins. The data in tax rolls and census records, for example, has suggested that African languages underpinned the development of Negerhollands, or Dutch Creole, among the St. Thomas population. One such study concluded that, contrary to popular notions of the enslaved,

> The strength and resourcefulness of the substrate population, the demography of the St. Thomas community, and perhaps the occasional humanity of the slave-owning population enabled the speakers of Akan, Eve and Ga who were transported to the Danish West Indies in the last quarter of the 17th century to survive long enough to begin to learn the language of their captors. In their struggle for survival as individuals and as a people, these long-forgotten men, women, and children created the language linguists have called Negerhollands.[16]

Oral Tradition

Scrutinizing Danish West Indian records through the lens of historical analysis reveals the layers of evidence that records may unconsciously yield about a community. At the same time, the more layers of community that are revealed, the more blurred become many issues surrounding the records-creating process. On the one hand, these are bureaucratic records created by a colonial administration operating within a colonial society; on the other, they reflect a completely different though parallel colonized society that exists both within and apart from the official one, a society that while it can be studied within the context of the records also exists in an entirely oral way that is only hinted at in the records.

Oral tradition adds yet another strata to our efforts to hear the authentic voices of a captive and writerless people. The importance of

---

16 Robin Sabino, "Towards a Phonology of Negerhollands: An Analysis of Phonological Variation" (PhD diss., University of Pennsylvania, 1990), 46.

oral tradition was emphasized by Olwig as an essential element in verifying the claims of the records and suggesting how the records were to be interrogated. She writes that in spite of the discontinuity between the written record and the spoken discourse of these separate but codependent populations, and in spite of the fact that "the slaves themselves were, by the nature of the institution of slavery, virtually barred from writing down their experiences and feelings and their reactions toward the situation in which they had been placed within the plantation society,"[17] historians and folklorists have suggested ways in which the written evidence and the oral tradition collide. Not only are administrative records and inscriptions, as well as material objects and artifacts, all sources of evidence that may never have been intended as part of the historical record but which still reflect the voices of both populations, but folk tales and stories of events handed down through the tradition augment historical evidence.

A Virgin Islands folklorist also points to the discrepancy between written and oral folk traditions stressing that even though many of the folk tales are written down, there are nuances in the physical movements and performance of the storyteller that "make the full story come alive."[18] In her research on folk story performance in the Virgin Islands, she urges thinking about the Virgin Islands tradition of storytelling as "not just a collection of simple folkstories but . . . a process, a creative/aesthetic performance process, involving the storyteller, the folkstories, the participants, and the setting through which it is generated and carried out in the community."[19]

Songs which are often interspersed within the stories add to their physical aspects. She explains that "long ago, the stories were told to educate the children, to learn about the history and values of the islands . . . today, even if the stories are not serving the same purpose, the children love to hear them and enjoy them, but most importantly they learn about their history and culture through them."

---

17 Olwig, *Cultural Adaptation*, 8.

18 The author is indebted to Virgin Islands folklorist, musician, and educator Lois Hassell Habteyes for sharing her insights, experience, and knowledge during an interview on St. Thomas in March 1999.

19 Lois Hassel Habteyes, "Tell Me a Story About Long Time: A Study of the Folkstory Performance Tradition in the United States Virgin Islands" (PhD diss., University of Illinois at Urbana-Champaign, 1985), 2.

When asked whether folk tales carried messages beyond the actual stories, specifically whether they conveyed historical lessons, the folklorist refers to a popular tale called "A Boar Hog wid Gol' Teeth," a story about a fat and ugly white boar hog who disguises himself as a wealthy farmer and courts a young girl who will only marry a suitor with gold teeth. A small boy sees through the disguise and exposes it by playing a magic tune on his flute. The story makes fun of the class pretensions of the girl as well as of aspects of plantation life in which "a gentleman is a boarhog."[20] Within the folktale, there are many historical references that give some idea of the environment, how people lived, what they did, and what they thought of each other.

For important historical events, however, a song alone would often tell the story because, as the folklorist suggests, "folk stories took on a completely different aura and these songs, the events were so historic and so important that the people did not want to put them into a make-believe component." The mockery and humor that was integral to folktales in which animals often assumed human characteristics may have been an effective way to teach moral behavior but was not considered an appropriate way to celebrate heroes. Virgin Islands oral tradition is filled with such heroic, history-telling songs as, for example, the song of "Queen Mary," a popular favorite with musical groups and schoolchildren today, which celebrates the courageous and semi-mythical woman, Mary Thomas, who led the "Fireburn," the St. Croix Labor Revolt of 1878.

The Place of Provenance

If the whispers in the records indeed reverberate throughout the entire society, how does the archivist account for them? How does the archivist reconcile or adapt accepted archival practices that focus around a specified record creator with a more nuanced understanding of who the record creator actually is. How does the archivist heed geographer Kenneth Foote's warning of the dangers in "assuming that collective memory is invested in any single type of human institution, such

---

20 Habteyes, "Tell Me a Story," 46, 134.

as the archives" and that the collective, interdependent nature of institutional memory "implies that the cultural role of the archives is hard to isolate from the contributions of other institutions and traditions."[21] For archivists, an answer may lie in the principle of provenance.

Archival provenance is a fundamental concept describing "the organization or individual that created, accumulated, and/or maintained and used records in the conduct of business prior to their transfer to a records center."[22] It is a principle that has undergirded archival practice since the late nineteenth century and relates to the maintenance of records within the environment in which they were created. Provenance is primarily concerned with identifying and safeguarding context. While there are numerous discussions and perspectives within the archival literature about the principle of provenance and its origins,[23] archivists would generally agree that provenance refers to the maintenance of records by their creator or source and that records from different creators must not be intermingled.

In the nineteenth century, archivists began to move away from a subject arrangement of archival materials to a contextual one, an arrangement based on the idea that archival documents were not discrete items but could be best understood in context of their creation and in relationship to other documents from the same source. Today, the principle of provenance has retained its essential core and remains the key organizational base of archival arrangement. If it has undergone any modification it has been in the direction of expanding and widening the definition of context.

Provenance may be expressed through individual creators, such as in a collection of personal papers, or through collective creators, as in

---

21 Kenneth E. Foote, "To Remember and Forget: Archives, Memory and Culture," *American Archivist* 53 (Summer, 1990): 380. In a subsequent book, *Shadowed Ground; America's Landscapes of Violence and Tragedy* (Austin, Tex.: University of Texas Press, 1997), Foote builds on the concept of collective memory as an aggregate of a variety of types of documentation when he explores the role of monuments, memorials, buildings, and the landscape itself in interpreting and constructing memories of tragic events.

22 The definition continues by stating that the principle of provenance also includes "the principle that records/archives of the same Provenance must not be intermingled with those of any other Provenance." Lewis J. Bellardo and Lynn Lady Bellardo, comps., *A Glossary for Archivists, Manuscript Curators, and Records Managers* (Chicago: Society of American Archivists, 1992), 27.

23 See for example the collection of essays in *The Principle of Provenance*, First Stockholm Conference on Archival Theory and the Principle of Provenance, 2–3 September 1993 (Sweden: Swedish National Archives, 1993); and Tom Nesmith, ed., *Canadian Archival Studies and the Rediscovery of Provenance* (Metuchen, N.J.: Scarecrow Press, 1993).

the papers of a family. The creator may also be an entity, such as an institution or government body which includes many creators working within one overarching context. But the context of creation is not limited to a person or institution. Provenance may likewise coalesce around an event or even a location.[24] As the complexity of modern records creation has put an ever-increasing burden on the principle of provenance, provenance itself has expanded to embrace both the specific processes of records production and the wider society within which the record was created. Canadian archivist Hugh Taylor noted in 1970 that

> archivists ought to focus more on why and how people have created documentation, rather than on their subject content. Archivists should extend their understanding of the provenance of documentation deeply in to the societal origins of human communication throughout history.[25]

Archivist Terry Cook envisions a "conceptual provenance," a provenance that "exists in the mind of the beholder." In his writings on appraisal, he suggests that in examining records and records structures,

> archivists would look at the reasons for and the nature of communication between citizen and state . . . this intellectual link to the creator thus shifts the central importance of provenance from the physical origin of the records in their creator's office to their original conceptual purpose in that same office.[26]

The principle of provenance dictates that, from an archival view, the records created by the Danish government through its colonial offices rightly belong within the context of those offices and that government. It is this rationale—governments as the creators of the records

---

24 In a 1980 report, for example, the consultative group on Canadian archives suggested adding to the principle of provenance. We would like to add to this principle a new corollary to the effect that any particular set of records should remain, as far as possible, in the locale or milieu in which it was generated. This may be called the extension of the principle of provenance (which aims at keeping the context of records intact) to a principle of territoriality (which envisages the locale or milieu of records as part of their context). Allied to the principle of provenance is the principle of unbroken custody.

25 Tom Nesmith, ed., *Canadian Archival Studies and the Rediscovery of Provenance* (Methuen, N.J.: Society of American Archivists, Association of Canadian Archivists and Scarecrow Press, 1993), 17.

26 Terry Cook, "Mind Over Matter: Towards a New Theory of Archival Appraisal," in *The Archival Imagination: Essays in Honour of Hugh Taylor,* ed. Barbara L. Craig (Ottawa: Association of Canadian Archivists, 1992).

and therefore the owners of the records—that gave Denmark official custody of the Danish West Indian records and the United States custody of the Virgin Islands records created after 1917. At the same time, too narrow a construction of ownership and of provenance runs the risk of not sufficiently recognizing those with equally valid, though less authoritative claims. Seen from the point of view of Cook's "conceptual provenance," however, the principle of provenance suggests an archival framework for understanding a records situation in which the native inhabitants of the Islands assume a more prominent role in both the context-creating and the record-creating process and thus might also lay a claim to at least a partial ownership of the records.

The demographics of the Danish West Indies since its early colonization indicate the predominance of enslaved Africans in the population. This majority group only increased, and in fact became the primary reason for the continued existence of the colony. Following emancipation in 1848, they formed the majority of its free citizenry. By 1917, the descendants of African slaves, creolized into native Virgin Islanders, were still the overwhelmingly majority population of the Danish West Indies/United States Virgin Islands as they had been all along. From an examination of the structure of the colonial offices as well as the records that were created, it is clear that the enslaved African population was involved in the record-creating process from the beginning. Whether as plantation statistics, transactions at the auction block, objects of punishment, manumission, property transfers, or wills, testifiers in court proceedings or on police blotters, subjects of administrative edicts or council debates, this population was a primary subject of record-creating functions and an integral part of the record-creating process.

As free citizens, the working class and the rising Black middle class continued to be a major subject of records creation. Looking at the Danish West Indian society in retrospect, it could be argued that from the point of view of context, the majority of the colonial records created in the Danish West Indies concerned the non-Danish, non-record-creating inhabitants and that the colonized society itself was the context.

Although the records were physically created by Danish clerks and other Danish officials during the daily functioning of their offices, the functions of those offices, as in any administrative office, indirectly reflected the transactions and serviced the needs of the whole society.

In this respect, therefore, the records were created by and within the entire colonial milieu. It could also be argued therefore that the entire colonial society within the specific locale of the Danish West Indian islands, rather than the colonial offices in Denmark, constitutes the larger context of the records. It could also be argued that in terms of ownership, the chain of custody does not necessarily begin with a central colonial office in Copenhagen, but possibly with a small records-creating function in St. Thomas, St. Croix, or St. John.

Extending the provenance of the creator to embrace the entire society presents, as Cook suggests, an entirely different view of the relationships between the community and its records, one that extends Marc Bloch's methodology so that the voiceless population is not the silent witness but a full partner in the record-creating process. In this societal construct, all layers of society are participants in the record-making process, and the entire community becomes the larger provenance of the records. Seen from this view, where the community consists both of records creators and records subject, all segments of the society have equal value.

Conclusion: "Go Back and Fetch It"

In conclusion, we turn to African tradition that suggests a way of encountering records that will allow us to embrace the entire process of records creation within a society, both the overt record and the whispers within it. "Sankofa" is a proverb from the Akan people of West Africa expressed in the Akan language as "se wo were fi na wosan kofa a yenki." Literally translated, it means "it is not taboo to go back and fetch what you forgot," or, in the shorter adaptation, "go back and fetch it." Sankofa teaches that people must go back to their roots in order to move forward, and that whatever they have "lost, forgotten, forgone or been stripped of can be reclaimed, revived, preserved and perpetuated." Visually and symbolically "Sankofa" is expressed as a mythic bird that flies forward while looking backward with an egg (symbolizing the future) in its mouth, or as a heart-like symbol.[27]

---

27 Definition of Sankofa is taken from http://www.mku95.com/sankofa.phtml, the web page of the Malika Kambe Umfazi Sorority, Inc. (October 28, 2002).

The concept of Sankofa was the inspiration for both the title and the content of a folklife conference held in the Virgin Islands in 1991.[28] Inspired by the Virgin Islands Folklife Festival sponsored by the Smithsonian Institution and held on the Mall in Washington, D.C., the previous year, panels and papers used many of the themes of the festival, such as crafts, folkways, and oral and music tradition to focus on defining the values of the past while at the same time acknowledging the necessity of having control of the past in order to shape the present. In its emphasis on the importance of remembering, possessing, and transforming culture and tradition, the dictum to "go back and fetch it" offers a particularly apt and fitting way to explore the nature of history in this Caribbean community where oral traditions are more accessible than the written word for above all, Sankofa reassures us that the past is there waiting to be discovered.

Our task is to reach back and bring it forward to be used in the present. The values inherent in understanding ourselves through our past speaks to the values of the collective memories that the community has garnered and carefully nurtured through the years. "Collective memory was stored in me," says a Virgin Islander talking about the influences that his grandmother and parents had on his understanding of his culture and society. Similarly, other Virgin Islanders reaffirm the importance of an oral memory handed down through family and through generations of "culture-bearers," those persons in the society such as folktale tellers and musicians who cultivate the oral traditions and teach them to the community.[29]

That Sankofa may not refer to oral tradition alone but may also symbolize a point of view about accessing the written past is suggested by the use of the Sankofa bird as a logo by the State Black Archives Research Center and Museum at the University of Alabama. For this archives, Sankofa "signifies the role that this repository plays in providing a dialogue between the present and the past."[30] How that dia-

---

28 The conference was also motivated to continue a dialogue about the value of tradition which had been inspired by a Virgin Islands Folklife Festival sponsored by the Smithsonian Institution held on the Washington Mall the previous year.

29 The Folklife Festival on the Mall concentrated on demonstrating the crafts, skills, and folkways of the Virgin Islands through its "culture-bearers."

30 Taken from the web page of the Alabama University State Black Archives Research Center and Museum, http//:archivemuseumcenter.mus.al.us (accessed October 3, 2002).

logue can occur in a former colonial society, how the descendents of enslaved peoples can "go back and fetch" their history from an archives filled with the records of former masters, offers challenges that speak to the very meaning and nature of the bonds between records and the communities that create them. Like the Sankofa bird, perhaps our mission as archivists is to see the entire past in all its layers and silences as retrievable for the present.

3

TITLE COMPANY V. COUNTY RECORDER: A CASE STUDY IN OPEN RECORDS LITIGATION, 1874–1918

Dwayne Cox

Prior to the mid-1870s, state appellate courts reported relatively few open records cases. During the 44 years between 1874 and 1918, however, the amount of litigation in this area increased dramatically. Several factors contributed to this trend, including a belief that open access to public records could reduce electoral fraud, discourage the misuse of public funds, and make government officials more accountable. This increase in litigation also represented an attack on the English common law tradition that restricted access to public records to those with a direct and tangible interest in the information, such as parties to a lawsuit. By the early twentieth century, state courts had established the notion that citizenship itself provided a sufficient justification for access to public records, a change that revolutionized legal thought on this subject.[1]

Interestingly enough, abstractors and insurers of real estate titles, whose interests were commercial, led the assault on the common law

An earlier version of this article appeared in *American Archivist* 67 (Spring/Summer 2004), 46–57.

1   42 Am. Dig. Cent. Ed. 698; Simon Greenleaf, *Treatise on the Law of Evidence* (Boston: Little, Brown, 1854), 329–30; "Inspection of Records," *American and English Encyclopedia of Law* (Northport, N.Y.: Edward Thompson, 1896–1905), 24: 182–186.

tradition that imposed the strict standard of direct and tangible inter-est. The cases initiated by these businessmen far outnumbered those concerning the misuse of public funds and honest elections, the next closest categories of cases. Title abstractors did more than any other single group to establish the assumption that public records are the public's business. Their efforts had an important impact on the profes-sional lives of subsequent generations of public records custodians, including archivists.

Traditionally, attorneys had verified chain of title for individual real estate transactions. During the late nineteenth century, however, rural-to-urban migration, the growth of cities, and the declining num-ber of Americans engaged in agriculture caused a dramatic increase in the buying, selling, and subdivision of real estate. Americans increas-ingly viewed land as a commodity rather than patrimony. Meanwhile, the methods that local governments employed to record and retrieve deeds, liens, and other information used to document chain of title had not kept pace with the fast-growing demand. Abstractors and insurers of real estate titles offered a solution to this problem.[2]

Typically, title companies sent employees to the offices of local government officials to duplicate records in mass, not for individual transactions, but in anticipation of future sales. Many firms prospered by this device, but they encountered opposition from the custodians of public records. County recorders of deeds, for example, voiced con-cerns not unlike those that modern archivists might raise: the hordes of abstract men who threatened to invade their offices would disrupt established procedures, interfere with the rights of others, and damage the materials in their custody. Furthermore, many local government officials depended on the fees they generated through title searches and duplication of records to pay salaries and office expenses. Title companies threatened this source of income, so the stage was set for litigation. The 1880s and 1890s brought a flurry of title company cases, which began to decline following the turn of the century and slowed to

---

2   Lawrence M. Friedman, *A History of American Law*, 2d ed. (New York: Simon & Schuster, 1985), 433–435; Michael J. Petrick, "Inspection of Public Records in the States: The Law and the News Media" (PhD diss., University of Wisconsin, 1970), 170–173; Harold L. Cross, *The People's Right to Know: Legal Access to Public Records and Proceedings* (New York: Columbia University Press, 1953), 28–29.

a trickle following World War I. By then, the battle over access to public records had been won.[3]

In 1874, the Georgia Supreme Court issued its decision in *Buck v. Collins,* the grandfather of title company cases, which typified a strict interpretation of the common law concept regarding access to public records. The dispute involved a title abstractor who wanted to station his employees in the Fulton County Registrar of Deeds Office, where they would remain for the duration of the time necessary to duplicate all county records relative to real estate. The plaintiff intended to create a set of title abstracts, planned to perform his search without the registrar's aid, and refused to pay the statutory search fee. The court ruled that the state created and maintained deeds out of necessity, but this did not imply the right to flaunt "private matters before public gaze." Furthermore, the registrar had a responsibility for the integrity of information in his custody. A full-time title abstractor may not have required assistance, but he did require supervision, which justified the fee. The Georgia Supreme Court subsequently upheld this decision in another Fulton County case, even though the plaintiff argued that the prohibitive cost would destroy the title abstract business in that state.[4]

Between 1877 and 1900, the New Jersey appellate courts issued a series of opinions regarding payment of statutory search fees. In the first instance, Harvey M. Lum's attorney sought to search a particular title without payment of the fee. The New Jersey Court of Errors and Appeals concluded that county clerks lacked the sole authority to conduct title searches and could not charge fees for those who undertook the work themselves. Later, the West Jersey Title & Guarantee Company asked for access to all land records in the custody of Robert L. Barber, the Camden County Clerk, in order to create a set of title abstracts. Based on the authority of the Lum case, the New Jersey Chancery Court ruled in favor of the company, but Barber appealed to the state supreme court, which reversed the decision. The Lum case had concerned an individual attorney searching a particular title, but

---

3 W.B. Martindale, *The Right to Inspect Public Records,* 22 Central Law Review 341 (April 1886); Ardemus Stewart, *The Right to Examine Public Records,* 37 Central Law Review 395 (July 1893); *Public Records, Inspection, Abstractor of Titles,* 35 American Law Register 721 (November 1896).

4 *Buck v. Collins,* 21 American Reports 236 (Ga. 1874); *Land-Title Warranty & Safety-Deposit Company v. Tanner,* 27 S.E. 727 (Ga. 1896).

West Jersey Title wanted to occupy the clerk's office, duplicate all the records, and establish a rival business—an entirely different situation.[5]

In 1900 the New Jersey Supreme Court ruled in *Fidelity Trust Company v. Clerk of the Supreme Court.* The facts were that the clerk kept two sets of indices to real estate judgments. One was volume by volume, as required by law, and the other cumulative and not required by law. When the clerk first undertook the cumulative index, he was not a salaried official, but had been compensated through fees, including those generated by searches of the cumulative index. In 1896, however, the clerk went on salary. Now, Fidelity Trust sought free access to the cumulative index, the clerk denied the request, and the company asked the supreme court for relief. In its decision, the court noted that the salaried clerk served two publics. The smaller one included Fidelity Trust and had an immediate interest in access to records in his custody; the larger taxpaying public had an interest in the revenue generated by the clerk's office; and the two were mutually exclusive. The court concluded that the larger interest of the taxpaying public governed the case. Fidelity Trust was denied free access to the cumulative index.[6]

In addition to the loss of revenue, local government officials also feared that title companies would disrupt others' access to the records in their custody. In 1883, for example, a representative of the New York Title Company approached Samuel Richards, the registrar for Kings County, New York, who had custody of approximately four thousand large books that contained records of real estate transactions. New York Title asked to station from twelve to twenty-five employees in the registrar's office in order to compile abstract books from these records. Richards responded that more than three Title Company employees would disrupt access by the general public and the court upheld his argument. The following year, the New York Supreme Court ruled that the Title Guarantee and Trust Company could consult records in the custody of the registrar of deeds for the city and county of New York, but noted that the local official had a duty to prevent the company from interfering with the rights of others.[7]

---

5   *Lum v. McCarty,* 10 Vroom 287 (N.J. 1877); *West Jersey Title v. Barber,* 24 A. 381 (N.J. 1892); *Barber v. West Jersey Title,* 32 A. 222 (N.J. 1895).

6   *Fidelity Trust Company v. Clerk of the Supreme Court,* 47 A. 451 (N.J. 1900).

7   *People v. Richards,* 1 N.E. 258 (N.Y. 1885); *People v. Reilly,* 38 Hun 429 (N.Y. 1886).

The Michigan Supreme Court devoted as much attention to title company litigation as any tribunal in the land. In 1880 that body heard the case of a title abstract company based in Jackson that sought access to records housed in the county registrar of deeds office. The registrar considered the proposal, but denied the company's request. Eventually, the case came before the Michigan Supreme Court, where the company claimed both a common law and a statutory right to inspect the records. The court disagreed. The common law limited this right to specific documents in which the applicant had a direct and tangible interest. This was not the case with a title company, which sought to duplicate large volumes of material for speculative purposes. The logical conclusion of complying with such a request could overwhelm public officials with similar demands. Furthermore, the statutory language provided no clear answer. Given the potential for disrupting public business, the court refused to accept the implication of the title company's right to inspect the records.[8]

Three years later, the Michigan Supreme Court heard arguments from the Delaware-based Diamond Match Company, which owned thirty thousand acres of pineland in Ontonagon County. Because of problems with conflicting titles, the company sought to occupy space in the county registrar's office in order to construct a complete abstract of all relevant documents housed there. The registrar of deeds denied the request, and the company sought a writ of *mandamus,* which would compel compliance. The Michigan Supreme Court declined the petition of Diamond Match, which it deemed a private, out-of-state corporation relying on state comity to support its request.[9]

Following the Diamond Match Company case, the Michigan state legislature enacted a law that gave the public broader access to records created by state and local officials. In 1889 attorney and businessman Clarence M. Burton tested the statute when he sought to gather information regarding tax liens that the city of Detroit held on private property. Thomas P. Tuite, the city treasurer and custodian of the books where the city tax collector recorded this information, refused to comply with Burton's request. The case eventually reached

---

8 *Webber v. Townley,* 5 N.W. 971 (Mich. 1880).
9 *Diamond Match Company v. Powers,* 16 N.W. 314 (Mich. 1883).

the Michigan Supreme Court, which upheld the new statute. The court's opinion noted that the plaintiff's motives exercised no bearing on the case. Attorneys routinely consulted these records for private gain and title companies should enjoy the same right. Excluding those motivated by private gain left records open only to buyers, sellers, and holders of particular lots, or their unpaid representatives. Three years later, the court upheld this decision in ruling that "a tax-title sharp" enjoyed the same right as any citizen to examine public records.[10]

In 1893 and again in 1894, the Michigan Supreme Court qualified its decision in the Burton case by emphasizing the obligation of officials to impose reasonable regulations on access to public records. The first dispute involved Homer A. Day, who requested access to records in the custody of James A. Button, registrar of deeds for Genesee County, in order to create a set of title abstract books. Button objected on the grounds that Day monopolized the limited space available in the registrar's office, hindered performance of official duties, and delayed access to the records by the general public. The court ruled in Day's favor, but noted that the title man's right to access did not permit him to monopolize space in the registrar's office.[11]

The second case again involved Clarence M. Burton, this time against Henry M. Reynolds, the clerk of Wayne County, who charged title companies twenty-five dollars per month to offset the cost of hiring additional help for the volume of requests generated by these businesses. Burton sought use of the special service without payment of the fee. Again, he asked the Wayne County Circuit Court to compel compliance with his request. The court refused and Burton appealed to the Michigan Supreme Court. This time the court ruled in favor of the county official. Reynolds had the right to establish reasonable regulations, which could include the payment of a fee for special services.[12]

Colorado followed a pattern similar to Michigan's: initial denial of access, passage of a statute that loosened the constraints, and finally emphasis of the county official's duty to protect records through reasonable regulations. The state supreme court first addressed this issue

10 *Burton v. Tuite,* 44 N.W. 282 (Mich. 1889); *Aitcheson v. Huebner,* 51 N.W. 634 (Mich. 1892).
11 *Day v. Button,* 56 N.W. 3 (Mich. 1893).
12 *Burton v. Reynolds,* 60 N.W. 452 (Mich. 1894).

in 1884, when a title company sought long-term quarters in the Gunnison County Clerk's Office in order to abstract land records in the custody of that official. The company argued that all records in the clerk's office were open to full public inspection, but the court disagreed. The opinion noted that granting access to one company could lead to similar requests from others, the endless multiplication of which would impose unreasonable expenses upon the clerk's office.[13]

Following the Gunnison County case, title abstractors persuaded the legislature to enact a statute that explicitly granted them access to county land records. Carlos W. Brooks tested the new law when he asked to consult records in the custody of Pitkin County Clerk Fred H. Stockman. Stockman refused and Brooks asked the district court for relief. The court complied and the clerk then appealed. The Colorado Supreme Court affirmed the district court decision, but noted that the clerk could implement reasonable regulations governing use of the documents in his custody.[14]

The Colorado Supreme Court reaffirmed local government's right to impose reasonable regulations when F.D. Catlin demanded access to the Montrose County Clerk's Office during all business hours in order to abstract and duplicate records housed there. County Clerk William Upton denied the request. The Montrose County Court ordered Upton to allow access on the basis requested by Catlin, and the clerk appealed to the Colorado Supreme Court. The court noted that the statute specifically granting title abstractors access to county land records had been upheld in the Stockman case. On the other hand, the clerk had a statutory responsibility for the safekeeping of the records, which implied a power to impose regulations. Those regulations should include supervision of third-party use, which because of limited staff was not possible during all business hours. Upton had posted written rules regarding access, which the court deemed a reasonable use of his discretionary power.[15]

In 1885 the Minnesota state legislature granted title abstractors the right to occupy portions of county buildings as offices, subject only to reasonable regulations. Title companies had lobbied for passage of this

---

13 *Bean v. People,* 2 P. 909 (Colo. 1884).
14 *Stockman v. Brooks,* 29 P. 746 (Colo. 1892).
15 *Upton v. Catlin,* 31 P. 172 (Colo. 1892).

act in order to circumvent uncooperative county officials. Two years later, the state supreme court upheld this law, but as in Michigan and Colorado later qualified its position. This occurred in 1901, when the Clay County Abstract Company requested access to records in the custody of G.D. McCubrey, clerk of the district court, in order to identify judgments affecting the titles to various lands. McCubrey offered to make the examination himself upon payment of the statutory fee. The title company then asked the Clay County District Court for a writ of *mandamus,* the court denied the request, and the company appealed.

The Minnesota Supreme Court's opinion noted that the district court clerk received no salary and depended on fees for the operation of his office. Furthermore, the clerk had statutory authority to charge a fee when searching for records of judgments affecting titles. The abstract company considered the statute unconstitutional because it deprived them of rights enjoyed by others; discriminated against those searching for judgments affecting titles; and deprived them of property without due process. The supreme court disagreed. The common law did not extend the right to examine public records to all citizens, but the state legislature had done so. The legislature further provided that such access was free of charge, except in case of statutory fees, which applied in this instance.[16]

In 1887 title cases first appeared on the dockets of appellate courts in North Carolina, Alabama, Kansas, and Wisconsin. The North Carolina Supreme Court ruled that no one enjoyed the right to duplicate records in the county registrar of deeds' custody without payment of a search fee, in part because the registrar was compensated through this device. The Alabama Supreme Court ruled that a county probate judge could limit the right of a title company to inspect public records because those engaged in such speculation often inhibited access by public officials. The Kansas Supreme Court ruled that unlimited access by title abstractors endangered the integrity of records in the custody of the county registrar of deeds, but the following year concluded that this limitation did not apply in the case of an individual who was investigating liens upon lands that belonged to his employer. In 1887 the Wisconsin Supreme Court ruled against the Waushara

---

16 *State v. Rahac,* 35 N.W. 7 (Minn. 1887); *State v. McCubrey,* 87 N.W. 1126 (Minn. 1901).

County registrar of deeds, who had argued that the right to inspect documents in his custody was limited to those interested in a particular item and did not extend to those concerned with private gain.[17]

Thirteen years later, the Wisconsin Supreme Court issued its opinion in another title company case that illustrated how far that state had moved toward more open access to public records. The facts were that in 1880 the Rock County Board of Supervisors decided to install a patented title abstract system in the county registrar of deeds' office. The board purchased the system and contracted with the county registrar to implement it. The registrar completed the task, the county accepted his work, and the board of supervisors established a fee schedule for private individuals who wished to obtain abstracts. Subsequently, the county board prohibited the registrar from allowing anyone "to make abstracts for sale from the county books." In 1909, however, a new registrar purchased several blank books from the county and began copying the abstracts with plans to enter that business when he left office.

Upon learning of this activity, the county board ordered the registrar to cease, offered to return the purchase price for the blank books, and sued in Rock County Circuit Court to recover the information that the registrar had duplicated up to that point. The circuit court ruled in favor of the defendant, the county appealed, and the Wisconsin Supreme Court affirmed the earlier decision. The county abstract books were public records subject to duplication by any citizen, even one who intended to create a rival set. Furthermore, the county could not recover the copies solely for the price that the registrar paid for the blank books, for he had expended $900 in transcribing information into them.[18]

Disputes between title abstract companies and local government officials became particularly bitter in Illinois, where in 1871 the Chicago fire had destroyed public records of land transactions in Cook County. In 1886 the board of commissioners instructed the county registrar, Wiley S. Scribner, to prohibit use of records in his custody by title abstract companies. Handy & Company asked the Cook County Superior Court for an injunction to prevent implemen-

---

17 *Newton v. Fisher,* 3 S.E. 822 (N.C. 1887); *Randolph v. State,* 2 So. 714 (Ala. 1887); *Cormack v. Wolcott,* 15 P. 245 (Kans. 1887); *Boylan v. Warren,* 18 P. 174 (Kans. 1888); *Hansen v. Eichstaedt,* 35 N.W. 30 (Wisc. 1887).

18 *Rock County v. Weirick,* 128 N.W. 94 (Wisc. 1910).

tation of this policy, the superior court agreed, and the county registrar took the case to the Illinois First District Court of Appeals. That
tribunal ruled in behalf of the registrar, for in granting the title company's request the superior court had circumscribed Scribner's statutory duty to prevent damage to the records in his custody.[19]

In 1887, following initiation of the Scribner case, Illinois passed
statutes that opened the county registrar's records to public inspection,
empowered these officials to create abstracts of real estate titles, and
authorized them to sell the information contained in the county
abstracts. Subsequently, the Abstract Construction Company duplicated Cook County abstract books that had been prepared since the
1887 statute, but in 1905 the registrar attempted to stop this practice.
Initially, the Illinois First District Appellate Court ruled in favor of
the local official. The relevant legislation clearly gave the title company
access to the original records used to compile the county abstract
books, but not the abstract books themselves. The court ruled on the
side of caution in saying that wholesale duplication of the latter might
interfere with use of the same by the recorder and the general public.
Abstract Construction continued to press its case and in 1908 the
Illinois Supreme Court ruled in its favor.[20]

Title company cases first appeared before other state appellate
courts during the last decade of the nineteenth century and the first
two decades of the twentieth. In 1890 Maryland upheld a statutory
search fee that supplemented the salary of a local government official.
In 1905 Florida struck down a search fee, but not without a strong dissenting opinion. The following year, the Nevada Supreme Court ruled
that a title company could examine free of charge records related to its
current business transactions, but could not copy all the records to create an independent set of abstract books. The question of whether a
title company could duplicate local government records wholesale still
varied from state to state, but was moving in the direction of more
open access in this and other areas.[21]

---

19 Friedman, *History of American Law*, 433–35; *Scribner v. Chase*, 27 Ill. App. 36 (1888).

20 *Davis v. Abstract Construction Company*, 121 Ill. App. 121 (1905); *Chicago Title & Trust
Company v. Danforth*, 137 Ill. App. 338 (1907); and 86 N.E. 364 (Ill. 1908).

21 *Belt v. Prince George's County Abstract Company*, 20 A. 982 (Md. 1890); *State v. McMillan*,
38 So. 666 (Fla. 1905); *State v. Grimes*, 84 P. 1061 (Nev. 1906).

In 1918 the Tennessee Supreme Court issued a ruling that illustrated the shift that had taken place since the 1874 Georgia decision in
Buck v. Collins. The facts were that the Shelby County Registrar of
Deeds allowed the Memphis Abstract Company to station two of its
full-time employees in his office. The registrar contended that this was
not an inconvenience and voiced no objection to the arrangement.
Nevertheless, Shelby County sued the title company to recover rent for
the space occupied, the court of civil appeals ruled in favor of the title
company, and the county appealed to the Tennessee Supreme Court,
which affirmed the previous ruling. The common law tradition had
been that only those with a direct and tangible interest in such records
had access to them. The Tennessee Supreme Court contended that this
policy applied only to a feudal society where land was entailed, not held
in fee simple. Present circumstances dictated an approach that allowed
for freer distribution of information regarding land holdings. Abstract
companies had a right to examine records under reasonable regulations
and the county could not charge rent for the space occupied, if the registrar of deeds supported the arrangement.[22]

Litigants seeking access to records documenting the misuse of
public funds instigated approximately 20 percent of the open records
cases reported during this period, but still ran a distant second to title
abstractors. An early and influential case arose in Alabama, when on
September 24, 1878, attorney Charles J. Watson entered the office of
Willis Brewer, state auditor, and demanded access to records documenting the work of his client, J.F. Boyles, who had served as tax collector in Monroe County. At the trial, it came to light that the state
auditor had accused the former Monroe County tax collector of making "erroneous allowances." Boyles had hired Watson to investigate the
charge. The Alabama Supreme Court acknowledged the common law
standard that officials could deny access to those who lacked a direct
and tangible interest in public records, but concluded that Boyles and
his attorney met that test. Other decisions denied access on the basis
of the same common law principle. In 1899 the Pennsylvania District
Court denied a journalist's request to consult financial records held by
the commissioners of Clearfield County. The court held that the com-

---

22 *Shelby County v. Memphis Abstract Company,* 203 S.W. 339 (Tenn. 1918).

missioners needed some degree of privacy in their deliberations and that public interest and public curiosity were not synonymous.[23]

Between 1903 and 1912, several state courts overruled the common law standard regarding access to public financial records. In 1903 the Tennessee Supreme Court held that political hostility did not warrant denial of access and directed the mayor of Memphis to allow inspection of municipal financial records by a political rival. Three years later, the Vermont Supreme Court ruled that a private citizen possessed the right to inspect records held by the state auditor of accounts. In 1910 the New Jersey Supreme Court declared that all citizens possessed an interest in railroad tax records held by the state board of assessors, in part because access to this material served the public interest. In 1912 New York rejected the common law tradition in ruling that a taxpayer enjoyed the right to inspect records documenting the process for awarding public contracts.[24]

Disputes regarding election records ran third behind public finance cases, but comprised less than ten percent of the open records decisions reported during this period. In 1885 the Missouri Supreme Court heard the case of an unsuccessful candidate for a St. Louis office, who had been denied access to poll books and registration lists needed to contest the election. The court ruled that allowing access to these materials did not compromise the secrecy of the ballot, for the information revealed only who voted and not how. In 1904 the West Virginia Supreme Court heard the case of J.M. Payne, who proposed to contest a bond issue vote, but had been denied access to the poll books and ballots. The court sympathized with Payne's request, but ruled against him on a technicality. Nevertheless, one member of the tribunal wrote a strong dissenting opinion. He argued that the common law rule, derived from a monarchical system, allowed the king and his officials to withhold information. The democratic rule, on the other hand, made public officials servants of the people, not the king. Individual citizens possessed a legitimate interest in honest elections.[25]

---

23 *Brewer v. Watson*, 61 Ala. 310 (1878); *Owens v. Woolridge*, 8 Pa. D. 305 (1899). The statistics used in this and subsequent paragraphs were derived from the cases cited in 42 Am. Dig. Cent. Ed. 698; 17 Dec. Dig. '06 1147; 19 2d Dec. Dig. 1084; and 23 3d Dec. Dig. 1176.

24 *Wellford v. Williams*, 75 S.W. 948 (Tenn. 1903); *Clement v. Graham*, 63 A. 146 (Vt. 1906); *Fagan v. Board of Assessors*, 77 A. 1023 (N.J. 1910); *Eagan v. Board of Water Supply*, 98 N.E. 467 (N.Y. 1912).

25 *Thomas v. Hoblitzelle*, 85 Mo. 620 (1885); *Payne v. Staunton*, 46 S.E. 927 (W. Va. 1904).

Parties concerned with misuse of public funds and honest elections appeared among the plaintiffs in open records litigation, but
abstractors and insurers of real estate titles dominated the scene during
these formative years. Title abstractors appeared as plaintiffs in more
than forty percent of the open records cases reported by state courts of
appeal; they lobbied state legislatures; they advocated their position in
law review articles; they demonstrated a consciousness of purpose that
transcended jurisdictional boundaries; and they dominated the few
federal open records cases that appeared between 1874 and 1918. They
also viewed themselves as reformers, fully in tune with the spirit of the
age. Title abstractors undoubtedly rejoiced when favorable court decisions thwarted petty local officials who stood in the way of the people's
right to know. The efforts of these businessmen fall neatly into the
well-worn grooves carved out by New Left historians of the Progressive
Era who argue that the so-called reforms of the period were merely
efforts to consolidate the strengths of various economic interests that
advocated them. In America the concept that public records existed to
protect public rights included the right of individual entrepreneurs to
make money at public expense.[26]

Many of the open records issues faced by late nineteenth- and
early twentieth- century custodians of public records sound familiar
to modern archivists. How can custodians of public records balance
the demands of access and the need for security? When should they
establish fee-for-service operations? To what extent can researchers
legitimately circumvent these fees? When does an individual's right
to privacy supersede the public's right to know? Between 1874 and
1918, state appellate courts answered these questions in part by saying
that custodians of public records had a responsibility to establish reasonable regulations that addressed these issues. Most importantly,
this chapter in the history of access to public records again demon-
strates that custody of such materials demands the acceptance of risks
and responsibilities all too familiar to modern archivists.

---

26 "Right of Inspection of Records," *Lawyer and Banker* 17 (September-October 1924): 297–300;
Gabriel Kolko, *The Triumph of Conservatism: A Reinterpretation of American History, 1900–1916*
(New York: Free Press, 1963), 3; James Weinstein, *The Corporate Ideal in the Liberal State,
1900–1918* (Boston: Beacon Press, 1968), ix; T.R. Schellenberg, *Modern Archives: Principles and
Techniques* (Chicago: University of Chicago Press, 1956), 5. Between 1874 and 1918, federal
courts reported nine cases regarding access to public records, four of which concerned title
companies: *Commonwealth Title Insurance v. Bell*, 87 F. 19 (1898); *Bell v. Commonwealth Title
Insurance*, 118 F. 828 (1901) and 189 U.S. 131 (1903); and *In re Chambers*, 44 F. 786 (1891).

4

GOVERNMENTAL RULE AND ARCHIVISTS: THE HISTORICAL EXPERIENCE OF THE 20ᵀᴴ CENTURY IN CENTRAL EUROPE

Friedrich Kahlenberg

Dedicated to Alexander Pensign

Introduction

I would like to begin by describing two incidents that occurred during my last year as president of the *Bundesarchiv* or Federal Archives of Germany.

Incident 1. Immediately after the change of government in the Federal Republic of Germany in October 1998, the incoming administrative assistants of the new Chancellor Gerhard Schröder discovered the loss of a remarkable amount of records, particularly the deletion of several gigabytes of electronic information in the *Bundeskanzleramt* (the Chancellor's Office), created during the time of the preceding Chancellor Helmut Kohl. Those days after the elections for the fourteenth *Deutscher Bundestag* on 27 September are called, in the language of the mass media, *Bundeslöschtage,* or days in which federal information is destroyed.

Soon after discovering the losses, the new government decided to entrust Burkhard Hirsch, an eminent former member of Parliament, whose liberal party had just taken up the role of official opposition, with the internal investigation. His report was used by lawyers in Bonn to examine whether there were grounds for accusing any individual of having acted illegally in destroying public records and electronic data. The judicial examination is still proceeding. Up to the present, neither my successor Hartmut Weber nor I were informed or involved in the investigation. This experience leads me to conclude that an active politician is better placed to research and highlight irregularities in governmental records administration than an archivist. It is clear that a parliamentarian can appeal to a wider audience with conviction.

Incident 2. On forming his first government in October 1998, Chancellor Schröder nominated Michael Naumann as Minister for Cultural and Media Affairs within the Chancellery. State *(Land)* governments in the Federal Republic of Germany (FRG), notably Bavaria, protested because this appointment appeared to disregard the constitutional principle that cultural affairs are within the province of the states, the *Länder*. Certainly, the nomination of a minister within the federal government inspired public discussion of cultural policy and events, and for the first time federal cultural activities had a public voice. When Naumann visited the *Bundesarchiv* Headquarters Office on 6 April 1999, he commented on the building and its installations in an aside, spoken with a sigh:

> What a pity that such an impressive, efficient building will be mainly useless within a brief time, probably within a decade, since archival information will then be totally digitized, and the bulk of the archival materials will be disposed of.

It was a surprise to find that this progressive intellectual, a dedicated promoter of cultural values in contemporary society, revealed himself to be an admirer of the new technologies as a dominant substitute for continuing archival tradition. Although I am sure he would have refused to imagine that the archives of Bismarck's period and the Weimar Republic or the private papers of politicians and academics should be destroyed, his spontaneous comment confirmed what I had experienced many times before—that politicians are far more ready to trust in new technologies than to improve on existing systems. Opportunities for innovation are more easily accepted the less they depend on traditional experience or the need to learn from history.

Background

From the earliest period, central European history has been characterized by an antagonism between central authority and the predecessors of the *Länder* of today. Centrifugal and centripetal powers have never ceased to be in active opposition to each other. This tradition of a vigorous federalism was significant not only for the Holy Roman Empire up to 1806 and the German Federation up to 1866, but also for Switzerland from the beginning of its history and for Austria at least since the mid-nineteenth century. In the *Reich* set up in 1871, the dominance of the Prussian monarchy seemed to favour centralist ideals, mainly supported by liberal parties, but federal values and goals never lost the esteem of a majority of citizens. Under these conditions, the central archives played only an ephemeral role; the archives of the states are the true treasuries of history in central Europe. They can boast of much more comprehensive archival source materials than the *Bundesarchiv*, at least up to 1867 or 1871.

I will start by considering the German experience since 1919, the year the *Reichsarchiv*, the predecessor of the *Bundesarchiv*, was set up. (The Austrian and the Swiss National Archives institutions share many similarities with the development of the state archives in the *Länder*, but those are not covered here.) Here, I concentrate on the central level.

What has been the nature of the central government interest in the activity of archivists in public service? What were the main fields of its activity? Where does my generation come from, who are we within government, and what was our role during the last four decades of the 20th century? My survey is divided into three sections covering the periods from 1919 to 1945, from 1949 to 1990, and since the reunification in 1990.

1

1919–1945

The *Reichsarchiv* was set up in 1919 because of the urgent need for an institution to serve as a collecting agency for the vast deluge of records of disbanded military and affiliated wartime organizations. The new institution was not born either from a public demand by historians or academic institutions or from the pressure of cultural or political considerations in the government of the Reich. So it is not at all surprising that the staff was made up nearly exclusively of former army officers, most of whom had served within the division for military history in the general staff, *Grosser Generalstab,* of the imperial army. Up to the late 1920s, the records taken over by the *Reichsarchiv* were for the most part of military origin. A small number of trained archivists entered the *Reichsarchiv* during the 1920s, but civilian historians remained a minority within the institution until 1935. In 1935, the military archives were separated from the *Reichsarchiv* and became the *Heeresarchiv Potsdam,* accompanied by the newly founded archives of the air force and of the navy (*Luftwaffe* and *Kriegsmarine*).

In the time immediately following the Great War and particularly after the signing of the Versailles Peace Treaty, there was in Germany, as elsewhere, a great deal of discussion and concern about the causes of the war. In 1919, the National Assembly in Weimar set up a commission to investigate the causes of the collapse of 1918, and the succeeding parliaments *(Reichstage)* continued this work. The Foreign Ministry decided to edit a selection of documents in order to defend the Reich's policy before the war, and refute the charge that they had caused the outbreak of the war in 1914. The important work, *Die grosse Politik der europäischen Kabinette 1871–1914: Sammlung der Akten des Auswärtiges Amtes, (The principal Policy of European Governments . . . Collection of Records of the German Foreign Office),* was published in a series of 40 volumes from 1922 to 1927, without the principal editors, J. Lepsius, A. Mendelssohn and F. Thimme, having any archival experience. In 1919 and for the following years, it is clear that the majority of the *Reichsarchiv* staff members were saddled with the preparation of the history of the Great War. *Der Weltkrieg 1914–1918,* edited by the

Reichsarchiv (Generalstab), was published from 1925 up to 1939, a remarkably slow production in comparison with the edition of documents by the foreign office *Auswärtiges Amt*. An accompanying series of monographs on the battles of the war, however, was started in 1921 and completed by a 36th volume in 1930, *Schlachten des Weltkriegs in Einzeldarstellungen (Battles of the World War in Monographs)*.

In spite of the military origin of the direction of its work, the *Reichsarchiv* as an institution was subordinated to the Ministry of the Interior (*Reichsministerium des Innern*). It was the intention of Erich Koch-Weser, Minister of the Interior, in June 1920, to strengthen the civilian element within the *Reichsarchiv*. He ordered the setting up of a commission of historians with chairs in various universities of the country, and this commission acted as an advisory board for the ministry as well as for the *Reichsarchiv*. Hermann Ritter Mertz von Quirnheim, president of the *Reichsarchiv*, and Paul Lehr, general director of the Prussian State Archives, were members ex officio. Other members were generals and university history professors. The majority were conservative, with some even having reservations about the republic. The influence of the Reichswehr (the remaining army of "one hundred thousand" as laid down in the Versailles peace treaty) and the War Ministry proved to be dominant in spite of the jurisdiction of the Ministry of the Interior, whose surveillance was performed only formally.

It is no exaggeration to say that the *Reichsarchiv* and its staff had no difficulties with the new government of the Nazi dictatorship starting in January 1933. A clear majority of the staff members believed in stab-in-the-back legend as the main cause of the 1918 defeat, and were convinced that Germany had been terribly violated by the peace settlement of 1919. Their opinion corresponded broadly with the sedulously fostered Nazi propaganda for a revision of the Versailles peace treaty and for rearmament without limitations, without any regard for the effects on neighbouring countries and the international community; they even supported the recovery of the former colonies. Some staff members shared the denunciation of the parliamentary system of the Weimar Republic. The small minority of dedicated democrats and liberal historians within the *Reichsarchiv* were either dismissed by the Nazi government or decided on their own to leave the civil service and emigrated. A few are known for their contributions to the development of archival science abroad. (In fact, their influence lasted up to the 1980s when a state archivist finally came to office in Israel whose mother tongue was *not* German.) Other archivists joined the resistance movement in later years.

To avoid misunderstandings, it must be noted that in spite of all political limitations and implications, and in spite of the burden of researching for monographs on military history, professional archival work developed. From the mid 1920s, records were taken over from more and more civil departments within government departments; archival appraisal, listing, and description were carried out. It is to the credit of the *Reichsarchiv* that a growing number of private papers was taken over, that vast collections of records of political parties, nationwide organizations, associations, and so forth were safeguarded and brought together to form an impressive documentation of contemporary history. Professional archival training became a precondition for service within the *Reichsarchiv* from 1935 on, after its separation from the military connection. Nevertheless, the staff of the *Reichsarchiv* at this period did not see themselves primarily as professional archivists. They saw themselves as historians, members of a learned academic society.

The general director of the Prussian State Archives, Albert Brackmann, acting for a brief time in 1935 as president of the *Reichsarchiv,* encouraged the research interests of the archivists. His successor Ernst Zipfel, who was a dedicated member of the Nazi party, fostered institutional cooperation with the *Reichsinstitut für Geschichte des neuen Deutschland,* set up in 1935 under Walter Frank. Eastern European history traditionally was a particular field of research in the Prussian State Archives. All archivists trained in the Prussian Institute for Science (IFA in Potsdam) had to learn Polish, for example. The *Ostforschung* flourished impressively from the mid-1930s not only within the archives, but also in research institutions within universities, heavily promoted by Nazi party agencies, by the military, and by the government.

In conclusion, we must remember that the *Reichsarchiv* was part of the public administration. Archivists served the governments of the time without any hesitation, and after 1933 more by personal inclination than before. They acted as efficient public servants for the needs of the moment. Archival professionalism and ethics were still developing and were not yet generally established. Almost nobody felt the need for archival legislation on access to records for public information, nor did historians ask for an archives law. There was marginal discussion during the 1920s on legislative protection for private archives, but this ended soon without any result. The authoritarian traditions before 1914, stretching back into the 19th century, seem to have survived strongly among the majority of historians and archivists. The imagination of the latter was far more attracted by academic historical studies than by archival theory and practice. We remember the archivists of that time chiefly by their individual publications, and not by their professional initiatives and procedures.

1949–1990

After the unconditional surrender of the *Wehrmacht* on 8 May 1945 and the arrest of the remaining members of the government of the Reich in Flensburg on 23 May, the four Allied Powers took over responsibility and divided the country into four zones of occupation on 5 June 1945. The eventual failure of the Allied Control Council, set up the same day to make decisions affecting the whole country, could not have been foreseen. The Allied powers had many good reasons to seize the records of the German government, the *Wehrmacht*, and the Nazi party organizations wherever they found them. Archives officers of the joint committee called the Military Intelligence Record Section, formed in March 1943, and intelligence units of the Soviet and French forces likewise confiscated current records as well as archival materials which had been evacuated during the war (for example into mines in Lower Saxony, Thuringia, etc.). Under Law No. 2 of 10 October 1945 of the Allied Control Council, providing for the liquidation of Nazi organizations, all relevant records were confiscated and assembled in collection points and document centres, where departmental and military records had arrived already. Special attention was given to documents concerning the horrible crimes of the Nazi dictatorship, which could serve as evidence in preparing for the International Military Tribunal of Nuremberg. By the end of 1949, the majority of confiscated records had been transferred to the United Kingdom, the United States, and the Soviet Union.

Immediately after the war, archivists in local and state archives were the first to start working again under the control of the allied military government in the different zones of occupation. The *Reichsarchiv* no longer existed, and no succeeding institution was yet available. The first initiative was taken by the Soviet military administration (SMAD). As early as October 1945, Soviet authorities ordered the German side to submit suggestions for the creation of a central archival institution for the Soviet zone. On the 8 May 1946, SMAD ordered the *Zentralarchiv für die Sowjetische Besatzungszone* to be created. Archivists of the new institution were recruited from former members of the *Reichsarchiv*, those who had not been arrested because of their Nazi careers or who were no longer prisoners of war. The expectation was that the new *Zentralarchiv* in Potsdam could be developed as a national archival institution for Germany as a whole. However, under the conditions after the outbreak of the Cold War, this plan could not work.

In the western occupation zones, the military governments did not feel the need for a new central archives institution, and the question was left for the German side. German archivists wanted to set up a professional association on the national level, and the first meeting of this association took place in April 1947. When the British military government invited the archivists to form an advisory council for archival affairs, the archivists hesitated. They feared that such a council could become the germ of a purely West German archives administration. The state archivists in particular opposed initiatives for centralization. They did not want the revitalization of something similar to the former Prussian archives administration. They had not forgotten the projects of the *Reichsarchiv* and the Reich Ministry of the Interior during the war to set up a national archival system covering all the state archives. Therefore, the state archivists refused the Allies' invitation to form an official representative committee, but they agreed to let the governing council of their society of archivists serve as an archives council (*Deutsche Archivausschuss*). In effect they behaved like true federalists, defending their independence as state archivists in the *Länder*, who were not willing to tolerate formal authority on a national level.

The setting up of the *Bundesarchiv* was decided by the cabinet of the federal government on 24 March 1950. This decision was strongly backed by the association of historians and by the *Deutsche Archivausschuss*. The reason for this unanimity—the new institution started work in 1952—was that in order to claim return of captured German records from the Allies, a receiving institution had to be created on the central level.

This is not the place to give a detailed report on the development of the central archives during the period of Germany's division, or its relations with the *Deutsches Zentralarchiv* in Potsdam, or on the settlement of the *Bundesarchiv* in Koblenz and its consequences on relations between the German Democratic Republic (GDR) and the Federal Republic of Germany (FRG). The main facts are known. In the GDR, the ideology of the Socialist Unity Party (SED) meant that archives and archivists had to be subordinated to the total control of the Party. Centralization was strictly enforced, and the *Länder* of Brandenburg, Mecklenburg, Sachsen-Anhalt, Sachsen, and Thuringia were dissolved in 1952. In a series of decrees in 1950, 1965, and 1976, the government of the GDR created the legal basis for a highly centralized archival system under the direction and control of the public archives administration (*Staatliche Archivverwaltung*) within the Ministry of the Interior.

From the beginning of the 1960s, this ministry followed a personnel policy which aimed at primarily placing politically reliable cadres (persons highly devoted to the security system of the GDR) into leading archival positions. In contrast, the *Bundesarchiv* in the FRG developed in accordance with the federalist tradition, marked by decentralization and a functionally differentiated pluralism. From 1950 on, there was a standing conference of the chiefs of the states' archives administrations (*Archivreferentenkonferenz der Länder*) which served as an instrument of cooperation, and the director of the *Bundesarchiv* joined the conference in 1952, as a matter of course. Archival legislation was discussed intensively beginning in the early 1980s, and from the beginning, there was no question but that legislation had to be prepared separately in each state as well as on the federal level. In the end, these discussions resulted in separate archives laws being passed from 1987 on by the *Bundestag* and the *Landtage,* the federal and the state parliaments. The federal archives act (*Bundesarchivgesetz*) of 6 January 1988 turned out to be the best preparation for the challenges of German unification in 1990.

Since Reunification in 1990

Looking back over the events since autumn 1989, archivists in all parts of Germany would agree that the process of change took place with unexpected rapidity. The fall of the Berlin Wall on 8 November 1989 marked the culmination of a movement of civil disobedience against a regime that had continuously disregarded the human and civil rights of its citizens. The efforts of citizens' committees (*Bürgerkomitees*) in Berlin and most other cities of the GDR for reformation and democratization were supported by individual members of the central archives and state archives as well. The archivists went on to establish an independent professional organisation of their own, something unimaginable during the preceding four decades. The *Verband der Archivare der DDR* was founded 12 May 1990. The time of the *Wend*—the process of transformation in Eastern Europe—brought about the disintegration of the Socialist Unity Party (SED) and of the political institutions of the GDR. Democratization and federalization were common aims of the citizens, complemented at the beginning of 1990 by the claim for unification (*"Wir sind das Volk, Wir sind ein Volk"*—we are the people, we are one people). On 18 March 1990, the parliament (*Volkskammer*) of the GDR was elected without any of the tricky manipulations that had been usual before; on 17 May 1990, self-government of the cities (*Kommunalverfassung*) was reinstated; and as early as 22 July 1990, the recreation of the *Länder* within the GDR was decided by the *Volkskammer*. Finally on 3 October 1990, these developments culminated in the dissolution of the second Germany by its decision to join the Federal Republic.

State archivists in eastern Germany saw the recreation of the *Länder* as a renaissance of their original historical traditions, of their true identity as keepers of the archival heritage of their region and homeland. They especially felt liberated from subjugation by the archives administration in the GDR Ministry of the Interior (*Staatliche Archivverwaltung*). They had finally escaped from constant regulation and interference. For four decades, they had been forced to act as functionaries of the network of information controls within the regime and had been dominated by the ideology of the almighty socialist unity party (SED). Fortunately, the majority of colleagues in public services of the GDR had acted as skilled, competent professional archivists, protected by a representative body in public affairs which was in accordance with socialist ideology. Although it was not easy for them to assimilate into Western society, they quickly learned the advantages of acting on their individual responsibility. In spite of the unimaginable challenges arising from the dissolution of former GDR authorities in the districts and of the industrial trusts (*Volkseigene Betriebe*), they had to deal with ever-increasing requests for information by citizens who had lost property or been prosecuted by the regime. The state archivists started to renew the research schemes of historical commissions and institutions for regional history (*Landesgeschichte*). They often joined the learned societies for regional and local history (*Landes- und Ortsgeschichte*) or even chaired them. They also started new series of publications and editions of documents very soon after reunification. State archivists efficiently helped move forward the process of reorienting historical memory of living generations. Government or party pressures on their activities had definitively ceased.

On the national, federal level, the former Central Archives of the GDR lost their institutional independence. The Federal Archives Law (*Bundesarchivgesetz*) was amended by the Unification Treaty Law of 23 September 1990. This law required the *Bundesarchiv* to take care of existing archival institutions on the central level including responsibility for their employees, buildings, and, of course, archival holdings in their repositories. From 3 October 1990, the day of German unity, the Central Archives of the GDR in Potsdam, the military archives under the Ministry of Defence in the same city, and the State Film Archives in Berlin under the Ministry of Culture, became outposts of the *Bundesarchiv* in Koblenz.

Although the details of the *Bundesarchiv's* accomplishments in the days of unification are not the subject here, two exceptional cases should be mentioned. First, it is regrettable that the unification treaty law of 23 September 1990 did not extend the scope of archives law (*Bundesarchivgesetz*) to the records of the Ministry for *Staatssicherheit,* the secret police of the GDR (*Stasi-Akten*). After a series of difficult discussions, government negotiators agreed on a special solution to this problem, resulting in the appointment of a special commissioner of the federal government (*Sonder-Bundesbeauftragter für die Unterlagen des*

Staatssicherheitsdiestes). By 24 August 1990, the *Volkskammer* had appointed Joachim Gauck as commissioner, but on 24 October Gauck also received a letter of appointment from the federal government. In 1995, he was reappointed by the *Deutscher Bundestag.* Curiously enough, the Unification Treaty instructed the president of the *Bundesarchiv* to act as the commissioner's deputy. This arrangement came to an end when the *Bundestag* passed the law of 20 December 1991 confirming the special status of the Stasi files (*Stasi-Unterlagen Gesetz*); however, this law did not even quote the *Bundesarchivgesetz,* the archives law. Undoubtedly, the reason for this was that the majority of members lacked trust in the *Volkskammer* and noted the administrative dependency of the *Bundesarchiv* within the Ministry of the Interior. This led them to give the special commissioner parliamentary status in August 1990. In principle, my view has always been that the balance between the public need to use records and the individual's need for privacy should be resolved by a consistent legal principle, irrespective of the provenance of the records concerned.

Second, the unification treaty law also disregarded the archival documents of the parties and mass organizations of the GDR. From the political point of view the most important question was that of the future of the archives of the Socialist Unity Party. This had constantly been discussed by the media since the end of 1989. But other parties and organizations were concerned as well, for example the trade union *Freier Deutscher Gewerkschaftsbund,* the *Kulturbund,* and so forth. On 13 March 1992, the Bundestag decided to amend the Federal Archives Act by adding a provision for a dependent foundation within the *Bundesarchiv* which would take care of all the documents concerned. A decree of the Minister of the Interior on 6 April 1992 set up this foundation and appointed a board of trustees *(Archiv der Parteien und Massenorganisationen der DDR in Bundesarchiv (SAPMO)).* Those organizations that were willing to transfer their archival documents or those of their predecessor institutions to the foundation were invited to take part in the work of the board.

This solution avoided any measure of expropriation, but required agreement between the owners and the *Bundesarchiv* concerning the foundation. There were immediate talks and a continuous series of deliberations, some of them confidential, with all parties who had representatives in parliament and also with civil servants in government departments as well. On 4 January 1993, the foundation started its work and was successful in nourishing a cooperative atmosphere among all the organizations concerned.

In closing, I am aware that I have neglected many more problems than I have included.

The archives of moving images, documentaries, and feature films, the collections of photographs, and of sound recordings, have been significant historical sources for the last century: they will gain growing appreciation by public and individual users. Are we giving a sufficient part of our professional attention to audiovisual archives?

I also did not consider the effects of the revolutionary information and computer technologies on the practice of archives. My personal observation is that the challenge of these technologies is almost overwhelming to many of my colleagues. Have we gone far enough or even a bit too far in adjusting our professional imagination and activities to these challenges? Do not our fundamental professional principles, methods, and responsibilities remain basically the same as in the previous generation?

Finally, I wish to emphasize that I never experienced serious pressure from the government as the president of the *Bundesarchiv.* I have to admit that I needed a lot of sympathy—or an appreciative responsiveness to the thinking within the government and the civil service—to allow me to represent the position of professional archivists and archival needs to them. Confidence in the mission to provide an authentic and comprehensive record of government activities in present times seemed to me the more limited the more far-reaching political responsibilities are. The preservation of archival documents as an essential part of cultural heritage is announced in Sunday speeches but has not yet been accepted as the basis for an archival policy deserving of the name. After my retirement, I sometimes feel tempted to dream of a *Bundesarchiv* independent of executive power, responsible directly to parliament. I realize that this is not at all a solid prospect, yet who knows? Since we mature as a democratic society in an increasingly united Europe in the 21st century, we have to see change as a constant challenge.

Access and the
Public Interest

5

"... AND GRANT GERMAN AND FOREIGN SCHOLARS ACCESS AT ALL TIMES": ARCHIVAL ACCESS IN WEST GERMANY DURING THE COLD WAR

Astrid M. Eckert

When Allied troops advanced into Germany in early 1945, they captured tons upon tons of German records. The historical records of the German Foreign Office dating back to 1867 fell into Allied hands. So did approximately ten million Nazi Party membership cards that would later become part of the Berlin Document Center. The British laid their hands on the papers of the German Navy; the Americans forwarded countless German military records to the United States. The documents were a priceless source for operational intelligence while the war lasted. They also provided crucial evidence for the trial of major war criminals and the subsequent proceedings in Nuremberg. Very soon, the unique historical value of the papers became evident as well.

This paper is based on archival research conducted for the author's book *Kampf um die Akten. Die Westalliierten und die Rückgabe von deutschem Archivgut nach dem Zweiten Weltkrieg* (Stuttgart: Steiner, 2004). The author wishes to thank Dr. Ari Sammartino, Oberlin College, for her comments on an earlier draft of this paper, and her brother Eike Eckert for his help with Polish language sources.

The seized records and archives became a bone of contention, once a West German government was formed and could reassert itself. In one of its very first resolutions, in October 1949, the West German parliament demanded the return of all captured records and archives.[1] The West German press, in sometimes nationalistic tones, joined in and held that the Allies had captured and carried away German national history. Chancellor Konrad Adenauer contacted the Allied High Commission and argued for the return of all records on the grounds that they were needed to write the history of the most recent past, the National Socialist period.[2] The ensuing negotiations lasted for years.[3] They turned out to be painstaking, and at times even nerve-wracking. Seven years after the West Germans had first asked for it, the American, British, and German governments signed an agreement that provided for the return of the diplomatic papers of the former German Foreign Ministry *(Auswärtiges Amt)*. Negotiations about the other papers—mostly military in character—began in January 1958. The bulk of the military documents and those of party organisations were returned by 1968. But up to this day, the return of captured German records is an ongoing process that might not even be finished in the near future.

The return of the diplomatic papers to Bonn in 1956 was accompanied by a German guarantee of future access to these papers for international scholars. The negotiations had made it all too clear that there was a too deeply seated mistrust on the Allied side, especially among British historians,[4] to return the archival records of the Nazi

---

1   The original resolution as introduced by members of the *Nationale Rechte*, a group of right-wingers, can be found in Bundestag, 1. Wahlperiode 1949, Drucksache Nr. 149, 27 October 1949. The resolution as it was finally adopted in Bundestag, 1. Wahlperiode 1949, Drucksache Nr. 844, 20 April 1950; also quoted in Josef Henke, "Das Schicksal deutscher zeitgeschichtlicher Quellen in Kriegs- und Nachkriegszeit. Beschlagnahme—Rückführung—Verbleib," in *Vierteljahrshefte für Zeitgeschichte* 30:4 (1982), 557-620, 585.
2   Konrad Adenauer to the Executive Chairman of the Allied High Commission, André François-Poncet, 17 June 1950, in *Konrad Adenauer, Briefe 1949–1951. Bearb. von Hans Peter Mensing. Rhöndorfer Ausgabe. Hg. von Rudolf Morsey und Hans-Peter Schwarz.* (Berlin: Siedler, 1985), Nr. 257, 232f.
3   The negotiations are partially covered in the article by Henke, *Schicksal deutscher zeit-geschichtlicher Quellen.* The article is based on sources from Bundesarchiv and does not fully acknowledge the international aspects of the negotiations.
4   On the role of the British historians, see D. C. Watt, "British Historians, the War Guilt Issue, and Post-War Germanophobia: A Documentary Note," in *Historical Journal* 36:1 (1993), 179-185; Sacha Zala, *Geschichte unter der Schere politischer Zensur. Amtliche Aktensammlungen im internationalen Vergleich* (München: Oldenbourg, 2001), 241-244.

past into the custody of the former perpetrator country. What would they do with the evidence of their worst crimes? The formal exchange of letters between the German Foreign Minister and the Allied Ambassadors that sealed the return deal therefore contained the following proposition:

> The Federal Government wishes on this occasion to renew again the declaration which it has repeatedly made, that it will keep the returned files in an orderly manner and grant German and foreign scholars access to the files at all times.[5]

As an added precaution, the Western Allies microfilmed most of the records prior to their return lest they conveniently disappear.[6]

The access guarantee is ambivalent in nature. The exchange of letters as such was not a formal contract according to international law. It was a letter of understanding, a mutual agreement. The access clause sounds like a self-obligation, voluntarily given. But in fact, it was an unnegotiable Allied condition for the return of any German documents. This was well understood on the German side. The central importance of the clause was rendered even more obvious by the fact that especially the Americans still held vast troves of records the return of which would be endangered by not abiding to the access guarantee.

---

5   The guarantee is contained in the Exchange of Letters between the Federal Government and the Governments of the United States, Great Britain, and France, 14 March 1956. See Walter Hallstein, signing for the German Foreign Minister [Heinrich von Brentano, CDU], to James B. Conant, American Ambassador, 14 March 1956, in PA/AA, B118, vol. 510. The letters are published in *US Treaties and Other International Agreement Series*, vol. 7:2, Nr. 3613, 2119–2124; *Exchange of Letters between the Government of the UK of Great Britain and Northern Ireland and the Government of the Federal Republic of Germany concerning the transfer to the Federal Republic of Archives of the former German Foreign Office (March 14), April 12 1956*, Germany Nr. 1 (1957) (London: Her Majesty's Stationery Office, 1957); see also Henke, *Schicksal deutscher Quellen*, 594f.

6   For financial and manpower reasons, the diplomatic records were only partially filmed. Those records held in Alexandria, Virginia, and administered by the Departmental Records Branch of the Adjutant General's Office were bulk-filmed by the American Historical Association. On the diplomatic files, see George O. Kent, "The German Foreign Ministry's Archives at Whaddon Hall, 1948–1958," *American Archivist* 24 (1961), 43–54, esp. 48f., 51–53. On microfilming at Alexandria, see Dagmar H. Perman, "Microfilming of German Records in the National Archives," *American Archivist*, 22 (1959), 433–443; Wilhelm Rohr, "Mikroverfilmung und Verzeichnung deutscher Akten in Alexandria, USA," in *Der Archivar* 19 (1966), 251–264; Gerhard L. Weinberg, "German Records Microfilmed at Alexandria, Virginia, in Collaboration with the American Historical Association," *Captured German and Related Records. A National Archives Conference (NA Conference 3)*, ed. Robert Wolfe (Athens, Ohio: Ohio University Press, 1974), 199–210.

The capture of such large quantities of enemy archives at the end of World War II was unprecedented in archival history. So was the access clause.[7] This essay examines the implementation of the access agreement after 1956–1958.[8] Implementing the agreement depended on a variety of factors that do not immediately suggest themselves as being interconnected: Cold War politics, German-Polish prewar relations, Germany's Nazi past, as well as providing for the needs of historians doing archival research. To show the interaction of these various factors, a case study is offered which focuses on the Political Archive of the German Foreign Ministry, the recipient of returned German diplomatic files.

This archive was soon caught in a web of conflicting interests. It became apparent that some German diplomats were reluctant to allow scholars from countries east of the Iron Curtain to work on the German diplomatic files. The motives for their behaviour, I argue, cannot simply be credited to the Cold War's East-West dichotomy. West German *Vergangenheitspolitik*—the politics of coming to terms with the Nazi past—played as much a role as did German-Polish prewar relations and the so-called West Campaigns of the German Democratic Republic (GDR) government. These GDR propaganda campaigns against former Nazi elites now in governmental positions in Bonn were gaining momentum in 1958. And, as historian Annette Weinke has shown, German records held in East Berlin as well as in Polish and Czech archives were central to the GDR plan to expose former Nazi perpetrators now in the Bonn government.[9] In thinking about archival access, then, West German officials feared that scholars

---

7   In 1951–1953, 1958 and in the early 1960s, the government of the United States returned diplomatic files and papers of private enterprises to the Japanese government. The files had been "borrowed" in 1945 for the International War Crimes Trial in Tokyo. In 1953, 1958 and on the occasion of later returns of files to Japan, an access clause was not included into the transfer agreement although the U.S. Army, Navy and Air Force had demanded future access as a primary condition when agreeing to the transfer. Apparently, this was an oversight by those U.S. government officials involved in the return. See James Bradsher, "A Brief Survey of the Disposition of Captured Japanese Records 1945-1962," (National Archives, unpublished typescript, 2000); and Bradsher's forthcoming detailed study of the history of Japanese records that came into American hands at the end of World War II.

8   The return agreement dated 14 March 1956. The first 100 tons of records arrived in Bonn from Whaddon Hall, Buckinghamshire, in autumn 1956. The reading room at the Political Archive of the German Foreign Ministry *(Politisches Archiv des Auswärtigen Amts)* reopened on 1 April 1957. The return was accomplished by 31 March 1958.

9   Annette Weinke, *Die Verfolgung von NS-Tätern im geteilten Deutschland. Vergangenheitsbewältigung 1949–1969, oder: Eine deutsch-deutsche Beziehungsgeschichte im Kalten Krieg,* (Paderborn: Schöningh, 2002), 209–224. See also Weinke, "Der Kampf um

from the Eastern Bloc would abuse the access privilege to collect further material for propaganda purposes.

Before having a closer look at the Political Archive, though, we need first to describe the reaction of German archivists to this strange new beast that had been thrust upon them. What did the access clause mean to them? In 1957, when the first diplomatic files returned to Bonn, the access guarantee was still a paper tiger. German archivists were keenly aware of the fact that they were being watched very closely from abroad. How would they deal with the files from the Nazi era? Would they attempt to cleanse the record? Clearly, the external expectations were outright negative. Especially at the Political Archive, those in charge knew that any *faux pas* might endanger the return of further records. There was no point in attempting to conceal anything because Allied microfilming had duplicated the records. Files you could not see in Bonn, you could examine in London or Washington instead. For archivists, then, the access clause coupled with the microfilming meant a loss of control over "their" records. The records of highest political offices that in other countries would be treated as *arcana,* and that were only between eleven and twenty-three years old, were laid open for scholars to see. The user guidelines had to be revised accordingly. At least in theory, any element of choice on the archivists' side had vanished.[10] The loss of control was a loss of power, and both were a sting for the professional pride.

Since the access clause was such a novelty, it produced initial insecurity among archivists. What were they still allowed to do? In an attempt to test the waters, the director of the Federal Archives suggested classifying records of the Reich Chancellery that had recently been returned from England. His colleague from the Political Archive, Johannes Ullrich, speaking on behalf of the German Foreign Ministry, reprimanded him immediately. His ministry expected complete access to

---

die Akten. Zur Kooperation zwischen MfS und osteuropäischen Sicherheitsorganen bei der Vorbereitung antifaschistischer Kampagnen," *Deutschland-Archiv* 32:4 (1999), 564–577. On the GDR West campaigns, see also Michael Lemke, "Kampagnen gegen Bonn. Die Systemkrise der DDR und die West-Propaganda der SED 1960–1963," *VfZ* 41 (1993), 153–174.

10 In its rigidity, this argument only applies to those files that had been confiscated by the Allies and were being returned by them. It does not apply to files that had remained on German territory after 1945 and had not been under Allied control. The various state, city, church, family, university, and company archives were not affected by the German access guarantee given to the Allied governments.

returning files, he held, lest the ongoing negotiations for the return of other records be disturbed. Even scholars from the "Soviet occupation zone" were welcome at the Political Archive. Especially with foreign users, Ullrich insisted, German archivists had to bend over backwards to accommodate them. Johannes Ullrich, the director of the Political Archive, was indeed a remarkable personality who held very liberal views on archival access—liberal even according to standards of his own time. In his opinion, it was not the archivists' job to regulate access in order to shape the kind of history that would be written. He believed that the open scholarly dispute on interpretations of history would set the record straight and bring about the one and only historical truth.[11] This attitude soon brought him into trouble with the Political Department of the German Foreign Ministry, his own Ministry.

With this in mind, the implementation of the access clause at the Political Archive will be examined. First, the issue of archival access to journalists which has a broader dimension than first meets the eye will be addressed, followed by the case of a Polish scholar, Karol Grünberg, who wanted to consult the returned files in 1961 but triggered something of a renegotiation of the access agreement instead.

The Political Archive's reading room had barely reopened in April 1957 when rumours about the re-classification and disappearance especially of personnel files began to appear. To counter such accusations, Ullrich made a point of welcoming any user at the archive, provided the person presented his or her scholarly credentials. The duplication of the records, he argued, rendered any other approach futile. No matter how carefully an archivist treated the access question, "unpleasant incidents" might always occur, even with *bona fide* scholars. Before long, the

---

11 Ullrich (1902–1965) received his PhD in 1929 from Berlin University where he was a student of Friedrich Meinecke. From April 1930 until September 1931, he studied to become an archivist at the Institute for Archival Science *(Institut für Archivwissenschaft, IfA)* that was connected to the Prussian Privy State Archive in Berlin-Dahlem. In June 1933, he became an assistant at the Political Archive of the German Foreign Ministry. Between 1938–1945 and again 1956–1965, he served as its director. The missing years he spent as a prisoner of war in the Soviet Union. Ullrich never joined the Nazi party although it had been "suggested" to him on several occasions. He was nonetheless promoted to *Legationsrat* in 1939 and became a civil servant for life *(Beamter auf Lebenszeit)*. As a non-party member, however, he was excluded from further promotions. See Niels Hansen, "Ein wahrer Held in seiner Zeit. Zum dreißigsten Todestag von Johannes Ullrich," *Historische Mitteilungen* 9 (1990), 95–109. Ullrich to Eugen Meyer, Saarbrücken, 1 September 1955, in LA Saarbrücken, NL MeyerE 23; Ullrich to Ernst Posner, 10 October 1956, in: NA RG 200, Posner Papers, Box 6.

Foreign Ministry had such an unpleasant incident. The Swedish daily newspaper *Dagens Nyheter* published an account of the role of King Gustav V during the Second World War, invoking the delicate issue of collaboration. German diplomats felt that the article had the potential to disturb German-Swedish relations. Ullrich thus had to defend his policy to grant access to journalists. In the given case, the journalist was even a professor of history. In his attempt to prevent the Political Department from banning journalists altogether, Ullrich argued along the lines of *quod est in actis, est in mundo.* He said that,

> the danger lies less in the way the material is presented in a news-paper than in the files themselves.... [To cause us trouble,] it does not take sensationalist journalistic style but the problem is caused by the sober language of the files themselves....If we were to pre-vent any embarrassing discussion, we would need to forbid the pub-lication of *every* file containing any hint towards collaboration.[12]

Although the Press Office of the Foreign Ministry sided with Ullrich, the Political Department prevailed and banned journalists from future use of the Political Archive. The access guarantee, they insisted, applied only to scholars, not to journalists.[13]

It is the timing of this decision—the year 1958—that requires fur-ther investigation. Although the Swedish article might have been the immediate trigger, it seems that this case was less about Sweden and more about a general attempt to curb any uncontrolled publicity on the Foreign Ministry, because the Ministry was entering difficult times. During the years 1957 to 1959, the Federal Republic became serious about prosecuting Nazi perpetrators. The trial against mem-bers of an operations unit *(Einsatzgruppenprozeß)* in the city of Ulm in 1957–1958 initiated a paradigmatic shift in the government's

---

12 The verbatim quote reads: *"[Der] Gefahrenpunkt [liegt] viel weniger in der Form und in dem Ort der Darstellung...als in dem Aktenmaterial selbst . . . Es bedarf also keineswegs etwa erst eines besonderen journalistischen Aufputzes, vielmehr liegt das als gravierend empfundene Moment in dem nüchternen Wortlaut der Akten . . . Wolle man alle peinlichen Erörterungen verhindern, müßte man also die Veröffentlichung des Inhaltes aller der Aktenstücke, die irgen-deine Spielart des Kollaborationismus zeigen, inhibieren."* See Ullrich, Memorandum on the question of archival access for journalists, 13 January 1958, PA/AA, B118, vol. 3. Emphasis in the original. See also Ullrich, Statement of Ref. 117 on the opinion of Ref. 200 on the question of archival access for journalists, 27 January 1958, in the same.

13 The head of administration decided for future reference that only "scholars" were allowed to use the PA. See Legationsrat Dirk Oncken to Referat 117 [Political Archive], 12 February 1958, in PA/AA, B118, vol. 474.

approach to former Nazi elites and lower-ranking perpetrators.[14] At the same time, the GDR propaganda campaigns against the "re-nazified Federal Republic" were gaining momentum.

In early 1956, the Foreign Ministry was targeted for the first time by East Berlin's Committee for German Unity. The campaign was directed against the head of the Eastern Department *(Ostabteilung)*, Otto Bräutigam. As a consequence of the revelations, Bräutigam was suspended from office.[15] In March 1959, a new campaign targeted a whole group of West German diplomats. In late 1958, the Foreign Office—expecting East German accusations—was already bracing itself against the propaganda onslaught. The GDR attacks as well as the Federal Republic's own nascent prosecution activities were taken very seriously in the Foreign Ministry because they dealt with nothing less than the participation of German diplomats in the persecution and murder of European Jewry. Under pressure, the Ministry's higher-ups finally made efforts to learn more about their diplomats' past. A researcher was dispatched to the Berlin Document Centre to gather information on Nazi party or SS membership. These details were treated as *acta personalia secreta* and disappeared in a vault.[16] Clearly, this was not meant to be an act of self-purging. The Foreign Ministry simply wanted to be prepared and in the position to anticipate the next volleys from East Berlin. The ban of journalists from the Political Archive thus came at a moment that was highly sensitive for the Foreign Ministry. They wanted anything but publicity.

Although in this case Ullrich had lost a battle, he still hoped to win the war. With journalists banned, he now fought his own ministry on

---

14 This shift is best illustrated in the founding of *Zentralstelle Ludwigsburg* in 1958. The Central Office was a clearinghouse set up by the Justice Departments of the German Federal States. Its task was to collect evidence on Nazi perpetrators and bring them to trial. On the founding of *Zentralstelle* see Weinke, *Verfolgung von NS-Tätern*, 82–93.

15 During the war, Bräutigam had served as proxy for the Eastern Ministry *(Ostministerium)* under Alfred Rosenberg. He was in charge of the Caucasus region. He also served as liaison officer between the Foreign Ministry and Army Group A, the latter occupying the said region. In early 1956, the East German Committee on German Unity published Bräutigam's War Diary in full. See H. D. Heilmann, "Aus dem Kriegstagebuch des Diplomaten Otto Bräutigam. Eingeleitet und kommentiert von H. D. Heilmann," in *Biedermann und die Schreibtischtäter. Materialien zur deutschen Täter-Biographie. (Beiträge zur nationalsozialistischen Gesundheits- und Sozialpolitik 4).* (Berlin: Rotbuch 1987), 123–130. Biographical data on Bräutigam in the same, 129f. For contemporary press reaction, see *Der Spiegel* Nr. 12 (21 March 1956), 21–24.

16 The researcher was Kurt Rheindorf (1897–1977), an unemployed historian with dubious "resistance" credentials. For the quote, see Johannes Ullrich, Confidential Memorandum, 16 January 1959, in PA/AA, B118, vol. 76.

the question of archival access for scholars from Eastern Europe and the GDR. Curiously, the access clause in the return agreement of 1956 that had at first been considered an unwelcome external interference now became his main weapon. But his position became untenable when the U.S. State Department, which had insisted on such a clause in the first place, agreed to a new reading of the access guarantee.

Even before the reading room of the Political Archive re-opened in April 1957, the first user request from a researcher in Leipzig had come in. Ullrich granted access on the basis of reciprocity since West German historians were also still allowed to work in East German archives. He did not want to give the other side any reason to worsen archival relations, or see the researchers travel to London instead of coming to Bonn.[17] In this case of spring 1957, the Political Department still agreed without a fuss. This might serve as an indicator that the aforementioned political pressure on the Foreign Ministry had not yet reached a painful level. However, in the following years a whole array of events changed the situation drastically: Relations with the GDR grew tense over the Berlin situation, culminating in the erection of the Berlin Wall; the propaganda campaigns against Bonn grew in size and precision; as a consequence, even a federal minister, Theodor Oberländer, resigned in 1960; a year later, the Eichmann trial opened in Jerusalem.

In this tense political atmosphere, the Polish desk and the desk for the Former German Territories in the East *(Referat für deutsche Ostfragen)* at the Bonn Foreign Ministry organized resistance against Ullrich's liberal agenda. Even the leading West German tabloid, *Bild Zeitung,* began to raise awkward questions: Was it really true that Polish scholars were allowed to use German diplomatic files?[18] State Secretary[19] Karl Carstens demanded a more cautious attitude towards

---

17 "It is supposedly in the German interest," Ullrich writes, "that *German* scholars, including those from the Eastern Zone, read files of German provenance in German, and not in foreign archives." *("Es dürfte auch im Interesse der Bundesrepublik liegen, daß deutsche Forscher, auch solche aus der Ostzone, Akten deutscher Provenienz in deutschen und nicht in fremden Archiven lesen.")* Ullrich to Political Department, 5 March 1957, in PA/AA, B118, vol. 504.

18 Ullrich, Memorandum on the use of the Political Archive by Polish scholars, 28 January 1960, in PA/AA, B118, vol. 163.

19 A State Secretary in the German Foreign Ministry is a high-level position comparable to a Deputy Secretary of State in the American State Department, or the Permanent Under-Secretary in the British Foreign Office. The American term Secretary of State is the equivalent of the Foreign Minister in the German system.

"scholars from the Soviet zone."[20] The Polish desk went even further and made an effort to end archival research visits from Poland entirely. They suggested the government should ask the Allies for a "security clause" that would change current access rules so as to allow for an effective exclusion of scholars from eastern countries. Those historians to whom archival visits had already been granted should only receive pre-selected materials.[21] A similar approach was demanded in 1965 in regard to users' requests from the GDR. The Political Archive was asked to send out negative replies claiming there were not enough seats available in the reading room.[22]

One could think that the developments described here were an outcome of generally worsening relations between East and West. The reasons, however, are a bit more specific and rather belong in the context of German-Polish relations prior to September 1939. To explain this further, the head of the desk for the Former German Territories in the East—the desk that was instrumental in attempting to exclude—was a man called Gotthold Starke. Starke's biography explains the vehemence with which he fought the access clause and its application to Polish users.[23] Starke was a *Volksdeutscher,* an ethnic German from Bromberg. This territory fell to Poland after 1919, and the German minority held Polish citizenship but mostly cherished its ethnic

---

20 State Secretary Karl Carstens, Minute, 12 October 1960, in PA/AA, B2, vol. 72: *"Ich bin der Meinung, dass wir grössere Vorsicht als bisher anwenden sollten und insbesondere Vorgänge der jüngsten Geschichte (wie: das deutsch-englische Verhältnis von 1939-1941) Benutzern aus der Sowjetzone nicht zugänglich machen sollten."*

21 Ullrich, Minute, The use of the Political Archive by Polish scholars and the introduction of a 'security clause' as suggested by *Referat* 705 (Ref. 701) in this connection, 24 April 1962, in PA/AA, B118, vol. 163.

22 Weinandy (on behalf of Ullrich), Memorandum (concept), Use of PA by historians from the Soviet Occupation Zone and the Eastern bloc countries, 14 January 1965, in PA/AA, B118, vol. 291.

23 Gotthold Starke (1896–1968) was born in Runowo near Bromberg. In 1914, he graduated from school *(Kriegsabitur)* ahead of schedule in order to join the German Army. He served at the front but was soon wounded and released from service. He turned to the study of law at the universities in Heidelberg, Berlin, and Göttingen. As a participant in the fighting against the newly drawn frontier between the German Reich and Poland in 1919, he had to leave the region for awhile and went to Berlin. There, he joined the *Juni Club* centred around Moeller van den Bruck. Starke kept his Polish citizenship which made him ineligible for Prussian judicial civil service. He returned to Bromberg in 1922, became editor-in-chief of the *Deutsche Rundschau in Polen,* a German language newspaper, and was one of the founders of the Kant Society in 1924. In 1939, he was interned by Polish authorities in an effort to control the leaders of the German minority. Once released, he joined the German diplomatic service. Between 1941 and 1945, he headed the Eastern European desk in the Press and News Department of the Berlin Foreign Ministry. For biographical data on Starke, see *Deutsche Biographische Enzyklopädie,* vol. 9, 453; Richard Breyer, "Gotthold Starke—ein Wortführer unserer Volksgruppe," in *Jahrbuch Weichsel-Warthe* 1970, 53–59.

German roots. All through the 1920s and 1930s, the German minority and the territory they inhabited were objects of German propaganda and Polish counterpropaganda, with both sides trying to bolster their claims to this territory.[24]

One of the Polish claims after the Second World War was that the German minority had acted as a fifth column for Hitler before the German invasion of 1939. This claim partly contributed to the post-war justification of expelling ethnic Germans from East Central Europe after 1945. The fifth column claim bothered Starke in particular. He had belonged to those prewar leaders of the German minority who had remained loyal to the Polish republic.[25] In his frame of reference, the archival visits by Polish scholars would only serve one purpose: The Poles would try to collect more "evidence" of the German minorities' alleged fifth-column activities, thus fortifying the Polish *ex-post* justification for their expulsion after the war. In other words, the way Starke handled the access issue had less to do with the Cold War realignment that placed Poland into the Eastern bloc than with German-Polish relations before the German invasion. Further developments suggest that he was indeed still very much wedded to the agenda of the prewar German minority in Poland.

---

24 In fact, German archivists had played a major role in revisionist German politics of the time and contributed a great deal to the so-called *Ostforschung*. The leading figure who actively shaped Ostforschung was Albert Brackmann, the director of the *Geheime Staatsarchiv* (Privy State Archive) in Berlin-Dahlem. On Brackmann, see Michael Burleigh, "Albert Brackmann (1871–1952). Ostforscher. The Years of Retirement," *Journal of Contemporary History* 23 (1988), 573–588. The role of historians, anthropologists, archivists, and so forth, in the German revisionist policies after Versailles (i.e., the German *Ostforschung* and *Westforschung*) called *Grenzforschung* has received major attention in recent years. To mention just a few titles: Michael Burleigh, *Germany Turns Eastwards. A Study of Ostforschung in the Third Reich*, (Cambridge: Cambridge University Press, 1988); Michael Fahlbusch, *Wissenschaft im Dienst der nationalsozialistischen Politik? Die "Volksdeutschen Forschungsgemeinschaften" von 1931–1945*, (Baden-Baden: Nomos, 1999); Ingo Haar, *Historiker im Nationalsozialismus. Deutsche Geschichtswissenschaft und der "Volkstumskampf" im Osten* (Göttingen: V&R, 2000); *Griff nach dem Westen. Die "Westforschung" der völkisch-nationalen Wissenschaften zum nordwesteuropäischen Raum (1919–1960)*, eds. Burkhard Dietz, Helmut Gabel, Ulrich Tiedau, 2 vols. (Münster, 2003).

25 Politically, the German minority split into two camps. The group of the more established leaders, the old local elite, had received their political initiation before the First World War and gathered in the German Union *(Deutsche Vereinigung)*. The German Union was set up in 1934 after the other camp, the Young German Party *(Jungdeutsche Partei)*, had begun to gain strength after 1933. The German Union preferred that the German minority in Poland remain loyal to the Polish republic. The Young Germans were open to National Socialist politics. Both sides, however, were financially dependent on money from the Reich. See Albert S. Kotowski, *Polens Politik gegenüber seiner deutschen Minderheit 1919–1939 (Studien der Forschungsstelle Ostmitteleuropa an der Universität Dortmund 23)* (Wiesbaden: Harrassowitz, 1998), 270–279; Joachim Rogall, *Die Deutschen in Posener Land und in Mittelpolen (Studienbuchreihe der Stiftung Ostdeutscher Kulturrat 3)* (Munich: Langen, 1993), 153–157.

In 1959, the first Polish users worked at the Political Archive.[26] Starke was particularly excited about the idea that they might get access to files of the former German consulates in Poland.[27] He was, however, not allowed to pass any orders to the Political Archive. But at least he could make Ullrich's life as difficult as possible. In June 1961, a senior Polish scholar recommended one of his advanced students, Karol Grünberg, to the Political Archive. Grünberg, who already held a PhD, wanted to write his second book on the *Social Structures of the German Population in Upper Silesia.*[28] Ullrich favored this visit and drafted a reply that offered Grünberg a seat for fall 1961.[29] Starke's department had to co-sign the reply, and since Ullrich anticipated trouble from those quarters, he pointed out that Polish archives were still forthcoming towards Western scholars.[30] For Starke, this was entirely irrelevant. He accused Ullrich of having acted against the explicit protest of Starke's desk in a previous case. The Polish historian Marian Wojciechowski from Thorun, Starke complained, had been allowed to take home hundreds of photocopies that were now being

---

26 Leon Grosfeld, Polish Academy of Science, Warsaw; Marian Wojciechowski, Historical Institute, Thorun; Dr. Kulak, West-Institute, Poznan; Dr. Jurkiewicz, Institute for International Relations, Warsaw.

27 The British had developed a three-step return schedule for the diplomatic files held in Whaddon Hall. The first consignment contained consular files but explicitly held back for the time being the consulates in Memel, Danzig, Poland, Switzerland, and Czechoslovakia. See the return schedule of August 1955 as devised by Kenneth Duke, in PRO FO 370/2431 LS5/82. Charles Henry Fone from the library of the Foreign Office names the consulates in a letter to Kit Barclay, British Embassy, Bonn, 30 September 1955, in PRO FO 370/2432 LS5/102: Bromberg, Brünn, Chust, Danzig, Eger, Genf, Kattowitz, Krakau, Lemberg, Lodz, Mährisch Ostrau, Memel, Pilsen, Poznan, Preschau, Reichenberg Teschen, Thorun, Warsaw, and Zurich.

   Although it is not sure whether Starke had a clear idea at the time what exactly the consulate files contained, recent scholarship has shown that the Security Police (*Sicherheitsdienst*, SD) and the Gestapo had used German consulates in Poland, especially Thorun, to recruit spies and saboteurs among the German minority. The German Foreign Office tried to curb these efforts but they nonetheless bore fruit, regionally in Polish Silesia, and politically among the Young German Party (*Jungdeutsche Partei*). See Kotowski, *Polens Politik,* 338–344.

28 Henryk Altmann, General Director of Polish Archives, Warsaw, to Ullrich, 21 June 1961, in PA/AA, B118, vol. 237. Altmann was the advisor for Grünberg's *Habilitation.* Grünberg, born 1923 in Drohobycze, finished his studies in history at University of Warsaw in 1951. He received his PhD in 1958 and did his *Habilitation* in 1968. Subsequently, he taught 19th and 20th-century history at Copernicus University in Thorun.

29 By that time, Ullrich must have already been aware that his archive would close down for organisational purposes from 1 November 1961 until 31 March 1962. See Ullrich to *Bundesarchiv,* 14 February 1962, in BA/K, B198, vol. 244/1. Ullrich obviously tried to accommodate Grünberg before the shut-down.

30 Ullrich to Altmann, 31 July 1961, carbon copy with handwritten note *"cesset!"* (not sent, not used). The carbon copy was submitted to Ref. 701 (desk for matters regarding the formerly

used for Polish propaganda against the Federal Republic.[31] "Freedom of science, yes, but not support of propaganda," he said.[32]

In East European countries, Starke argued, there simply was no such thing as free science in a Western sense. In the pending case of Karol Grünberg, Starke conceded that the topic sounded harmless enough, but "unfortunately, it is very likely that Dr. Grünberg will feel compelled to collect evidence for the utterly false thesis of 'fifth column' activities by the loyal German population in pre-war Poland."[33] Starke was aware of the fact that Grünberg could also travel to London and see the German files there. In that case, though, the Germans would at least not contribute to the ensuing attacks themselves.[34] Having said all this, Starke asked Ullrich not to invite Grünberg for September 1961 but offer him a seat six months later. Postponing his visit would yield time to prepare for the visitor: "The material for Mr. Grünberg could be pre-selected."[35]

Ullrich made every effort to retain his independence in granting access to the Political Archive. He had to accommodate Starke to some degree, though. Thus he agreed to offer Grünberg a seat only for April 1962, six months after originally envisioned.[36] For Grünberg, this offer came too late. As far as it can be determined, he never set foot in the

German territories) and Ref. 705 (Polish desk) to co-sign. Ullrich had previously sought background information on Grünberg and had contacted West German scholars for Eastern Europe. See Ullrich to Werner Philipp, Director, Eastern European Institute, Free University Berlin, 11 July 1961, in the same. That West German scholars were still able to work in Polish archives in the late 1950s and early 1960s also becomes clear from a survey conducted by the Federal Archives *(Bundesarchiv)* in 1969. Hans Ulrich Wehler, Cologne, and Gottfried Schramm, Freiburg, reported about their trips and the forthcoming attitude of Polish archivists. The survey is documented in BA/K, B198, vol. 1638.

31 Wojciechowski visited the Political Archive in 1959 and worked on German-Polish relations between 1933 and 1939. See Ullrich, Note on archival access for Polish scholars, 28 January 1960, in PA/AA, B118, vol. 163.

32 "Die Freiheit der Wissenschaft in Ehren, aber *nur* die Freiheit der *Wissenschaft*, nicht die Unterstützung der gegnerischen Propaganda!" VLR Starke, Ref. 701 to Ref. 705, Re. Study of archival material by Dr. Karol Grünberg, 8 August 1961, in PA/AA, B118, vol. 237. Emphasis in the original.

33 *Es ist "leider keineswegs von der Hand zu weisen, daß sich Herr Dr. Grünberg berufen fühlt, zum Nachweis der durchaus falschen These von der 'Fünften Kolonne,' die das vorbildlich loyale Deutschtum in Vorkriegspolen gebildet haben soll, eine oberschlesische Ergänzung...zu schaffen."*

34 *Dies sei "für die deutsche Seite aber insofern leichter ertragbar, als sie dann nicht selbst die Rute schneidet, mit der man sie schlagen will."*

35 See note 32.

36 Ullrich to Henryk Altmann, Warsaw, 11 August 1961; Altmann to Ullrich, 19 October 1961, both in PA/AA, B118, vol. 237.

Political Archive. Starke had won.[37] Yet at no point did Ullrich ever agree to present pre-selected or otherwise tampered-with material. Such a trick, he felt, could be easily detected by comparison with the microfilms in London or Washington. The proof of political censorship by the Archive, and, by implication, the German Foreign Ministry, would cause much more damage than the files by themselves ever could. Similarly, Ullrich felt that a security clause against users from Eastern countries, as demanded by the Polish desk, could not be hidden from the public view forever but would surface eventually and cause a scandal.[38]

Ullrich was particularly averse to any renegotiation of the German access guarantee with the Western Allies. But this was exactly what Starke and the Polish desk had in mind. Ullrich felt that any modification of the access clause might weaken German chances of receiving further captured material that was being held in the United States.[39] The State Secretary decided against him, though, and ruled that the access clause should be taken up again at least with the Americans. He could count on their support: The State Department signalled that Ullrich's reading of the access clause was "perhaps somewhat broader than we had proposed. . . ." What they had meant at the time was access "to qualified researchers of *friendly* allied powers."[40]

The State Department itself herewith effectively undermined Ullrich's effort to keep the files accessible for scholars of all nations.[41] Henceforth, the Polish desk time and again reminded Ullrich of "an American suggestion to prevent archival access by administrative

37 Grünberg eventually published his findings in a book, *Nazi-Front Schlesien. Niemieckie organizacje politicyczne w wojeództwie śląskim w latach 1933–1939,* (Katowice/Kattowitz: Śląsk 1963). *(The Nazi-Front Schlesien: German Political Organisations in the Silesian Voivodship during 1933–1939).*

38 Ullrich, Statement on the immigration request by the Polish citizen Karol Grünberg, 22 January 1962, in the same. See also Ullrich, Memorandum, 24 April 1962, PA/AA, B118, vol. 163.

39 Ullrich, Memorandum, 24 April 1962, PA/AA, B118, vol. 163. See also Ullrich, Memorandum re. access of the Political Archive by Polish scholars, 28 January 1960, PA/AA, B118, vol. 163.

40 Bernard Noble, Director, Historical Office, State Department to Fritz T. Epstein, Editor of the Documents on German Foreign Policy at the German Foreign Ministry in Bonn, 27 July 1961, PA/AA, B118, vol. 123. Emphasis mine.

41 This is not the only case in which the State Department itself undermined the access guarantee. In an argument between the Flick industrial corporation of Duesseldorf and the German Federal Government over files of the Flick corporation, the German Foreign Office, the Ministry of the Interior as well as the *Bundesarchiv* and Political Archive tried to employ the access guarantee in order to prevent Flick regaining its files. They had been confiscated by American occupational forces for use in the Nuernberg Industrial Trials, and were being returned from U.S. custody together with German governmental files in

measures."[42] In 1964, this American "suggestion" was employed against a Czech and a Yugoslavian user; the latter was even explicitly re-routed to London.[43] When, indeed, he showed up at the Public Record Office, the British were not amused. They did not share the American distinction between friendly and not-so-friendly powers. In fact, when the head of the Foreign Office's library learned about the incident, he demanded that the Bonn government keep adhering strictly to the access guarantee of 1956, regardless of the users' nationality.[44] This was the kind of reaction that, in turn, strengthened Ullrich's position again. He would make a point of reminding the Polish desk in every new access dispute of the unpleasant consequences that had followed the exclusion of these two scholars.[45] However, his lonely efforts could not halt the increasing deterioration of archival relations between East and West during the 1960s.

March 1960. With the return of the documents in sight, the company announced that it would treat its returning property as it saw fit, including destroying files it no longer deemed important. The government agencies involved, however, argued that the access guarantee given by the federal government to the Western Allies also covered the Flick papers, and that these papers were being returned to the federal government and not to a private company. The goal was to keep the papers accessible for prosecutional activities of *Zentralstelle Ludwigsburg* and for historical research. Flick threatened to sue the federal government if it did not hand over the files that were temporarily stored at the *Bundesarchiv* in Koblenz. The federal position became untenable when the State Department informed Flick's lawyer "that the United States Government does not insist that such a condition [making them available for inspection; A.E.] be imposed on those seized German records returned from the United States which the German Federal Government decides to give back to private owners." The files were returned to Flick in November 1962. The case is documented in PA/AA, B118, vol. 203.

42 Referat 11.5 to ZB 8, 3 July 1964, "Study of archival material at Political Archive by scholars from communist countries," PA/AA, B118, vol. 237. Referat 11.5 was the new abbreviation for the Polish desk after an internal reorganisation of the Foreign Ministry. Likewise, ZB8 denominates the Political Archive.

43 The scholars were Bohumil Cerny, Prague, and Tone Ferenc from the Institute for the History of the Labor Movement, Ljubljana. Ferenc was working on a dissertation on ethnic policies in Yugoslavia under the German occupation during World War II. The head of the Political Department (D II) declined Ferenc's user request while Johannes Ullrich was on vacation leave. Ferenc received the negative reply via the Swedish Embassy. Sweden represented the Yugoslav interests in the Federal Republic since the two states had no offical diplomatic relations. See Note Verbale, 25 November 1963, PA/AA, B118, vol. 237.

44 R. W. Mason, FO Library, to Ullrich, 29 April 1964, PA/AA, B118, vol. 237. In October 1965, Ferenc was finally allowed to work at the Political Archive for five days. See Weinandy to Ferenc, 16 September 1965, in the same.

45 Weinandy acting for Ullrich (later signed by Ullrich) Memorandum, Use of the Political Archive by historians from the Soviet Occupation Zone (SBZ) and countries of the Eastern Bloc, 14 January 1965, PA/AA, B118, vol. 291. The memorandum considered the user requests of the East German scholars Gerhart Haß, A. Anderle, Fritz Klein and Johanna Schellenberg.

In conclusion, it should be noted that the issue of archival access during the Cold War—and, for that matter, archival politics during that era in general—is still largely an unmapped territory.[46] What is known thus far about the issue does not allow us to place blame on either side, or to clearly distinguish between action and reaction in a spiral of worsening archival relations. The material for this case study does not include Polish sources and it is, therefore, not possible to make determinations about the scholarly and political intentions involved on that side. It would be useful to know the degree to which Polish history writing was put to political use and followed or was pressed to follow an agenda that was drawn up outside of scholarly circles.[47] In other words, it is not yet possible to say whether Starke's fears about Grünberg's study were warranted. The fact is, however, that by the beginning of the Cold War, both sides of the Iron Curtain had already realized that historical research and archival access were an "inexpensive resource in the battle of the political systems."[48] They

---

46 One aspect of archival politics during the Cold War, the exchange of archival material between the Federal Republic and the GDR, is discussed by Reinhard Kluge and Klaus Oldenhage, "Archive im innerdeutschen Dialog. Zur Geschichte der Rückkehr deutscher Akten und Urkunden in deren Heimatarchive im Rahmen des innerdeutschen Kulturabkommens vom 6. Mai 1986," in *Archivistica docet. Beiträge zur Archivwissenschaft und ihres interdisziplinären Umfelds,* eds. Friedrich Beck, Wolfgang Hempel, and Eckart Henning (Potsdam: Verlag für Berlin und Brandenburg, 1999), 189–203; Klaus Oldenhage, "Archivbeziehungen ZUR DDR," in *Aus der Arbeit der Archive. Beiträge zum Archivwesen, zur Quellenkunde und zur Geschichte. Festschrift für Hans Booms,* ed. Friedrich P. Kahlenberg (Boppard/Rh.: Harald Boldt, 1989), 130–141. To the best of my knowledge, there is no more literature on the general field.

47 While we still do not know much about Polish *Westforschung* (historical, archeological, anthropological and ethnological research on what became Poland's Western territories in 1919 and again in 1945), the continuities of its equivalent, the (West) German Ostforschung, are meanwhile being examined. See Jörg Hackmann, "An einem neuen Anfang der Ostforschung. Bruch und Kontinuität in der ostdeutschen Landeshistorie nach dem Zweiten Weltkrieg," in *Westfälische Forschungen* 46 (1996), 232–258; Wolfgang Kessler, *Fünfzig Jahre Forschung zur Geschichte der Deutschen in Polen. Die Historisch-Landeskundliche Kommission für Posen und das Deutschtum in Polen und die Kommission für die Geschichte der Deutschen in Polen 1950-2000* (Herne: Stiftung Martin-Opitz-Bibliothek, 2001); Eduard Mühle, "Ostforschung. Beobachtungen zu Aufstieg und Niedergang eines geschichtswissenschaftlichen Paradigmas," in *Zeitschrift für Ostmitteleuropa-Forschung* 46:3 (1997), 317–350; Eduard Mühle, "Institutionelle Grundlegung und wissenschaftliche Programmatik der westdeutschen Beschäftigung mit 'deutscher Geschichte' im östlichen Mitteleuropa (1945-1959)," in *Erfahrungen der Vergangenheit. Deutsche in Ostmitteleuropa in der Historiographie nach 1945,* ed. Mühle, Jerzey Kłoczowski, Witold Matwiejczyk (Tagungen zur Ostmitteleuropa Forschung 9). (Lublin-Marburg: Verlag Herder Institut, 2000), 25–64.

48 "Kostengünstige Resource im Systemkonflikt." See Edgar Wolfrum, *Geschichtspolitik der Bundesrepublik Deutschland. Der Weg zur bundesrepublikanischen Erinnerung 1948–1990,* (Darmstadt: WBG, 1999), 36.

were simply deemed too important to be left to historians and archivists alone. By the end of the 1960s, active and reactive politics on all sides had effectively ruined the possibility of archival access.[49] The issue had been politicized to a degree that could only be detrimental to historical research. If archival access was granted to scholars from the respective "other side," political motives were usually not far removed.

49 The deteriorating archival relations are well documented in BA/K, B198, vol. 1638.

6

OFFICIAL SECRECY AND THE RIGHT TO A FAIR TRIAL: THE CASE OF HMS THETIS

Maureen Spencer

One important ingredient of a fair trial is the right of the parties to produce all relevant evidence. They should also be able to call on third parties to produce whatever relevant evidence they may have. This right of access to evidence is part of the more general right of access to justice. If the ability to produce evidence is limited, there is a danger that the outcome may not be factually accurate and that procedural justice is denied. As a result, confidence in the machinery of justice may be undermined. However, access to evidence has never been an absolute right. One of the most significant limitations of that right is the court's capacity to refuse to order disclosure of material which it is not in the wider public interest to disclose.

In 1942, the House of Lords laid down two important rules in the landmark case *Duncan v. Cammell Laird* [1942] AC 624. The case was a result of the sinking of HMS *Thetis* submarine in Liverpool Bay in June 1939 with a loss of 99 lives. The 1942 hearing arose from a request for a preliminary ruling on disclosure of evidence before the substantive suit for negligence was heard. The House of Lords held that relevant documents must not be disclosed if a public interest, such as national security, required that they be withheld. It also held that Ministers of the Crown were to be the sole arbiters of what the public interest was. A certificate or affidavit from the responsible Minister, or the permanent head of the department in the Minister's absence, would be accepted by the court as conclusive.

It has been widely accepted that the actual decision for non-disclosure in *Duncan v. Cammell Laird* was a correct one in light of the wartime need to preserve naval secrets, although the reasoning behind the decision and administrative abuse of it in subsequent years have been condemned. In their authoritative text *Administrative Law*, Wade and Forsyth claim that after the war it was revealed that the *Thetis* had a new type of torpedo tube which in 1942 was still secret. They write: "The case is a good example of the most genuine type where it seems plain that the interests of litigants must be sacrificed in order to preserve secrets of state." This view accords with that of Lord Reid in *Conway v. Rimmer* [1968] AC 910, 938.[1] Indeed, the ruling may well be explained in part by the extreme exigencies of wartime conditions. It meant that the plaintiffs, dependants of the victims, suing naval personnel, and builders of the submarine, Cammell Laird, were, initially at least, denied materials which they argued were necessary for their case. However wartime files of the Treasury Solicitor's Office show that government insistence on secrecy was due less to the need to protect the nation's defences than to an entrenched bureaucratic approach which

---

1   H.W.R. Wade and C.F. Forsyth, *Administrative Law*, 8th ed. (Oxford: Oxford University Press, 2000), 827. The House of Lords in *Conway and Rimmer* asserted the court's right to look behind the Minister's affidavit and inspect the documents themselves. It thus finally overruled *Duncan v. Cammell Laird* on this point. In doing so, Lord Reid, for one, seems to have adopted the conventional view of the *Thetis* case: He said [1968] AC 910, 938: "I have no doubt that the case of *Duncan v. Cammell Laird & Co. Ltd.* [1942] A.C. 624 was rightly decided. The plaintiff sought discovery of documents relating to the submarine "Thetis" including a contract for the hull and machinery and plans and specifications. The First Lord of the Admiralty had stated that 'it would be injurious to the public interest that any of the said documents should be disclosed to any person.' Any of these documents might well have given valuable information, or at least clues, to the skilled eye of an agent of a foreign power. But Lord Simon L.C. took the opportunity to deal with the whole question of the right of the Crown to prevent production of documents in litigation. Yet a study of his speech leaves me with the strong impression that throughout he had primarily in mind cases where discovery or disclosure would involve a danger of real prejudice to the national interest. I find it difficult to believe that his speech would have been the same if the case had related, as the present case does, to discovery of routine reports on a probationer constable."

saw the litigants as an intrusive inconvenience, and which prompted resistance to any request for assistance from the administration. The crucial outcome of the case as far as the government and civil service were concerned was that the precedent was clearly established—that the courts could not look behind a claim for non-disclosure on the grounds of public interest if made by a Minister in the proper form. In fact, having achieved this victory but having failed to stop the substantive litigation proceeding, the government, of its own volition, made the documents which were the subject of the 1942 case available to the same litigants a year later. Actually, revealing the documents was acceptable as long as the principle was maintained that it was the government and not the court which had the final word. The story of *Duncan v. Cammell Laird* therefore is one of the interrelationships between the archival record and the development of the important legal principle known as Crown Immunity.[2]

HMS *Thetis* sank on her maiden dive in the afternoon of 1 June 1939, carrying over fifty passengers in addition to her naval complement. Many civilian visitors were on board, including employees of the shipbuilder, subcontractors, and even catering staff. These had not chosen to disembark, as expected, to a waiting tug before the dive. At the initial diving position, HMS *Thetis* was at first very reluctant to dive, and for nearly an hour the submarine was submerging very slowly and on an even keel. Then suddenly she dived, completely disappeared within one minute, and sank with her bows in the mud about 160 feet from the surface. The crew spent the rest of the day and all night in a failed and increasingly desperate attempt to refloat her. Eventually some eighteen feet of the stern on the 270-foot submarine was above the water. The decision was made that four men should escape early the next morning using the special underwater apparatus, and try to get assistance. The four succeeded in reaching the surface, but all rescue attempts failed, in part because of slow Admiralty reaction to the disaster. All left on board perished, probably by the end of the second day. The supply of air which would have been sufficient for the crew for three days was used up by the excess of passengers.

---

2 Subsequently, the courts recognised that claims for non-disclosure in the public interest could be claimed by bodies other than central government departments and the doctrine was renamed Public Interest Immunity.

The catastrophe was initiated in the forepart of the submarine. There, six torpedo tubes were contained in separate compartments, with bow caps which could be opened to the sea at one end, while at the rear end, the collision bulkhead formed a strong watertight compartment, dividing the torpedo space from the stowage department by six watertight rear doors. Obviously, a bow cap and a rear door should never be open at the same time or the stowage would be flooded, but there were no safety arrangements in place preventing such an occurrence. In the torpedo space, there were levers controlling the supply of power to the bow caps. These could be set in three positions: open, neutral, or shut. In the neutral position, the power was locked in whatever direction the lever had previously pointed, whether open or shut, and so was not a clear indication of the existing state of the bow cap door. In addition, there were six mechanical bow cap indicators whose design was such that the dials were difficult to see. Apart from the position of the bow cap levers and the indicators, there were two other methods of assessing whether a torpedo tube was filled with water and thus that the bow caps had been opened. The rear tube doors were fitted with a small test cock which could be opened by a lever. If a jet of water came through the hole, this indicated that the tube was full and the water under pressure. To check the working of the test cock, a rimer (a needle-like rod) was provided to poke through the hole and clear any obstruction. Another more reliable test was provided by a drain valve where a rush of water would indicate that the bow caps were open.

The initial slowness of the *Thetis* to dive had indicated to those on board that she was too light and that errors had been made in calculating the amount of water needed in her tanks for the dive. First Lieutenant Woods, who was in control of preparations for the dive, was ordered by the captain of the submarine, Commander Bolus, to check on the state of the torpedo tubes. He used the test cocks to check if the holes were blocked but did not use either the rimer or the drain. He reported that the No. 6 tube contained water but that no water had come from the No. 5 tube. There followed some difference of opinion between the Cammell Laird foreman and the Admiralty personnel about whether these tubes should be full of water.

Woods was ordered to recheck the tubes, performed the same operations on the test cocks, and reported the same results. He then decided to inspect the inside of the tubes but did not inform the control room. He inspected the bow cap indicators and was satisfied that they were all shut; he asked Leading Seaman Hambrook to check the position of the bow cap operating levers, received a satisfactory reply, and again opened the test cocks. He next ordered Hambrook to open the rear doors and inspected the insides of the Numbers 1, 2, 3, and 4 tubes, which were all empty. On opening the No. 5 rear door, however, an enormous rush of water flooded in; the door could not be re-closed, and with difficulty the men retreated to the stowage compartment, which in turn was flooded. They finally closed its watertight door and escaped to the accommodation space. The flooding and consequential imbalance caused the *Thetis's* sudden dive. The four who escaped the next morning included Woods but not Hambrook or Bolus.[3]

In September the *Thetis* was raised; it was discovered that the bow cap of the No. 5 torpedo tube was fully open to the sea, its mechanical indicator was at "open," all the bow cap levers were at neutral, and the test cock aperture of the No. 5 door was blocked by a small plug of the bitumastic enamel which had been used to paint the doors in dock at Cammell Laird. The blockage had not been noticed by the Admiralty overseer, Edward Grundy, who was responsible for checking the work before the launch of the submarine and who had not been on board during the fatal dive. An internal naval inquiry and then a judicial public inquiry chaired by His Honour Judge Bucknill had been set up in June. In August 1939, supported by their unions, relatives of civilians on board initiated legal action against Woods, against the estates of Hambrook and Bolus, and against Cammell Laird. Later, the subcontractors who carried out the enamelling, Wailes Dove Bitumastic, were joined as defendants.[4] As the law stood then, the Crown was immune from legal liability in negligence, but by custom the government departments defended their personnel who were sued for acts committed in the course of their duties. Only relatives of the dead civilians sued since no liability existed for acts committed against serving naval or military personnel.

---

3 For a very detailed account of the sinking of the *Thetis* see C. Warren and J. Benson, *Thetis: Disaster in Liverpool Bay: 'the Admiralty Regrets . . .'* (Higher Bebington: Avid Publications, 1997). There seems no doubt that Woods demonstrated considerable bravery during the attempts to refloat the submarine and in volunteering to embark on the hazardous escape. He returned to active service and was awarded the Distinguished Service Cross in August 1940.

4 It is not clear from the papers why Edward Grundy was not joined as a defendant.

The government law officers in the Office of the Treasury Solicitor had the task of providing legal assistance to the public inquiry and to Woods and the representatives of Bolus and Hambrook. They worked closely with the Admiralty personnel. Although privately acknowledging that the plaintiffs might succeed, officials were contemptuous of the plaintiffs' motives and took a largely uncritical view of the evidence of Lieutenant Woods, influenced in their view of the facts by his undoubted bravery after the disaster. Indeed, the facts were complex and capable of differing interpretations, and it is arguable that the final 1946 House of Lords decision in the substantive negligence case exonerating all the defendants was the correct one.[5] Irrespective of whether the final decision was a fair one or not, it is illuminating to review the influence of civil servants in generating the cultural climate of secrecy which accelerated the development of judicial deference to the executive.

The official position that no liability for the tragedy should lie with any individual was set within a month of its occurrence. The internal naval inquiry interviewed 51 witnesses including Woods, Cammell Laird employees, and naval experts and presented its report at the end of June.[6] Woods, under questioning, gave the following account: he had tried the test cocks without using the rimer to clear the apertures, he had seen the No. 5 bow cap indicator at the "shut" position, he had asked Hambrook if the levers themselves were in the shut" position, and he got the answer "yes." The report commented on his responsibility for the accident:

> [T]here was no adequate reason for Lieutenant Woods opening the rear doors and he was not justified in doing so without instructions.[7]

However, despite this criticism, the Admiralty inspectors appeared to be so impressed with Woods's honesty and courage that they discounted the possibility that he had mistakenly read the bow cap indicators. This initial interpretation of events was to dominate perceptions

---

5   *Duncan and Others v. Cammell Laird* [1946] AC 401.

6   I am grateful to maritime historian David Roberts for drawing my attention to the papers of the Internal Naval Inquiry which are held in the archives of the Submarine Museum at Fort Gosport. The papers of the Inquiry are to be found in files A1939/023 and A1939/5. David Robert's book, HMS *Thetis, Secrets and Scandal* (Bebington: Avid Publications, 1999), draws on archival research and on interviews with relatives of the survivors.

7   Report of Internal Naval Inquiry. Gosport A 1939/5.

of the tragedy in the years which followed, even in the face of emerging contrary evidence. The internal inquiry report concluded:

> We are of the opinion that the behaviour of all in the submarine—naval personnel and civilians—was exemplary and in accordance with the best traditions of the Naval Service and the British Race.[8]

An honest and brave witness, however, can still be a mistaken one. Woods was later to testify at the High Court trial in 1943 that the question he had asked Hambrook about the bow cap levers was not whether they were shut but, more ambiguously, whether they were "correct."[9] This change from his earlier testimony did not shake the consistent official view that he was a highly reliable and convincing witness.

The proceedings of the Bucknill inquiry were held in public from July to December 1939 and the report was presented in February 1940. On receiving the report, the First Sea Lord, Winston Churchill noted (with perhaps a rather an unfortunate choice of metaphor from this master of the English language):

> All interest in this tragedy has been submerged by the war. I should deprecate any disciplinary action unless some definite act can be traced to an individual. Indeed I should be glad if Lieutenant Woods' mind could be set at rest.[10]

The Second Sea Lord Admiral Sir Charles Little presented an internal memorandum on the Bucknill Report. He wrote, "I am in favour of publication as owing to the incidence of war it will receive the least notice at the present time." He noted the responsibility of both Woods and Grundy for the disaster:

> [T]he door of the torpedo tube is fitted to admit offloading or withdrawing the torpedo: it is not intended as a means for observing whether the tube is full or empty of water. For this purpose a drain clock is specially fitted at the forward and after ends of the tube underneath and the special fitting referred to with the timer attachment is placed on the rear door for the same purpose. In my opinion no discreet or experienced submarine officer would have tested the tube for this purpose and especially under the circumstances of the trial dive, by the rear door. Mr Grundy, the Admiralty overseer who

---

8   Ibid.
9   PRO TS32/113 report of Court of Appeal hearing, 7 July 1944.
10 PRO ADM 116/4115 Personal Minute by First Lord of the Admiralty, 12 February 1940.

inspected the internal painting of the tube, is also not free from blame as he failed to make a thorough and secure inspection.[11]

However, the public position was to avoid allocating individual blame, and this was the conclusion of the Bucknill Report itself, which was welcomed by the Admiralty. Little noted:

> It is clear that the action of these two (Lieutenant Woods and Mr Grundy) only forms part of a series of what the judge calls "perverse mishaps" in the report of the Tribunal. It is suggested that an official letter should be sent to their superior authorities to the effect that, after considering the reports of the Naval Board of Inquiry and of the Public Tribunal, their Lordships have come to the conclusion that the loss of "HMS Thetis" is to be attributed to a combination of mischances, and that it has not been possible to discover the whole facts; in the circumstances, it is to be put on record that their Lordships will not hold Lieutenant Woods or Mr Grundy to blame for the disaster, and that in this respect the matter is to be regarded as closed.[12]

This official perception of Woods as a brave hero contrasts with the administration's view of the relatives of the civilian litigants who were pictured as self-seeking and unpatriotic litigants manipulated by their unions and unscrupulous solicitors, although at the same time it was conceded that they could have a winnable case. Twenty-six actions were eventually initiated, of which the vast majority were sponsored by the trade unions to which the dead men had belonged, namely the Amalgamated Engineering Union (AEU), which supported fourteen cases, and the Electrical Trade Union supporting five.[13] Eventually, it

---

11 PRO ADM 116/4115 Memorandum by Second Sea Lord, 16 February 1940.

12 Ibid.

13 The litigation on the negligence suit was not completed until February 1946. After the final judgement of the House of Lords, Treasury Solicitor's assistant F. Lawton drafted a table for the Admiralty showing the outcomes of the various hearings (PRO TS 32/110: "HMS Thetis, Actions for Damages," 27 February 1946). It reads as follows:

	Wrottesley J	Court of Appeal (3 JUDGES)	House of Lords (5 JUDGES)
Woods	Not liable	Liable	Not liable
Hambrook	Not liable	Not liable	Not liable
Bolus	Not liable	No appeal	———
Cammell Laird	Liable	Not liable	Not liable
Wailes Dove	Not liable	Not liable	Not liable

Lawton noted: "The final result is that the Plaintiffs are held to be disentitled to recover against any one of the Defendants, Lt Cmdr Woods; Mrs Bolus (as representing the late

was agreed that the cases of two widows, Mrs. Duncan and Mrs. Ankers, should form test cases. The defendants' cases were prepared by Liverpool solicitors, Evill and Coleman.

Initially the Treasury Solicitor's staff tried to discredit the plaintiffs by arguing that they were acting unlawfully. At the time, the ancient offence of maintenance (third-party financing of litigation) had not been fully repealed, though its scope was steadily narrowing. The Treasury Solicitor's department took a traditionalist stance. Legal Assistant F.A.K. Ridley drafted a long memorandum arguing that consideration should be given to whether the unions were committing this offence and the solicitors breaching Law Society rules. He suggested that "any sort of stand against the accident claims racket would be salutary."[14]

> It ought not to be very difficult to make it clear to reasonably minded persons that what really lies behind these claims is not so much the desire of the claimants to obtain redress for their wrongs but the desire of the A.E.U. to embarrass the government and of the solicitors to make money out of a national calamity . . . it could be shown that the claimants have exhibited no great willingness to prefer claims but have been pressed to do so by Evill and Coleman. This contention would be reinforced if it could be shown that the proceedings were illegally maintained and that the solicitors' action in touting the claims has been the subject of disciplinary action by the Law Society.[15]

He went on to point out that the litigants were doubly undeserving since they were receiving payments from the charitable fund established in November 1939 under the direction of the Archbishop of Canterbury, which collected £150,000 in donations from the public:

> It would probably be possible to carry the matter further by showing that no real hardship would be suffered by the claimants if they were unable to recover these claims, since they have not only workmen's compensation but in addition a large fund has been raised by public subscription and it is not to be supposed that this fund would have been subscribed if it had been known that the persons

---

> Cmdr Colus (sic); Mrs Hambrook (as representing the late leading Seaman Hambrook); Cammell Laird & Co Ltd; Wailes Dove Bitumastic Ltd, a result that I think you will agree is most satisfactory. I have not sufficient information to make any reliable estimate of the sum that might have been recovered if damages were awarded but a total in the neighbourhood of £100,000 would not surprise me."

14 PRO TS32/110 *"Thetis*. Claims for Damages," E.A.K. Ridley to F.W. Lawton, 21 September 1939.

15 Ibid.

to benefit from it were looking to the Admiralty for full compensation, nothing having been said about this while the fund was being collected. It would probably be possible to get out some figures to show how much each might expect to get from the fund and it could no doubt be shown that the result of their getting both benefits from the fund and damages would be to confer on them much greater benefits as a result of the death of the person in respect of whom they were claiming than the law regards as the proper measure of damages—in other words that they have already been adequately compensated. A further point might be made that this is quite unlike the case of persons being killed by the unforeseen act of a stranger and that here they have voluntarily, or for the purposes of employment, submitted themselves to very definite risks of exactly the nature which resulted in their deaths. . . .

The real objection to these claims is, of course, that they would never have arisen but for the touting of the solicitors and I don't think there can be much doubt but that it was the solicitors who instigated the A.E.U. to act as they have done, though we have nothing at present but the letters to establish this. That leaves the other main question to be considered from the point of view of policy—namely what actions, if any, should be taken against the A.E.U. and/or the solicitors. . . . To establish illegal maintenance is not going to help us in dealing with the claims and the question of maintenance seems to be one for the DPP. On the other hand, I suggest that there is ample justification for bringing the solicitors' conduct to the notice of the Law Society. . . . No doubt the solicitors will assert that they acted on the instructions of A.E.U. (which may or may not help them) and the Law Society have not hitherto shown much zeal in dealing with the touting evil.[16]

The Attorney General, Sir Donald Somervell, however, doubted whether much could be made (1) of "the question of the impropriety of the Solicitors' action and maintenance with regard to the Union." (2) The existing cases left "the position of Unions in some doubt" and "as the potential plaintiffs are probably all poor the maintenance could be refused on the ground that it was an act of charity."[17] He wrote later that "the financing of claims by a Union is well known and recognised—particularly of course in Workmen's Compensation cases—and, so far as I know, has never been objected to on this ground."[18] One way forward was to try and settle out of court, and the Treasury

16 Ibid.
17 PRO TS32/110, Somervell to Lawton, 4 October 1939.
18 PRO TS32/110 "The *Thetis* Claims," Somervell, 6 November 1940.

Solicitor's Office prepared a memorandum for the Admiralty. There was, it was felt, "some risk of the actions being successful."[19] One solution was to try and reach an out of court settlement.

> [It] may be that the various Plaintiffs, if properly approached, might be prepared to come to a reasonable settlement. Many of the plaintiffs may feel it distasteful, now that the country is at war, to prosecute the claims for negligence against deceased naval personnel.[20]

Secret informal negotiations took place during 1940 between William Jowitt, Solicitor General, and trade union leaders, including the General Secretary of the Trades Union Congress, Sir Walter Citrine.[21] To underline the government's position, Somervell stressed that

> [t]he actions were felt to be objectionable partly because of the circumstances of the case and the unpleasantness of pursuing with a claim for negligence the executors of dead men who were not there to give evidence and deal with allegations made against them. Lieutenant Woods is alive, so this objection did not apply to his case, but it would I think seem distasteful to many to pursue him in this way. In his case and the other cases one's mind is affected by the very large sum of money (I believe about £150,000) raised by the public in order that the Workmen's Compensation and other payments should be supplemented. On the other hand, of course, one must be careful of adopting the position of suggesting that people are not entitled to enforce their legal rights.[22]

The Attorney-General considered that the litigants had an arguable case.

> I think myself that a finding that Lieutenant Woods and Able Seaman Hambrouk [sic] were negligent is a possible result and perhaps a not unlikely one. They were jointly engaged in opening the rear doors and in fact one bow cap was open and the levers were in the neutral and not in the shut position. When an accident happens in circumstances such as this, however fortuitous the group of circumstances which lead to the disaster, the Court rarely, if ever, finds that it was accidental.[23]

---

19 PRO TS32/110 Memorandum to Secretary, Admiralty. "The Thetis," undated.
20 Ibid.
21 See papers in TS32/110.
22 PRO TS32/110 "The *Thetis* Claims," Somervell, 6 November 1940.
23 Ibid.

Somervell also took up the link between the litigation and the Charitable Fund asking whether

> It might be a good idea to discover from the Trustees of the Fund what payments are being made to these people. I feel that this should and might affect the mind of the court and I also feel that from the point of view of any injustice by delay it would be satisfactory to know.

He was sent a list of payments in January 1941. Mrs. Rose Duncan was getting £1 a week and Mrs. Hannah Ankers £1.10.[24]

The negotiations however came to nought, in part because the government offer was limited to making a token contribution of £10,000 to the charitable fund, and because of the intransigent position of Cammell Laird.[25] During this time, solicitors for the parties continued to prepare their cases for trial. In June 1940, 16 documents in total were requested by solicitors acting for the plaintiffs. The list included the 1936 contract between the Admiralty and Cammell Laird. Many of these documents, including the contract and also the notebook of the Cammell Laird foreman in charge of the painting of the doors, had been available to the Bucknill Inquiry. However, F.W. Lawton, Assistant Treasury Solicitor, recommended resisting disclosure. He wrote:

> The Crown's claim for privilege which has at all times been jealously guarded, is based solely upon considerations of general public interest. I regard it as of very great importance that in no case should there be any relaxation of the direct application of the principle where it properly applies.[26]

He advocated claiming Crown Immunity for all except three items which related to the findings of the condition of the stricken submarine. The contract and the foreman's notebook were among those which should not be disclosed. He added that he did not think "that the war should be expressly relied on as a ground for refusal to admit disclosure since the actions may not come on for trial until after the war." He concluded:

---

24 PRO TS32/110, Somervell to Sir Thomas Barnes, 17 January 1940; Barnes to Attorney General, 17 January 1940.

25 See PRO TS32/110.

26 PRO TS32/110 "*Thetis.* Claims for Damages," Lawton, July 1940.

> In my view, whatever importance is attached to the documents either by the solicitors or by the court, the claim for privilege if made by the First Lord in the proper manner cannot be challenged successfully in or by the court and it is unlikely that anything further will be required from the First Lord than an affidavit in which the claim is made formally.[27]

The Admiralty acted on Lawton's advice, and in February 1941 the Minister's affidavit was presented to court. It read:

> All the said documents were considered by me with the assistance of my technical advisers and I formed the opinion that it would be injurious to the public interest that any of the said documents should be disclosed to any person.[28]

The High Court and the Court of Appeal both gave judgements in favour of non-disclosure and in early 1942 the plaintiffs' appeal reached the House of Lords. It was unanimously rejected. Despite this setback, the plaintiffs continued the litigation on the substantive issue of negligence. The government, which still wanted the trial to be in secret, proposed that the transcripts of the Bucknill Inquiry should be used as evidence instead of direct testimony, except that Woods would be called in person. The problem was that it would be difficult for the court to follow the transcript without having sight of the documents which were available to the public inquiry, and Counsel for Cammell Laird wanted to refer to the contract documents. The Admiralty then effected a complete about-turn. The First Lord directed that the matter should proceed on the following lines:

(a) [T]he Admiralty should not press for the trial to be held in camera;

(b) [T]he exhibits for which privilege was claimed by the First Lord in 1940 should be shown to the Judge and Counsel only;

(c) [A]n Admiralty representative should be present in Court with authority to advise the Judge and Attorney General when he considers that for reasons of security the public should be cleared from the Court.[29]

---

27 Ibid.
28 See text in *Duncan v. Cammell Laird* [1942] AC 624, p. 626.
29 PRO TS32/110, 13 September 1943.

As Counsel for Wailes-Dove put it

> [N]otwithstanding the journey to the House of Lords (!) the First
> Lord is now prepared to allow copies of the documents for which
> privilege was successfully claimed to be made available for use of the
> Judge and Counsel. [30]

When the trial opened in the Kings Bench Division in September
1943, the Attorney-General explained to the court that the real point
of the 1942 House of Lords hearing was executive privilege. He said,
referring to the 1941 affidavit:

> The First Lord of the Admiralty, having looked at [the documents]
> filed an affidavit in the terms referred to saying that it was not in
> the public interest that they should be disclosed. That was taken to
> the House of Lords really on the point as to whether that was a
> matter for the First Lord or for the Courts. When arrangements
> were made some time later . . . that this case should be tried on the
> transcript [of the Bucknill Inquiry] we communicated with the
> First Lord and we also communicated with my learned friend, who
> said that these documents should be available for Counsel and the
> Judge and if required by anyone for the purpose of seeing that all
> proper issues were brought before your Lordship.[31]

Counsel for the plaintiffs, Mr. Wallington KC was scornful.

> The position was this, that this matter of production and indeed
> the question whether it would be injurious to the public interest
> that any of the said documents should be disclosed to any person, as
> the first Lord swore it would be, went to the House of Lords,
> despite the fact that in each Court on our way up to the House of
> Lords and in the House of Lords what we were saying was: 'Let the
> Judge look at the documents; let him be the judge of whether this is
> unjust or not and at all events let some direction be given that the
> Judge himself and Counsel may see the documents.' But that was
> rejected and right up to the House of Lords the position was main-
> tained against us that nobody must see them and the affidavit of the
> First Lord was final and conclusive about it.... What I feel and
> what I want to present to your Lordship on the case now is that the
> House of Lords ruled, as they did, that none of these are to be seen

---

30 PRO TS32/110 Streatfield to Parker, 17 September 1943.
31 PRO TS32/110, Transcript of Mr.Wallington's opening speech in Kings Bench Division,
    22 September 1943.

by anybody because the First Lord so said, it is not now open to the Attorney-General to be magnanimous and say, 'Well, now in 1943, although there has been no change in circumstances, what the First Lord swore in 1941 no longer holds and you may see them, although we refused to allow you to see them in 1941.'[32]

In the event, the contract was inspected and referred to in court. Although it is arguable that the national security position had changed between 1940 and 1943, it is clear that the overriding objective of the administration had been to assert its authority over the courts on the decision on disclosure; the content of the actual documents was less important. As the Attorney-General told the court, "everybody has been told" what is in the contract. He continued,

> The real point in the Cammell Laird issue which was decided was whether . . . the question of non-disclosure in the public interest was a matter for the Judge or a matter for the Crown. That was the issue and the House of Lords did not make any Order that the First Lord of the Admiralty could never at any time allow anybody to see it.[33]

There is also a suggestion in the papers that the administration had hoped that their earlier obstructive tactics would halt the litigation. This is apparent in the discussion concerning a request made by Wallington to inspect a submarine similar to the *Thetis*. In December 1940, the request had been refused, but the government's approach had changed by the summer of 1943. The Admiralty official noted:

> When application was made in December 1940 for Mr Wallington KC to be permitted to inspect a submarine similar to the Thetis we were hoping to arrange for the threatened legal action to be withdrawn. The Attorney-General was not in favour of granting the facilities; we took the hint from him and refused to grant them 'under present conditions' without giving any reason. The papers show that the actual reason was expediency and not considerations of public interest and security since representatives of the Press were constantly being given facilities to visit submarines. . . . The circumstances have changed. The plaintiffs have now got their case together and obtained a date for the trial; the Attorney-General considers it would be desirable, if at all possible, that facilities should be granted to the

---

32 Ibid.
33 Ibid.

plaintiffs' counsel and also the counsel for Cammell Laird, to inspect a 'comparable submarine.'[34]

This time, the visit was arranged.

The archive record also dispels another myth about the 1942 case: that the plaintiffs were cheated of victory in the substantive case by the government's withholding of evidence. In fact, the plaintiffs were eventually able to inspect contested material (since the court had not ordered that they could not do so, and it suited the government to reveal it). The 1942 House of Lords decision was to be enormously influential. It initiated a period of over 25 years when government departments routinely and successfully claimed Crown Privilege even for low-level and uncontroversial documents, and the courts did not look behind the claims. As Wade and Forsyth put it, "It is not surprising that the Crown, having been given a blank cheque, yielded to the temptation to overdraw."[35]

---

34 PRO TS32/110 Morrison, 5 July 1943.

35 Wade and Forsyth, *Administrative Law*. My thanks to the staff of the National Archives Kew and to Mr. Malcolmson, Archivist at the Royal Naval Submarine Museum Gosport, for their generous assistance.

See also Maureen Spencer, "Bureaucracy, National Security and Access to Justice: New Light on *Duncan v. Cammell Laird*," *Northern Ireland Legal Quarterly* 55:3 (2004).

7

THE TUSKEGEE SYPHILIS STUDY: ACCESS AND CONTROL OVER CONTROVERSIAL RECORDS

Tywanna Whorley

As the nation's archives, the National Archives and Records Administration (NARA) preserves and provides access to records that document how the government conducts business on behalf of the American people, past and present. For the American citizen, NARA provides a form of accountability through the records in its custody, which affect the nation's collective memory. Many of these records, however, contain evidence of the federal government's misconduct in episodes in American history, and these have affected public trust. The Tuskegee Syphilis Study records are a prime example of records in the custody of NARA that continue to have a lasting effect on public trust in the federal government. Even though NARA has made available administrative records which document the government's role in the study, the Tuskegee Syphilis Study records continue to challenge the archival institution on a variety of issues, such as access, privacy, collective memory, and accountability. The administrative role of the National Archives in maintaining and providing access to the Tuskegee Syphilis Study records, especially the restricted information, will be examined here.

In 1932, the United States Public Health Service (PHS) began a study that would observe the natural course of syphilis in 399 African-American men in Tuskegee, Alabama, until they died, in order to determine whether there were any racial differences in the natural history of the disease. As a control, there was a comparable group of 200 African-American men without syphilis who were observed. The infected men were never told that they had syphilis. They were merely told that they had "bad blood." Throughout the study, the men never received any kind of formal medical treatment for their disease. With the cooperation of state and local physicians, the researchers managed to prevent these men from receiving any kind of treatment or discovering what "bad blood" meant. As a result of this concealed effort, the study continued for 40 years. Often called the "longest non-therapeutic experiment on human beings in medical history," the study was exposed to the world on 25 July 1972. This controversial and unethical study ended officially in November 1972.

The exposure of the study has engendered a much closer scrutiny of many aspects of governmental and overall research practices, specifically creating safeguards for those who participate in research experiments. The survivors and their families have received compensation from the federal government as well as free medical care for life. More importantly, on 16 May 1997, they received a long-awaited government apology.

The records generated from the 40-year study underscore the informational and evidentiary value in holding the U.S. government accountable. The voluminous documents revealed that PHS physicians knew from the inception of the study that the participants believed they were in a treatment programme. The files consisted of records created during the course of the study that related to: 1) individual patients; 2) publications based on findings of the study; 3) correspondence between medical personnel; 4) administrative records; 5) photographs of various medical tests or procedures; and 6) minutes. More importantly, the documents reveal how meticulous these physicians were in carrying out the initial steps of the study in the early years.

Today, the original records are in the custody of the National Archives Southeast Region Center in Atlanta, Georgia. These records also include affidavits relating to: 1) the ensuing federal court case; 2) agendas and committee hearings; and 3) materials relating to the public scrutiny to which the study and the agency were subjected once the study was exposed. Currently, there are 40 boxes of administrative files. Of the 40 boxes, boxes 1–20 and 20(a) are open to the public. The remaining boxes, an additional 1–3, and 21–35 and 32(a), which contain information about individual patients and the court case, are restricted until the year 2030, in order to protect the personal privacy of the participants. In addition, there are 47 boxes of medical files which are restricted until the year 2030. Thus, there are a total of 87 boxes pertaining to the Tuskegee Syphilis Study. It would seem obvious that protection of the Tuskegee participants' medical records is non-negotiable, given the humiliation these men and their families have already endured. However, it is not that simple. Access to all the Tuskegee Syphilis Study records is a hotly contested issue between NARA, researchers, and African Americans.

The significance of archival records cannot be overstated. Archival records serve as instruments of accountability and building blocks of collective memory. John McDonald notes the connection between records and accountability as follows: "Without records, there can be no demonstration of accountability. Without evidence of accountability, society cannot trust in its public institutions."[1] Thus, the records within the custody of the National Archives are the bedrock for holding the federal government accountable to its citizens. As a result, the National Archives continues to function as the important collective memory of our society. However, records within the custody of the National Archives that enable us to confront our recent past "provide evidence of actions, decisions, and intentions, both legal and illegal, proper and improper," which is "an inherent part of the accountability function and recordkeeping systems."[2] For records that reveal illegal and improper governmental actions, archivists must not hesitate in exposing the existence of such records. As Kent Haworth states, "The essence of archives are the records in our care," and "the purpose of the archivist is to hold in trust for society the evidence of the truth, the evidence of justice and injustice in the society our archives document."[3]

1 John McDonald, "Accountability in government in an electronic age," www.irmt.org/resources/maljm2.doc (accessed July 2003, no longer available).
2 Richard J. Cox and David A. Wallace, eds., *Archives and the Public Good: Accountability and Records in Modern Society* (Westport, Conn.: Quorum Books, 2002), 4, 11.
3 Kent Haworth, "The Principles Speak for Themselves: Articulating a Language of Purpose for Archives," in *The Archival Imagination: Essays in Honour of Hugh Taylor,* ed. Barbara L. Craig (Ottawa: Association of Canadian Archivists, 1992).

The Tuskegee Syphilis Study continues to be a high-profile incident in recent years. More importantly, the records themselves are critical to revealing government misconduct that gave rise to this
notorious episode of American history. In their recent edited volume,
Richard Cox and David Wallace concur that, as archivists, "We need
to remember that records are critical to societal awareness and the
memory of pivotal events, and that their use may be part of controver-
sies forcing archivists to take stands on access to records."[4] Such is the
case with the Tuskegee Syphilis Study records, where restricted access
to medical records has become a controversial issue.

Scholars interested in medical records for historical research purposes face many obstacles, which include confronting access and confidentiality issues relating to their research agendas. Medical records
raise special problems for archives having such records in their custody.
Providing access to sensitive material has been and continues to be a
constant struggle for archivists. Thus, the challenge for repositories,
which have holdings containing medical information, has been protecting individual privacy interests while providing access to the intellectual content of the material.

Even though the National Archives contains documented evidence of "the rights of American citizens, the actions of Federal officials, and the national experience," it is bound by federal laws that
prohibit the release of certain information, especially sensitive or personal information. As a result, it would seem that the right to be
informed, to know, to have access to important information, is anti-
thetical to the right to privacy. For archivists working at the National
Archives, administering access to records that contain personal information is a challenge, given the nuances of the federal statutes they
must follow, specifically the Privacy Act and the Freedom of
Information Act (FOIA). As Heather MacNeil points out, for government archivists "personal information collected and maintained by
government agencies eventually ends up in their custody, leaving them
with the unenviable task of reconciling legitimate but conflicting
interests—the individual's right to privacy and society's need for
knowledge."[5] Hence, the most apposite example to examine how the

---

4   Cox and Wallace, *Archives and the Public Good*, 11.
5   Heather MacNeil, *Without Consent: the Ethics of Disclosing Personal Information in Public
    Archives* (Metuchen, N.J.: Scarecrow Press, 1992), 5.

National Archives balances between these two competing interests is the Tuskegee Syphilis Study records case.

In 1990, before the National Archives could take custody of the Tuskegee Syphilis Study records from the Centers for Disease Control (CDC), a written agreement was prepared between the two agencies.[6] The agreement, which was attached to the accession record, stated that:

> The National Archives and Records Administration will be responsible for preserving and maintaining the records in accordance with the approved CDC Records Control Schedule, item 101 (records will be preserved in perpetuity for future historical research).
>
> Because of the sensitive nature of the information contained in these medical records of Tuskegee Study Health Benefit Recipients, and the potential negative effects on the subject individuals and their families, disclosure is not permitted to the general public, including researchers, per 5 U.S.C. § 552 (b)(6), until the year 2030.
>
> The National Archives will become the responsible party regarding maintaining the records in accordance with the requirements of the Freedom of Information Act and the Privacy Act.[7]

According to the records manager at the Centers for Disease Control (CDC), those working for the Tuskegee Study Health Benefits Program were reluctant to turn over custody of the records to NARA despite the Centers for Disease Control records retention schedule that required the transfer. Some CDC officials did not trust NARA to preserve the records. Furthermore, they did not want anyone to have access to the medical information. However, the voluminous amount of FOIA requests interfered with their duties with the Tuskegee Benefits Program. When responding to requests by researchers or the general public who desired to see patient information, the CDC FOIA office told requesters that they could not see this information due to 5 U.S.C § 552(b)(6), otherwise known as Exemption 6 of the federal Freedom of Information Act. Exemption 6 permits federal agencies to withhold

---

6   Custody defined by the National Archives and Records Administration is "guardianship, or control, of records, including both physical possession (physical custody) and legal responsibility (legal custody), unless one or the other is specified," in National Archives and Records Administration, *Disposition of Federal Records: a Records Management Handbook* (Washington, D.C.: NARA, 1992), D-4.

7   National Archives and Records Administration, "Transfer, Approval, and Receipt of Records to National Archives of the United States," RG442. Tuskegee Syphilis Study Administrative Records, Accession Nos. 4NN-442-90-01, 1992.

"personnel, medical, and similar files whose disclosure would constitute a clearly unwarranted invasion of personal privacy (see 5 U.S.C. § 552(b)(6))." Requests would end there, especially when researchers were not familiar with the legal nuances of FOIA and the Privacy Act.[8] Therefore, for the CDC, Exemption 6 proved to be the shield against the public interest in the right to know what the government was up to when it conducted the Tuskegee Syphilis Study.

The National Archives managed to get custody of the Tuskegee Syphilis Study records by making a number of assurances to and entering the aforementioned agreement with the CDC. Even though NARA is federally mandated to take custody of records from governmental agencies, exercising this authority continues to be a challenge. There have been a number of reported cases where governmental agencies have failed to turn over records to the National Archives, especially records with sensitive information. MacNeil points out that the transfer of records to a governmental archive is a challenge when "even in jurisdictions [mandated by legislation] archivists are often refused access to records containing sensitive personal information which are either maintained by the record-creating agency in perpetuity or destroyed before archivists have had an opportunity to determine whether they have archival value."[9] Thus, if the Tuskegee Health Benefits Program were not inundated with FOIA requests, NARA might not have received the records when scheduled. The non-receipt of these records would have undermined further public accountability of the Tuskegee Syphilis Study.

The written agreement between the two agencies is inconsistent with the spirit of FOIA and the values that the statute espouses, such as promoting public discourse on matters of public interest. For example, Exemption 6 and NARA regulations issued under FOIA do not allow NARA to decide categorically to withhold medical records without weighing the public interests in disclosure against the personal privacy interests at stake. NARA FOIA regulations on restricting the use of records are contained in the Code of Federal Regulations, Volume 36, Section 1256. NARA interprets information that would invade the privacy of an individual as follows:

---

8 For information on these federal statutes, see The Freedom of Information Act (FOIA), 5 USC §552a, as amended.

9 MacNeil, *Without Consent*, 193.

Records containing information about a living individual which reveal details of a highly personal nature that the individual could reasonably assert a claim to withhold from the public to avoid a clearly unwarranted invasion of privacy, including but not limited to information about the physical or mental health or the medical or psychiatric care or treatment of the individual, and that contain personal information not known to have been previously made public, and relate to events less than 75 years old.[10]

The issue of withholding records in order to protect an individual's privacy interest becomes more complicated when that individual is deceased. Furthermore, Section 1256.4 (a)(4) states that "NARA will not grant access contrary to a specific restriction to records which have specific restrictions on access imposed by the agency or origin." In the case of the Tuskegee Syphilis Study medical records, NARA agreed to restrict access until 2030.

Although these two regulations would seem to prohibit NARA from releasing archival records containing personal information such as the Tuskegee Syphilis Study medical records, Section 1256.4 (a)(2) provides that "if NARA is able to make a copy of such records with all personal identifiers masked or deleted, NARA will make such a 'sanitized' copy of the record available to all researchers with part 1254 of this chapter." Therefore, NARA may be able to redact any personal identifiers such as names and addresses and still grant access to the Tuskegee medical files. For researchers unfamiliar with the National Archives FOIA regulations, they would not know that access to records containing personal information is possible.

The statutory language of Exemption 6 does not provide guidance on whether the privacy interests protected by FOIA diminish upon the death of the person mentioned in the record. In this case, the privacy interests to be protected by FOIA may depend on the relationships that third parties had with the deceased. A number of federal courts have suggested that these privacy interests either disappear or are reduced in that case. The National Archives is now facing this issue with the Tuskegee medical files. The Tuskegee records are the only records in the custody of NARA that have restrictions, even though most of the participants in the study are deceased. Generally, NARA releases records about an individual after the individual's death.

---

10 See National Archives regulations under General Restrictions 36 CFR§1256.16(a)(1)(2).

Another controversy surrounding the Tuskegee Syphilis Study records is identifying participants by name who were a part of the study. Under the previously mentioned regulations, NARA will not release any archival records that contain personal information, including names. This is definitely the case with the Tuskegee Syphilis Study records. However, the names of the participants are in the public domain. Fred Gray, a civil rights attorney, who sued the government on behalf of the participants, has written a book about the lawsuit, where he names 625 men who were part of the study. In addition, some of the men and their family members have given public interviews, as well as participated in events associated with the public outcry over the study. Thus, this confidentiality asserted by the CDC and NARA, which has been the hallmark of the management of these records, has been circumspectly challenged.

The Tuskegee Syphilis Study records document the longest non-therapeutic study in American history. The records illuminate government misconduct and allow an additional opportunity for the public to hold the federal government accountable for this misconduct. These records exemplify a National Archives archival policy on restricting archival records that contain personal information without reconciling the right to know versus the right to privacy. The National Archives entered an agreement with the CDC intended to insulate the participants from the public by forbidding the disclosure of their identities. However, that information has made it into the public domain. In addition, a researcher can challenge the release of all or partial disclosure of the medical information based on the FOIA and NARA regulations issued under that statute. Richard Cox and David Wallace state that "records frequently provide the scaffolding for the stories relayed and sometime they even play central roles, yet they are rarely explicitly surfaced as objects receiving concentrated attention."[11]

Due to public demand for accessibility, the Tuskegee Syphilis Study records are now receiving such attention. Unfortunately, a blanket withholding of the underlying medical records of the Tuskegee Syphilis Study may have contributed to a growing distrust among African Americans regarding generally accepted medical practices,

---

11 Cox and Wallace, *Archives and the Public Good*, 2.

such as organ donations and participation in research studies. Thus, there will continue to be distrust until the government grants access to all the information it has on the study. The National Archives and Records Administration's management of the Tuskegee Syphilis Study records has not changed over time, despite the public's increased demand for government accountability. Consequently, restricted access policies may have continued to perpetuate myths and misconceptions about the study. As a result, there is no guarantee that access to the restricted medical records will be open to the public in the year 2030, creating serious implications for future access.

8

THE ROLE OF PRIVATE ARCHIVAL CENTRES IN STORING, PRESERVING AND PROVIDING ACCESS TO POLITICAL RECORDS IN BELGIUM

Godfried Kwanten

One of the essential tasks of a democratic state is to pay attention to records and to preserve them. This particularly applies to political records. Indeed, all records—political or otherwise—can provide support for the basic rights of citizens. Well-managed records contribute to higher standards in politics and to a basic continuity in policy. They encourage transparency and openness in political dealings. Whenever politicians and their policies, whether in the short- or long-term, have to be called to account—an essential mark of every democratic regime—their records are indispensable in creating some degree of clarity about events in the past. Finally, records also supply the building blocks for scholarly historical research on political themes.

However, political authorities can fall short in various ways in the care of records. Clearly, they can abuse them for political motives. They can, for example, either openly or surreptitiously, put pressure on archival institutions or personnel. They can monitor archivists and force them into interventions that contravene their professional ethics. A government may deliberately destroy records, or may selectively preserve them or even falsify them. Sometimes the threat is less dramatic and may be the result of carelessness or of a systematic neglect of records by the political authorities. Obviously, dictatorial regimes are not alone in abusing or deliberately destroying records; democratic countries too can make many errors on that score. Indeed, a lack of attention to records and the indifference of politicians are perhaps as damaging for records as overt abuse. Those responsible for policy may fail to implement proper legislation concerning the care of records, or they may fail to provide the sector with adequate support, personnel, and infrastructure. They may make little or no provision for the acquisition and accessibility of records, or for the professional training of archivists.

Obviously, the indifference of the authorities to the archival sector in general also affects political records. The decades-long neglect of political records in Belgium came to light some years ago and became painfully clear during the investigations by a parliamentary commission into the death of the first prime minister of the newly independent Congo, Patrice Lumumba, in 1960. Some years ago, the committee had to reconstruct the circumstances of his death and determine the role played by various Belgian agencies. For this, the commission called on four experts, four academically trained history professors. They consulted dozens of records, including the records of the head of state, of the National Security Service, of various ministers at the time, and of the big colonial companies and businesses.

The actual content of the investigation's conclusions are not of importance here. What should be noted, however, is that the investigators were confronted with the appalling neglect in the preservation of essential sources from the 1960s. Many files had been lost, surviving records were often in very poor condition, and there was hardly any access available to key records concerning the country's political history. In its final report, the parliamentary investigative commission pointed very explicitly to this neglect of records; they stated that "important official records, including those of the head of state, were in danger of being lost if the appropriate steps were not taken."[1] They

---

1   L. De Vos, E. Gerard, J. Gerard-Libois, and Ph. Raxhon, *Parlementair onderzoek met het oog op het vaststellen van de precieze omstandigheden waarin Patrice Lumumba werd vermoord en van de eventuele betrokkenheid daarbij van Belgische politici. Verslag namens de onderzoekscommissie uitgebracht door de Heren Daniel Bacquelaine en Ferdy Willems en Mevrouw Marie-Thérèse Coenen.* Belgische Kamer van Volksvertegenwoordigers. Doc. 50 0312/006-Doc. 50 0312/007, 16 November 2001.

attributed the neglect to a lack of resources in the area of infrastructure as well as that of equipment and personnel. In its recommendations, the commission "invited the government to implement all the measures necessary to locate, make an inventory and safeguard the records of the various state bodies and in particular those of the head of state, by providing an appropriate allocation of personnel and financial resources." The commission likewise advised that "the legislation with regard to the care of records should be evaluated and if necessary adapted so that the state's archival heritage could be preserved in an appropriate way." Finally, they asked for a redefinition of the regulations concerning the accessibility of government records.

The commission's report caused a minor shock in Belgium among policymakers, the media, and the general public. The problem of political records and of archives in general was a central point of interest in the debate, but only for a short while; the report had only a temporary effect. Following a very brief general outcry, it resulted in hardly any concrete measures being adopted; nor was there an improvement in preserving political records and in making them accessible and available for inspection. However, the report's conclusions were indisputable: Before 1980, the condition of many of Belgium's political records was in fact disastrous. This was to be attributed as much to the creator of the records as to the absence of an archival policy worthy of the name and to the attitude and policy of the public archival institutions.

Indeed, political parties and their public representatives paid hardly any attention to their own records. They were totally lacking in any historical understanding, and the historical value of their records escaped them completely. This lack of interest in their own political records was not so much due to a deliberate policy of negligence; rather it was the result of indifference and complete carelessness. Because of this lack of interest, the records of parties, parliamentary groups, policy study-groups, and politicians were neglected and sometimes even destroyed. The problem was most acute with regard to the records of the executive, of ministers, and of their staff.[2]

---

2   On the problem of ministerial records in Belgium, see B. Hellinck, "Gezocht: papier! Over kabinetten en kabinetsarchieven," *Brood & Rozen*, 1 (2000), 82–87; B. Hellinck, "Doorgaans maar niet altijd. . . . Ervaringen met kabinetten en kabinetsarchieven," *Bibliotheek- & Archiefgids*, 3 (2000), 7–13. I. Schoups, "De archivistiek toegepast op kabinetsarchieven," *Bibliotheek- & Archiefgids*, 5 (2000) 18; B. Hellinck, *Bibliotheek- & Archiefgids*, 6 (2000), 29; *Kabinetsarchieven. Rapport van het Stadsarchief Antwerpen* (2002), 50.

In Belgian politics, ministers surround themselves with personal assistants, often dozens, to help with drawing up and executing policy. They produce records of crucial importance for getting information about executive policy and decision-making mechanisms. In the past, however, these important records were mostly lost. Indeed, even their status was not clear: Were they public or private records? The politicians concerned considered them to be personal records, and in the best instances, they preserved those files or sections of them. More often, however, these important collections were neglected and sometimes even deliberately destroyed.

There are many stories about the systematic burning of ministerial records in the decades after the Second World War. Whenever a new government took office, politicians of all persuasions preferred not to leave any records behind for their successors, and certainly not if they were of another political hue. Even less did they want to transfer what they saw as their own private records to a public archival service; in any case, they were not legally obliged to do so. Even today, the status of these ministerial records remains ambiguous. There is indeed a consensus among archivists themselves about the necessity of depositing such records in a public archive or in a state-recognized archival centre. The problem lies mostly with the politicians who even still continue to see their ministerial records as personal files which they have no desire to transfer to the public archives.

It should be noted, however, that in the past the state archives also evinced only limited interest in the category of ministerial records. They made little effort to acquire them and offered few facilities to make their storage more attractive for the donor. The state archives preserved only a few personal records of great statesmen and had hardly any interest in other political records, such as those of administrations, national and regional party groupings, parliamentary factions, less important political figures, political study-groups and training institutions, or youth organisations. Not only did the state archives not evince any interest in this category of records, they also lacked adequate financial resources to implement a balanced and comprehensive policy for this sector. Moreover, following the recent reforms to make Belgium into a federal state, it is often not clear which governmental level should be responsible for storing the records of politicians who were active in the various executive bodies.

The large-scale neglect of political records in the past has led to the loss of crucial information. Consequently, it becomes difficult to reconstruct the political decision-making process of the past. A shortage of archival sources renders a serious investigation of the political past and an adequate and democratically necessary openness almost impossible. After all, scholarly historical research is possible only on the basis of well-preserved, accessible files; easily accessible records contribute in a fundamental way to the democratic calibre of a society. Of course, access must be reasonable and subject to definite rules. The political agency may require that particular files be treated with a certain confidentiality and even be kept secret for a defined period. The accessibility of political records may not clash with respect for personal privacy. What we can state, however, is that the destruction or neglect of political records, even if not deliberate, damages the democratic quality of the political order. It is a matter of regret that such was the case in Belgium for so many decades.

From the end of the 1970s and the beginning of the 80s, however, Belgium broke with this trend in the preservation of political records. At that time, four private archival centres were set up in the Dutch-speaking part of Belgium.[3] The four new centres were offshoots of the major ideological currents in Belgian society: the socialist, the Catholic or Christian democratic, the liberal, and the Flemish nationalist. From the last quarter of the nineteenth century, these ideological movements had built up networks of their own organisations, such as trade unions, cooperatives, social groupings, schools, hospitals, sports clubs, youth organisations, libraries, and so on. The political party was often the cornerstone of such a network, each of which functioned independently of the state and was clearly separate from the other ideological networks. Researchers speak of this phenomenon in terms of "pillars" and "pillarisation." The four private archival centres brought about a shift in the attitude to political records and played a pioneering

---

3   Information about records, inventories, records management, and the selection process of the four private archival and documentation centres is available in their annual reports, their magazines (*KADOC-Nieuwsbrief, AMSAB-Tijdingen, ADVN-Mededelingen*), and/or on their websites (http://www.kadoc.kuleuven.ac.be; http://www.amsab.be; http://www.advn.be, and http://www.liberaalarchief.be).

role in their preservation. With each centre working for its own pillar or network, they arranged for the wholesale conservation of political and other records, and for making them publicly available. There is no doubt that they also brought about a widespread change of attitude towards the care of political records.

Initially, the newly founded centres functioned exclusively thanks to contributions from private donors, universities, and organisations. These private financial contributions enabled them to offer an outstanding physical infrastructure for storing records and for making them available for public consultation. In 1985, the Flemish government gave official recognition to the four institutions, and from then on, they received annual government subsidies. Their precise assignment was to be responsible for the care of records belonging to the ideological sector in which they were active, including its political records. That official recognition yielded a large and very diverse harvest of political records. Old and hidden records were centralised and made available for public inspection. Agreements were made with agencies of the political parties and with politicians (who were active on a European, national, regional, provincial, and local level) to transfer records on a regular basis. In this way, the still-surviving records of the four political groups were put into safekeeping: the Catholic or Christian democrat, the socialist, the liberal, and the Flemish nationalist. The four centres also acquired the records of party chairmen and employees, of parliamentary groupings, of less well-known politicians, of policy study-groups, youth organisations, lobbying groups, and training institutes. They also had a very strong interest in political publications, magazines, and audiovisual material (photos, films, posters, and audiotapes). In a number of cases, extensive and thoroughly prepared interviews were held with former politicians, the texts of which were given archival status and are available for consultation in the centres.

This rich harvest of records was only possible thanks to the trust built up between these centres and the political world. Direct contacts were established between the two sides; flexible contractual agreements provided for the transfer and preservation of records. Within a few years, the private centres were storing political records on a large scale and making them available for inspection. These included the records of top politicians such as Jean-Luc Dehaene, a long-time prime minister who also held ministerial office many times, Willy Claes, a top minister and former secretary general of NATO, and Mark Eyskens, a former prime minister and minister for foreign affairs.

Inspired by foreign initiatives, including the British National Register of Archives, the four centres are also working hard on developing the "Flanders Archival Database," a computerised register of private records in Flanders.[4] This database will also identify the *political* records of persons and organisations that are in private hands in various places and will register them in accordance with internationally recognised rules of description. Undoubtedly, this national registration is a first, important precondition for improving the preservation of records and raising awareness of their value, and is at the same time a first step towards greater openness and use.

The four institutions are scholarly, independent centres. Even though their names point to the ideological field in which they are active, nevertheless they remain completely autonomous in relation to the political agencies and figures whose records they manage. Academics and professional archivists sit on their boards of management. Their staff are highly educated and experienced. With regard to the various aspects of records management (acquiring, storing, ensuring accessibility, selecting, describing, and so on), they adhere to the professional and ethical criteria that operate in the national and international archival field. Over the past 20 years, they have often made positive suggestions in a number of areas relating to political records and have made political files available for public inspection in a quick and superior manner. Acquisitions were publicly announced in a timely manner. New information and communication technology has been put to remarkable use so as to make political records quickly accessible for research; objective and widely accepted rules of access were applied.

The four centres have also ensured that the results of their work with political records reaches a broad public by intensive outreach campaigns (on the Internet, and in their own magazines, exhibitions, and

---

4 On the Flanders Archival Database, see *Archiefbank Vlaanderen. Blauwdruk voor een geautomatiseerd register van het Vlaams privaat archivalisch erfgoed.* [A publication of ADVN, Amsab (Institute for Social History), KADOC (Documentation and Research Centre for Religion, Culture and Society) and Liberaal Archief (Liberal Archives), commissioned by Bert Anciaux, Minister of Culture in the Flemish Government]. (Antwerp-Ghent-Leuven, 2002), 78; see also www.archiefbank.be.

publications). All this has led to the greater involvement of researchers and of a wider public. Political records now are among the most consulted files. The work of the four centres has then made an important contribution in creating more transparency in politics, and in providing fuller insight into the political decision-making process, the genesis of laws and decisions, the formation of cabinets, and the evolution of past political conflicts. They have given a significant impetus to scholarly research. Sometimes this research has been carried out by historians and political scientists from outside the centres; sometimes the four institutions themselves have undertaken extensive research initiatives that were carried out completely independently. In any case, by attracting and making available such a large collection of political records, the centres have given a significant boost to research and provided source material that often opens up new avenues of research.

The four centres have put an important section of the political heritage of the twentieth century into safekeeping for preservation and research. However, not only have they made a decisive contribution to the maintenance of strictly political records, they also were quick to anticipate new needs in the archival field, more quickly at least than the state archives. In recent years they have attached considerable importance to the archives of the so-called "new social movements." These organisations do not have as pronounced an ideological character, are often pluralistic by nature, and serve as pressure groups in areas such as the environment, human rights, animal rights, the peace movement, cultural minorities, or developmental co-operation. This is a very broad area with diverse associations of activists, pacifists, ecologists, anti-globalist protesters, and so forth. Even though they are neutral politically, their activities undoubtedly have a political dimension; through their actions they have influenced public opinion and have exercised political influence. The four private archival institutions have evinced interest in the records of these groups in Belgium and have already taken dozens of their important files into custody and made them available to the public.

The work of the four centres in the area of political records has not been without consequence. They have brought about a change in attitude towards political records, not only among political authorities but also in public archival institutions and among the general public.

Under their influence, the state archives have shown more interest in this area since 1987 and have embarked on a systematic study of the creators of political records. Moreover, the state archives have increasingly been acquiring the records of ministers, government administrators, and politicians; they have drawn up and published important archival guides and have created access tools. The problem of political records was brought up for discussion many times in the archival field and in professional publications which urged the government to draw up archival legislation. The issue even came increasingly to the fore in the press and media.

Finally, political parties and politicians became more conscious of the importance and value of their records. By contrast to the decades before 1980, they no longer dared to destroy records on a large scale. They also saw in a proper preservation of their records the possibility of ensuring their own place in historical research and in history. They were less distrustful of their personal records being stored in public depositories and of scholarly historical research being carried out on them. The overall situation of political records has thus significantly improved in just a few years. In this, the private centres undoubtedly played a crucial role.

In conclusion, the contribution of private institutions to the storing of political records in Belgium has been decisively significant. It was and is to their credit that they broke with historical trends. A combination of governmental resources and private efforts has put a definitive end to the thoughtless handling of political records. The initiatives undertaken by the private centres in the area of political records have also led to greater involvement by the state archives, though they remain inadequately equipped to become properly engaged. Still, although much progress has been achieved in the past twenty years in preserving and evaluating political records, the situation continues to be far from ideal. Belgian archivists therefore look above all to politicians in the expectation of archives legislation that is modern, comprehensive, and sound.

Ethical Dilemmas in the
Public Service

9

ETHICS ISSUES FOR CREATORS, MANAGERS, AND USERS OF RECORDS

Rick Barry

Provided here is a brief account and commentary on some of the grow-ing number of cases involving records and recordkeeping violations being reported in the public media internationally, often under circum-stances involving improper political pressure, and to draw appropriate lessons. These are cases that result from ethical and possibly legal lapses of one kind or another or which pose ethical problems for creators, managers, and users of records. A practical, case-study approach is used, following that of *Ethics, Lies, and Archives*[1] (although cases used there are hypothetical). Its editor Stephen Yorke wrote, "In my experi-ence, broad discussions about ethics in a group context or treating ethics as theory gets nowhere . . . [C]ase studies . . . actively engage an audience no matter how reluctant initially."[2] Media accounts, often the only current sources for case information, can help augment actual case studies now available.[3] Questions are also raised about the teaching of

The author will publish updated versions of this article as significant changes in the status of the cases become known. Visit http://mybestdocs.com/barry-r-eth-iss0307-lucas.htm.

1   *Ethics, Lies and Archives: Proceedings of a One-Day Seminar by the Canberra Branch of the Australian Society of Archivists,* 1993, eds. Stephen Yorke and others, 1994.
2   Stephen Yorke, in a letter to R. Barry dated 16 June 1997.
3   For example, see Richard J. Cox and David A. Wallace, eds., *Archives and the Public Good: Accountability and Records in Modern Society* (Westport, Conn.: Quorum Books, 2002), and

ethics in graduate archives and records management (ARM) programmes, for this purpose assuming that both branches of the recordkeeping professions are involved to an equal degree, although in some
countries there is a formal distinction between the management of
archives and of records.

The Union Bank of Switzerland

On 17 January 1997 the New York Times reported that a 28-year-old
Swiss security guard at the Union Bank of Switzerland (UBS) in
Zurich, Christoph Meili, "was startled to find two bins filled with
papers ready for shredding: old ledgers, lists of mortgaged buildings in
Germany in the 1930s and 1940s—the years of Nazi rule."[4] Bearing in
mind news reports about the millions of Holocaust victims who had
had their real estate, art works, and other "Nazi gold" assets forcibly
transferred by the Nazi state, and allegations that many Holocaust victims still had unrepatriated business and personal accounts in banks,
including those in Switzerland, he returned to the shredding room and
removed whatever documents he could hide inside his jacket. Many
more records that were in the full carts he had left behind presumably
were shredded. "It didn't seem right to have these books in this room.
These were historical papers," he said. At home, he and his wife agreed
to make their knowledge public and did.[5]

A week later, UBS officials announced that staff had mistakenly
destroyed Nazi-era records that might shed light on financial transactions and related Nazi gold issues, despite a government ban a month
earlier on the destruction of such records—while there was an investigation of the extent to which Swiss banks may have colluded with the
Nazis to launder Nazi gold.[6] Meili was made the subject of a criminal
investigation for violation of bank secrecy laws and dismissed from his

---

Karen M. Benedict, *Ethics and the Archival Profession: Introduction and Case Studies*
(Chicago: Society of American Archivists, 2003).

4   "Swiss Bank Guard: A Document Hero," *New York Times,* 17 January 1997.

5   Chelsea J. Carter, "For Swiss Bank Whistle-Blower, the Aftermath Is Bittersweet,"
    Washington Post, 4 March 2001, A12.

6   "Swiss Bank Says Worker Mistakenly Discarded Archives," *Washington Post,* 15 January
    1997, A14. See http://pqasb.pqarchiver.com/washingtonpost/search.html.

job. Later, news and other accounts revealed that the documents included German Reichsbank wartime records.[7] Meili fled Switzerland with his family in April 1997, stating that he had received threats from neo-Nazi groups. The investigation was subsequently dropped, as was the investigation of the UBS chief archivist who had authorized the shredding of the litigious archives in violation of the government ban and UBS's own stated policy.[8]

The following year, a settlement was reached between Holocaust survivors and their successors and the Swiss banks. Barbara Hafer, Pennsylvania Treasurer, one of the financial officers involved in the return of Nazi gold assets to Holocaust victims remarked, "The Swiss never would have negotiated a settlement. They never would have agreed to pay $1.25 billion. And the Germans would not be at the negotiating table right now if it were not for the selfless and truly heroic actions of one brave young man . . . Christoph Meili."[9] Christoph Meili became the first Swiss citizen to be granted political asylum in the United States, where he lives today. Meili says he doesn't regret his decision in the shredding room. "First, you are a hero. Then, you are suspected. . . . Then, you are forgotten. But nobody forgets what you did."[10]

This case, like others to follow, illustrates the vital importance of strong, well-enforced, whistleblower laws. In the absence of these, only the most extraordinary courage of individuals in stepping forward is effective. Strong, well-enforced, whistleblower laws act as a deterrent to misdeeds and encourage people to reveal the truth rather than become complicit in ethical improprieties. They also protect employing or record-creating agencies from charges of impropriety in carrying out their records management procedures. As the inviolateness of records is often at stake, archives and records management professionals and their associations should be among the strongest advocates of tough whistle blowing legislation.

---

7   Stuart E. Eizenstat, *Imperfect Justice: Looted Assets, Slave Labor and the Unfinished Business of World War II* (New York: Public Affairs, 2003). See also, Tom Bower, *Nazi Gold: The Full Story of the Fifty-Year Swiss-Nazi Conspiracy to Steal Billions from Europe's Jews and Holocaust Survivors* (New York: HarperPerennial, 1998).

8   "Swiss End Bank Guard Investigation," *Washington Post*, 2 October 1997, A20.

9   Barbara Hafer, "Statement of Pennsylvania Treasurer Barbara Hafer in honor of Christoph Meili," 8 March 1999, Kollel Jewish Learning Center, Pittsburgh, Pennsylvania.

10 Carter, "For Swiss Bank Whistle-Blower, the Aftermath is Bittersweet," A12.

The Heiner Case ("Shreddergate")[11]

In 1996, following a keynote presentation to the Records Management Association of Australia (RMAA), I received an e-mail message from Kevin Lindeberg, a former official of the Professional Officers' Association whose members were public servants of the State government of Queensland, Australia. He asked if historical value was the only criterion used by archivists in the process of determining if and for how long public records should be kept and for making decisions on requests to destroy them. I assured him that historical value was one but by no means the only value that had to be taken into account in appraising records. From the ensuing e-mail exchange, I soon learned about the Heiner affair and that Lindeberg was a principal victim in the case.[11]

In November 1989, a retired Queensland stipendiary magistrate, Noel Heiner, was appointed to conduct an investigation into alleged malfeasance at a government-operated youth detention centre. Heiner withdrew from the case in January 1990 and turned the incomplete investigative materials over to the Queensland Department of Family Services and Aboriginal and Islander Affairs. When requests were made by trade union representative Kevin Lindeberg on behalf of the centre's manager to obtain copies of relevant records regarding the allegations, including the Heiner investigative records, he was informed that the records had been destroyed. It was subsequently revealed that the records had not been destroyed at the time of his request, but later, when the government allegedly knew they were required in evidence for a foreshadowed judicial proceeding.

The Queensland Cabinet requested that the state archivist make a judgment on whether the records relating to the probe had any long-term historical value and, if not, whether they could be destroyed. In their letter, they failed to inform her that the records were known to be

---

11 See the *Proceedings of the 17th Conference of the Samuel Griffith Society,* 8–10 April 2005, Chapter One, "The Heiner Affair," by Kevin Lindeberg (http://samuelgriffith.org.au/papers/html/volume17/v17contents.htm). See also Kevin Lindeberg's "The Rule of Law: Model Archival Legislation in the Wake of the Heiner Affair," *Archives and Manuscripts* 31 (May 2003). See also Chris Hurley's essay in this volume; and his chapter, "Records and the Public Interest: The Heiner Affair in Queensland Australia," in *Archives and the Public Good,* eds. R. Cox and D. Wallace; the University of Queensland Justice Project, http://justiceproject.net/content/ShreddingStoryOverview.asp.

required in evidence for a future court proceeding. Some years later, it was further alleged that the Queensland Cabinet also knew that the records contained evidence about the abuse of children in state care. Despite this, the decision was made to destroy the records reportedly to prevent the gathered evidence from being used against the centre staff. The archivist was asked to make a decision within 24 hours and did so, authorizing the shredding of the records, which was carried out shortly thereafter by a senior staff archivist together with a government department officer.

Repeated requests by Lindeberg for access to those records resulted in his being fired. The manager on whose behalf he was seeking the records withdrew his request after being reassigned to a new post and receiving payments for what the government said were unrelated reasons. The propriety of the payments and whether they might have been considered "hush money" has come into question. Lindeberg continued his efforts to seek justice in various forums and through law enforcement authorities, claiming that the shredding was an illegal act. It is once again the subject of a Parliamentary investigation thirteen years after the fact, and is still seen as highly relevant to the practice of public record-keeping and the administration of justice.

The Australian Society of Archivists (ASA) was not invited by any of the investigating authorities to comment on professional or procedural aspects of the case. By the time ASA gained consensus on a position, it had been bypassed in the investigative deliberations. Kevin Lindeberg unsuccessfully appealed to the International Council on Archives (ICA) to consider a statement he had prepared on the subject.

As with other cases that gain public interest, the focus of public discourse is understandably on the content of records (in this case child abuse) but unfortunately often to the exclusion of the also egregious and illegal nature of their treatment or destruction.

The Heiner case contains a catalogue of ethical challenges, including:

- allegations of complicity by the state criminal justice system and Cabinet in the inappropriate and illegal destruction of public records;

- an urgent request by the governing law enforcement agency to approve destruction of records for lack of historical value, while the Cabinet withheld information on the litigious nature of the records;
- an agreement (tacit or otherwise) to carry out an appraisal of the documents within 24 hours;
- *ad hoc* decision-making to dispose of records independently of like records in the same functional area and subject to the same retention schedule;
- destruction of other related original records without the archivist's approval;
- political interference with the inviolate nature of public records; and
- failure of official inquiries to consult independent professional archivists or to request the testimony of the state archivist, staff archivist and department officer who carried out the shredding, requesting agency's records managers, former manager of the youth detention center, or Kevin Lindeberg.

According to Lindeberg, in August 2004 the Australian House of Representatives Standing Committee on Legal and Constitutional Affairs tabled its report into its investigation into the Heiner affair. Unprecedented in Australian political history, the Committee recommended, *inter alia,* that criminal charges be brought against all members of the Queensland Cabinet of 5 March 1990 who ordered the destruction of the Heiner Inquiry documents to prevent their use as evidence in a judicial proceeding, and that an independent Special Prosecutor be appointed by the Queensland Government to fully investigate all aspects of the affair.[12] This report, reflecting the situation as of this writing in early June 2005, was still under review by the Australian Government. While the Queensland Government has declined to take up its recommendations, the affair has since come under consideration by the Governor of Queensland by the exercise of her constitutional discretion to be informed.[13]

---

12 See Australian House of Representatives Standing Committee on Legal and Constitutional Affairs Report into the Heiner affair: http://www.aph.gov.au/house/committee/laca/crimeinthecommunity/report.htm.

13 See Question on Notice Queensland Legislative Assembly: http://www.parliament.qld.gov.au/view/legislativeAssembly/questionsAnswers/2005/47-2005.pdf.

Professional associations may be reluctant to make comments on these questions because they do not wish to appear to be judging or calling their own professionals to account. Individuals are also reluctant to speak out. State/provincial and national archivists do not do so because they feel that they do not have a mandate to speak for the profession or because doing so might create a conflict of interest.

In part, the lessons of the Heiner case suggest the need for written questions for future archivists to pose to those requesting the urgent destruction of records. They should be asked to:

- state the basis for urgency and what risks might arise from taking a more measured disposition decision;
- certify that there is nothing litigious about the records that could be expected, imminently or in the reasonably foreseeable future, to become the subject of an internal investigation or court case, including consideration of cases that have arisen elsewhere with like classes of records;
- inform if and when the records have been the subject of a freedom-of-information request and if such requests have been honoured; and
- consider why the records concerned should not be dealt with under the terms of an approved retention schedule.

The Heiner case has in part been responsible for further discussion in professional circles and professional literature. In 1993, the Canberra branch of the ASA held a seminar on "Ethics, Lies and Archives." The ASA e-mail discussion list archive records much debate on its response to Heiner.[14]

New York City Mayoral Records

In some governments, senior elected and appointed officials are allowed to remove personal records when they leave their posts. In others, the

---

14 For examples of discussion threads on the ASA List see http://www.asap.unimelb.edu.au/asa/aus-archivists/threads.html#03073 for an index of discussion threads by subject line. A word search on the page for <Heiner> will reveal numerous threads on the subject.

papers created by elected officials are considered public records and are subject to the custodianship of the agency concerned. In the United States, the latter approach is usual at national, state, and local levels of government. Records of senior officials at all levels are typically regarded as among the most important organizational records.

Before New York City Mayor Rudy Giuliani left office, December 31, 2001, he moved a considerable collection of the records of his time in office, including those of the September 11, 2001 tragedy, to a private archive. This decision caused a public outcry. Charges were made that Giuliani was attempting to keep the records in order to write his memoirs for considerable financial gain at the expense of the public. He replied that the city archives organization was not in good enough condition to properly maintain the records. This of course gave rise to the question: Why, after all his time in office, was the archive's organization in such poor condition, and why was it not improved? Eventually, the American Civil Liberties Union (ACLU) reached an agreement with Giuliani that the records would be returned to the city's Municipal Archives and Department of Records and Information Services.[15]

The crisis might have been avoided had the city had a clear policy on the matter in advance. During the negotiations with the ACLU and Giuliani, the city, under the new Mayor Michael R. Bloomberg, passed a law in March 2003 clearly establishing that future mayors will be barred from having a say on the disposition of their papers and that the papers will be retained and controlled by the city archives.[16]

Because of the New York City case and a similar case in the Commonwealth of Virginia, historians and archivists are concerned that if records are maintained outside a trustworthy recordkeeping environment for a long period of time that their completeness and integrity, when repatriated to proper custody, are open to serious question.

If senior elected and appointed officials use as a defence for removing public records that the archives and records management unit was

---

15 Richard Cox, "Former President Giuliani and His Library?" February 2002, in the guest author section of www.mybestdocs.com.

16 ACLU archivist, Janet Linde, received an award from the the Archivists Round Table of Metropolitan New York for her work in drafting the new city law. In an unrelated matter, Ms. Linde resigned from her ACLU post in May 2005 after her warnings to management over the improper shredding of ACLU documents went unheeded. (See Stephanie Strom, "Concerns at A.C.L.U. Over Document Shredding," *New York Times*, 5 June 2005.)

not of sufficient quality to deserve receiving them, then they are acknowledging that they themselves failed in their duty to ensure a trustworthy recordkeeping environment in their own organizations while they were in office. This is a dangerous claim for their successors to inherit, for any subsequent legal action against the organization would be able to use such statements as evidence that the recordkeeping system is not trustworthy—and in the process bring into doubt the trustworthiness of *any* records the organization may bring to its defence.

The more senior the official who tries to remove public records, the more difficult it is to take him or her to task. It is also often the case that senior officials wish to keep significant portions of their substantive business records (especially their e-mail) from the eyes of administrative staff and treat such records as private. This can become an unspoken barrier to full implementation of electronic records policies and systems. The main point is to ensure that appropriate laws, regulations, and policies are in place *before* the system is challenged.

ENRON and the Sarbanes-Oxley Act

The tragic crash of the oil company Enron revealed the role of the audit company, Arthur Andersen, which advised Enron on its records retention schedules. There were allegations that Enron had falsified records and that Arthur Andersen had provided dubious retention schedules that would cover the matter up. During u.s. Congressional hearings on the case, Representative James C. Greenwood scoffed at the idea of Andersen's "overtime" defense. "It doesn't seem to us it takes a lot of overtime to retain documents," he said. Based on the Victim and Witness Protection Act, which makes it a crime for one party to knowingly, corruptly persuade another to destroy documents, Andersen was indicted and in 2002 was found guilty of obstruction of justice charges with criminal intent when it allowed many of Enron's accounting papers to be destroyed. The conviction was upheld by the United States Court of Appeals for the Fifth Circuit, in New Orleans. On further appeal to the Supreme Court,[17] and to the sur-

---

17 *Arthur Andersen v. United States* (No. 04-368).

prise of many not close to the case, the Court unanimously overturned the conviction and returned the case to the Court of Appeals, leaving the Justice Department free to seek a retrial under new jury instructions.[18] Barbara Ley Toffler's *The Final Accounting: Ambition, Greed, and the Fall of Arthur Andersen,* gives a graphic account.[19]

Other similar cases have brought about the financial destruction of small investors, a loss of confidence in the free enterprise system, and an unwillingness on the part of small traders to trade. Because of these reactions, Congress and the Securities Exchange Commission (SEC) have significantly tightened up regulations, principally by means of the Sarbanes-Oxley Act.

This Act applies not just to organizations in the financial sector that are regulated by the SEC. It is important to recognize that even though this is a U.S. law, its implications reach out globally, to multinationals and others doing business in the United States or who trade on the U.S. stock market. A footnote in the Act states that "publicly traded companies with at least $75 million in revenue are subject to section 404 of the Sarbanes-Oxley regulations in June 2004. Other smaller companies and foreign entities are impacted in April 2005."

The Act tightens auditing/accounting practices and requires public corporations and their audit committees to implement confidential, anonymous whistleblower complaint procedures through which employees can report malfeasance to the SEC. (SEC is also requiring the keeping of e-mail records for at least three years.) The Act has also spawned new consulting services and systems development products aimed at helping affected companies to become compliant.

After this, financial organizations should be careful to ensure that archives and records management professionals are key players in the business of retention scheduling and that they are listened to. Without strong input from them, scheduling can easily devolve into an exercise of simply protecting the organization by prematurely destroying records in the name of established retention scheduling policy.

---

18 Linda Greenhouse, "Justices Unanimously Overturn Conviction of Arthur Andersen," *New York Times,* 31 May 2005, and Kurt Eischenwald, "Analysis: Reversal of Andersen Conviction," *New York Times,* 1 June 2005.

19 Barbara Ley Toffler, *Final Accounting: Ambition, Greed, and the Fall of Arthur Andersen* (New York: Broadway Books, 2003).

British American Tobacco

A similar situation developed in the British American Tobacco Australian Service (BATAS) case where external legal counsel recommended unreasonably short retention periods for documents that were clearly litigious because they revealed the organization's prior knowledge of the dangerous health effects of tobacco.

The majority of organizations are presumed to operate in a reputable, upright manner and understand that records are not just there to indict an organization, but to come to its defence against misrepresentations. Furthermore, legacy records are increasingly being seen as principal document representations of organizational knowledge. Destroying records prematurely also destroys the intellectual capital of the organization.

The Texas Legislature Case

A political fundraising committee, Texans for a Republican Majority (TRMPAC), organized by U.S. House of Representatives Majority Leader Tom DeLay (R-Tex.) succeeded in creating the first Republican majority in the Texas State House in 130 years. Over the course of the summer of 2003, the new Republican majority of the Texas state legislature attempted to change its voting boundaries. The stakes were very high because state legislature districting decisions are the basis for defining the state voting districts for the U.S. Congress. Texas Democratic state legislators attempted to freeze the process by leaving the state at the time of the critical vote, thus depriving the state legislature of the two-thirds majority required to suspend rules to consider new legislation. Various federal departments were called up to investigate the whereabouts of the missing legislators in a manner the media questioned as abuse of power. Much of the pressure to gain access to and make inappropriate use of records and services of federal agencies, which had no jurisdiction in the matter, alledgedly came from the staff of the U.S. House Majority Leader, a possible successor to the post of Speaker in a Republican-dominated House later on in the decade. Their planned redistribution was achieved, resulting in the loss of Texas-based Democratic seats and four additional Republican seats, significantly contributing to a Republican Party majority in the u.s. House of Representatives.

The case is still very much alive. The *Washington Post* reported a 26 May 2005 state judge ruling on a civil case that the TRMPAC treasurer "violated the state's election law by failing to report $684,507 in contributions from corporations and other donors in 2002. . . . Separate criminal charges related to that issue, including indictments of three political associates of DeLay and four of the corporations that provided contributions, are pending in another Texas court."[20]

This case underscores the potential for abuses of government records for purely political reasons and the need for sound non-partisan policies to avoid such cases. It also emphasizes the importance of having independent accounting offices or other investigative bodies in government that can examine such cases and come to conclusions that are not driven by a desire to avoid embarrassment to the government but rather to protect the rights of citizens and to minimize the potential for political pressure on unwitting or low-level officials who are most subject to such pressure.

The Weapons of Mass Destruction (WMD) Case

In President George W. Bush's State of the Union Address on 28 January 2003, he declared: "The British government has learned that Saddam Hussein recently sought significant quantities of uranium from Africa." Some critics suggested that the intelligence was falsified or exaggerated in order to support a decision that had already been made.

In May 2003, a group of retired CIA and state department intelligence analysts circulated a memorandum indicating that there was "growing mistrust and cynicism" among intelligence professionals concerning "intelligence cited by you and your chief advisers to justify the war against Iraq." It stated that, in the past, intelligence reports had been "warped for political purposes but never before has such warping

---

20 Sylvia Moreno and R. Jeffrey Smith, "Treasurer of DeLay Group Broke Texas Election Law," *Washington Post*, 27 May 2005, A1. See also, Mike Allen, "GOP Worries Ethics Issue May Hurt Party in '06," *Washington Post*, 6 June 2005, A1.

been used in such a systematic way to mislead our elected representatives into voting to authorize launching a war." Serving CIA analysts also complained that they felt pressured by administration policymakers before the war concerning their assessment of Iraq's arms programmes.[21] In December 2003, the President's Foreign Intelligence Advisory Board inquiry called the intelligence "dead wrong" and:

> concluded that the White House made a questionable claim in January's State of the Union address about Saddam Hussein's efforts to obtain nuclear materials because of its desperation to show that Hussein had an active program to develop nuclear weapons, according to a well-placed source familiar with the board's findings. . . . Although the president's intelligence board keeps its findings secret, the Senate panel plans to make public details of its inquiry in a report, which is being drafted and is expected to be released next spring, according to congressional sources.[22]

Intelligence analysts in Britain and Australia put forth similar theories about their own governments.[23] Since that time, investigations into the matter have concluded that no such weapons were still being maintained in Iraq. The President's Commission on the subject concluded that the intelligence used by the President in making decisions on the Iraq war was faulty. The report states: "On the brink of war, and in front of the whole world, the United States government asserted that Saddam Hussein had reconstituted his nuclear weapons program, had biological weapons and mobile biological weapon production facilities, and had stockpiled and was producing chemical weapons. All of this was based on the assessments of the U.S. Intelligence Community. And not one bit of it could be confirmed when the war was over. While the intelligence services of many other nations also thought that Iraq had weapons of mass destruction, in the end it was the United States that put its credibility on the line, making this one of the most public—and most damaging—intelligence failures in recent American history."[24]

---

21 "Tenet Defends Iraq Intelligence. CIA Chief Rebuts Allegations of Pressure from Administration Before the War," *Washington Post*, 31 May 2003, A1.

22 Walter Pincus, "White House Faulted on Uranium Claim, Intelligence Warnings Disregarded, President's Advisory Board Says," *Washington Post*, 24 December 2003, A1.

23 "Blair Tries to Rein in Kelly Judge over Scope of Inquiry," *Daily Telegraph*, 22 July 2003.

24 The Commission on the Intelligence Capabilities of the United Staes Regarding Weapons of Mass Destruction, 31 March 2005, http://www.wmd.gov/report/index.html (accessed 22 June 2005).

A principal lesson for recordkeepers is that users may not be independent of biased interests.[25] For executives, the lesson is to avoid politicizing information and records by telegraphing wished-for information to support policy decisions. This lesson was underscored in the so-called "Downing Street memo" that was published by the *Sunday Times* (Britain) reporting on the "IRAQ: Prime Minister's Meeting 23 July" (2002). Among other things, the report recounts a visit by a top British intelligence executives' meeting in Washington. In it, he is quoted as stating that, in Washington, "the intelligence and facts were being fixed around the policy."[26]

Teaching Ethics in University Courses

The following information results from an informal communication with faculty heads and members of graduate archives and records management programmes. This was not a scientific or complete survey, but it at least offers a taking-off point for further discussion among educators in the archives and records management field. My line of inquiry is summarized in a posting to the Australian *Aus-archivist* discussion list.

> I raise . . . a question to ARM educators more broadly: what importance is attached to preparing ARM professionals to deal with the real world ethics and social issues that arise in recordkeeping, and how that is made explicit in course offerings . . . I wonder in what other ways our concerns about these aspects of recordkeeping are manifested in ARM graduate programs—the degree to which graduate students are encouraged and actually do take ethics courses as electives, how frequently ethical and social issues relating to ARM are the subject of theses/dissertations, etc.[27]

None of my correspondents responded that they offered a separate course on archives and records management ethics. All indicated they included ethics issues in course work where it seemed appropriate. All of those contacted said they felt the subject was deserving of more time.

---

25 "Officials Knew of Dodgy Iraq File," *Sydney Morning Herald*, 11 July 2003.

26 David Manning, "The Secret Downing Street memo," *Sunday Times*, 01 May 2005, http://www.timesonline.co.uk/article/0,,2087-1593607_1,00.html (accessed 22 June 2005).

27 Rick Barry, 23 March 2001, posting to the *Aus-archivists* list.

Asked if they would allow or encourage students to take a traditional ethics course from the philosophy programme as an elective, the consensus was that they would agree in principle but did not particularly encourage such an elective. They thought that general ethics courses would not have sufficient direct relevance to the needs of their graduate students. Reasons for *not* offering a separate ethics course included:

- There was insufficient room in existing programmes for added subject coverage in ethics because of other new demands—especially those related to electronic records;
- Real-life case material specifically oriented to information and records management was not easily accessible; and
- More can be achieved by addressing ethical issues integral to the subject discussed in specific archives courses than by looking at case studies.

With the seeming burgeoning of cases and the presence of case-based texts,[28] it may be timely to now revisit the adequacy of the coverage of ethics and the reasons for not addressing actual ethics-based cases more directly. Demands for coverage of new materials in existing programmes are always difficult to meet. Needs always exceed demands, and choices have to be made. For those institutions where a separate ethics course is not seen as feasible, other alternatives might include the following steps:

- Follow the Monash University model in which at least a few if not most required courses have ethics coverage.
- Begin or end several courses with periods dedicated to examining a specific case in all its dimensions, rather than just the dimension most relevant to the course.
- Follow the University of Pittsburgh model that has a long-standing Information Ethics course, which is not part of the ARM program but includes a segment given by the head of its ARM graduate program.[29]

---

28 For example, Cox and Wallace, *Archives and the Public Good;* Benedict, *Ethics and the Archival Profession;* and other titles dealing with computer ethics, for example, Marsha Cook Woodbury, *Computer and Information Ethics* (Champaign, Ill.: Stipes Publishing, 2002).

29 University of Pittsburgh, Module description for "Information Ethics, Spring 2003" http://www.sis.pitt.edu/~ethics/syllabus.html (accessed 22 June 2005).

- Encourage an information ethics course as an elective for the ARM graduate degree program.
- Encourage ARM ethics as an important area for student research.
- Include ethics in all course descriptions.

The University of Pittsburgh Information Ethics curriculum defines the term "ethics" as: "The art and science that seeks to bring sensitivity and method to the discernment of moral values."[30] In the context of archives and records management, ethics has to do with decision-making when a personal stand or decision is required to identify and resolve conflicting choices of action in the workplace.

How does one know when one is facing an ethical dilemma? An ethical issue arises when there is a decision involving one or more of the following factors:

- There is a reasonable likelihood of inappropriate personal financial or other gain, or there are other inappropriate conflicts of interest for the individual or the individual's superiors or subordinates;
- A proposed action contradicts established regulations, laws, professional codes, or organizational policies;
- A proposed action would jeopardize one's professional standing;
- There is a direction that offends a professional's personal sense of right.

In most cases, an ethical issue will take the form of a conflict between personal and organizational values. The Code of Ethics of the Australian Society of Archives puts it this way: "Archivists distinguish clearly in their actions and statements between their personal beliefs and attitudes and those of employing institution or professional body."[31] The problem is usually not in recognizing the distinction but in deciding what to do about it.

---

30 University of Pittsburgh Information Ethics pages, http://www.sis.pitt.edu/~ethics/ (accessed 22 June 2005).

31 Australian Society of Archivists Code of Ethics, http://www.archivists.org.au/about/ ethics.html (accessed 22 June 2005).

Avoiding Practices with Potential Ethical Risks

The best strategy for addressing ethical risks in the workplace is to avoid such situations in the first place. Examples of situations that carry some ethical risks are:

- Poorly trained front-line ARM staff
- Risky organizational arrangements (not providing a buffer against political interference)[32]
- Failure to disclose the existence of potentially contentious or litigious records
- Augmenting budget resources with private funds
- Overzealousness in forcing efficiencies (e.g., outsourcing high-risk aspects of recordkeeping)

The Role of Professional Societies and Associations

There are many roles that professional societies can carry out to support membership in the area of ethics. Most such organizations produce codes of ethics. For example, the Institute of Certified Records Managers and the Dutch Archivists Society have policies on the subject of compliance with their codes. It is difficult, however, to find any organization that has actually tried to enforce such a role. Additional areas for consideration ask, does the association/society:

- Have a code of ethics and an ombudsman/woman or other system for fast-track handling of complaints or members seeking ethical help?
- Recognize and reward exceptional ethical conduct?
- Monitor and report to members on international cases?

---

32 Some state/provincial archives have an advisory or management board that includes members from the legislative and judicial branches of government. If the archivist is requested to carry out a questionable action, s/he can indicate that such matters have to be brought before the board and do so. Examples are the state/provincial archives in: New South Wales, Australia; Saskatchewan, Canada; and Kentucky, U.S.A.

- Share information and case studies with the international professional community?
- Perform independent evaluations and publish statements of findings or lessons learned when there are complaints?
- Foster greater accountability for its own members?

A principal task of professional societies in fostering a high level of ethics is to be or become relevant players in cases that arise. Speed of response is likely to be crucial.

Is the likelihood of facing ethical dilemmas on the rise? Is the rise in cases such as those described here because things are worse in the United States, or because there is a stronger and more aggressive free press there? What are some of the signs that more such cases are likely?

- Increasing global political and economic tensions
- Less user-friendly job climates
- A sharp rise in information and records originated in digital form

A valuable step that could be taken by professional associations would be to acknowledge and celebrate the work of those who have undertaken significant action in support of an ethical principle, especially when this action has resulted in personal disadvantage, such as those examples mentioned earlier. Some general principles can be drawn from the cases presented here:

- Ethical cases are not rare phenomena, but occur in all countries and sectors, in governments at all levels, and in large and small businesses, universities, and religious groups.
- The importance of strong recordkeeping, freedom-of-information, and whistleblower legislation is substantial. These laws offer vital defences against improper political pressures upon recordkeeping.
- It is essential to take strong action against those who clearly defy established ethical rules, and to provide real support for highly ethical conduct, including genuine whistleblowing.

- The importance of a powerful, diverse, aggressive, and independent press cannot be overemphasized as an essential means for protecting public interests.
- The absence of sound recordkeeping policies and practices makes for a climate in which ethical violations will occur. The information and records management professional is a complicit partner of the violators in such cases for not having carried out necessary policymaking tasks.
- Codes of ethics are needed and should be elaborated on to cover recurring situations. They are not enough, however, in the absence of mechanisms for the ARM community to address serious ethical violations in a timely manner that is credible to the public.

10

THE ROLE OF THE ARCHIVES IN PROTECTING THE RECORD FROM POLITICAL PRESSURE

Chris Hurley

I would like to share two stories in which I have been personally involved and deliver two lessons based on these experiences. For this discussion, I treat the term "the record" as being synonymous with "public record in a free democracy." I could extend the discussion to other political systems and non-government enterprises, even to personal recordkeeping, but because both my stories deal with records destruction, that is what I focus on. The issues are the same, however, for all aspects of the making and keeping of records.

The Nordlinger Affair

THE FIRST STORY TAKES PLACE IN VICTORIA (AUSTRALIA) IN 1990

Australia is a federation of six states that make up a national or "Commonwealth" government. In addition to federal law, each of these states has its own archival legislation making a State Archivist responsible, *inter alia,* for authorising the disposal of all records. Records cannot, by law, be disposed of until this authorisation is given.

In 1990, I had been the State Archivist of Victoria for nearly ten years. The State Archives was called the Public Record Office (PRO), and my title was Keeper of Public Records.

From time to time, it is the common experience of government archives authorities that cases of unauthorised disposal come to notice—often in the pages of newspapers and mentioned incidentally in connection with stories which have another focus. It is then normal practice for the Archives to write to the offending department or agency, obtain a reply acknowledging awareness of their obligations under archives legislation, explaining that the reported occurrence (if true) was regrettable, and that steps have been taken to see it doesn't happen again. The Archives then usually files the reply, and nothing further eventuates. This is sometimes waggishly called "enforcing" the Act.

In 1988, the Cain Labor Government was going to the polls. It might be an understatement to say that they had an unusually strong desire to control media reporting of their performance. In the lead-up to the election, a story erupted concerning the dismissal of a senior bureaucrat, Nordlinger, who had been an embarrassment to them.

Nordlinger decided he was not going to go quietly. He argued his dismissal was improper. The press reports referred to an interview between Nordlinger and Chairman of the Victorian Public Service Board, Maurice Keppel. Reports said that Nordlinger had observed Keppel making notes during the interview and had lodged a Freedom of Information (FOI) request to see them. He was informed that they had been destroyed.

As Keeper of Public Records, I wrote to Maurice Keppel asking him what authority he had under the Public Records Act for destroying the notes of the interview. I received a reply that I regarded as evasive and unsatisfactory—according to the benchmark we habitually apply in similar cases of unauthorised destruction. The correspondence continued (unsatisfactorily) throughout the election campaign.

Although it was not publicised, everyone involved was aware of the potential for political embarrassment. Nordlinger was out to make trouble. The State Premier was personally involved in his firing and was on the record as supporting the Chairman. The tenor of Keppel's replies to me (I believed) was that the disposition of the notes of the interview and the public records issues surrounding the record of the meeting were none of my business. I found this unsatisfactory. It was not a reply I would have accepted from any other agency or any other public servant. The reply I would have accepted (and then filed) would have said that a mistake had been made and it wouldn't happen again.

The problem for the Government was that the Public Records Act laid an obligation on all public offices to make and keep a full and accurate record of the business of the office. If a record of the interview existed, Nordlinger would be entitled to it under FOI. The Government had said he couldn't have it because no record existed. However, it had been publicly reported that notes had been taken. Therefore, either the notes (or a record of the meeting based on the notes) had to be made available to Nordlinger or, if neither the notes nor a full and accurate record based on them could be produced, a breach of the Public Records Act would appear to have occurred.

After Keppel's second or third reply, I was summoned to the office of the head of the department within which the PRO operated. I was asked to take the matter no further; it was potentially damaging to the Government in an election campaign. Under no circumstances would Keppel supply the response I was seeking. If the issue became public, it would do neither the PRO nor me any good. If, on the other hand, I abandoned my pursuit of the matter, I was promised that after the election the acting head of department would personally urge an augmentation of my powers as Keeper and seek to obtain the support and resources for us to pursue such matters more effectively.

I should say that I placed no reliance whatsoever in these promises, but thought the implied threats were real.[1] I replied that I had no wish to make a public fuss during an election campaign, but that I felt obliged to pursue the same course of action in this case that we would pursue (and had pursued) in all similar cases. I made the point that if

---

1 I had observed the treatment handed out to a former departmental colleague, Victoria's Chief Electoral Officer. He came under pressure when exercising statutory discretion as to whether or not to prosecute a government minister for electoral fraud (the Nunawading Affair). He sought legal advice and was told that the Minister should be prosecuted. The department "suggested" that prudence required he seek a second opinion, then a third, then a fourth, and so on. Each opinion recommended prosecution. Finally, one was received which said there was a possibility that the prosecution would not succeed. On the basis of this, he was advised not to proceed. Afterwards, he resigned, a broken man.

we were seen to pursue a different course of action in a case involving the Premier and the Chairman personally, it would expose us all to greater criticism than if the PRO was seen to treat everyone in the same manner. I even alluded to Watergate and the analogy that harm comes not from the offence but the attempt to cover it up. To no avail.

As a matter of prudence, and to avoid the possibility of unnecessary publicity in the heat of an election campaign, I agreed to hold off replying to Keppel's latest unresponsive letter until two days before the election and to keep the papers locked in my desk until then. This was done.

After the election, I was again summoned to the office of the acting head of department, told there would be no reply from Keppel to my latest letter, instructed not to write to him again on that matter, instructed further to write no letters of any kind to any departments except with the approval of the head of my own department, and (for good measure) asked why I hadn't solved the problems of electronic recordkeeping. I was told my failure to do so might now be viewed as a performance issue. (For some years prior to this, I had been drawing attention, in my annual reports to Parliament, that like archives programmes everywhere we were concerned about the problems of electronic recordkeeping.) The impracticality of having all our correspondence with government departments vetted at departmental level quickly became apparent even to those who had issued this instruction. During the next two years, we gradually re-established that the PRO could correspond with government agencies on routine matters, but any correspondence on unauthorised disposal still had to be vetted by higher authority.

In Victoria, the Minister is advised by a statutory body called the Public Records Advisory Council, which I attended. During this period, I gradually gathered evidence of instances of unauthorized disposal which came to our notice. On average, there are about half a dozen of these every year in every jurisdiction in Australia which get reported in some way in the media. I discussed with some members what, if anything, our responsibilities were—theirs, mine, and the Minister's—in dealing with such reports. Some of those I spoke with were uncomfortable, then alarmed, and eventually concluded (as I had hoped) that if everyone went on effectively ignoring the reported breaches of statutory obligations then everyone, the Minister, the Keeper, and they themselves would be open to blame.

When I thought they were in a receptive frame of mind, I prepared a report for the next Advisory Council meeting recommending that they advise the Minister to adopt a more proactive stance towards reported breaches of the Act. At this time, I was required to submit papers to a departmental official who sat as a member of the Council. Although there was no formal instruction to delay despatch to other members until after this official had vetted them, this was in fact what usually happened. As expected, I was summoned, asked to withdraw the report, and (when I refused) instructed not to send out the papers. I replied that it was too late and that they had already gone out. In fact, they were stamped and waiting for me downstairs, so I personally mailed them immediately upon my return to the office.

Two months later, I was removed as Keeper and transferred sideways to the non-job of "Chief Archivist," especially created for me and never filled again after I left it. Meanwhile, the statutory position of Keeper was occupied by acting arrangements for the next two years before it was finally filled just before the 1992 election.[2] For the succeeding six years, I was left with virtually no duties of any kind, but being paid at my former salary level. That period became a most fruitful time in my career for research and publishing. So far as I am aware, the Victorian Government has not been made uncomfortable since then in the matter of unauthorised disposal of public records.

What should the archivist do in the face of political pressure? In this case, by my own admission, I lied and disobeyed a lawful order. Does the archivist have professional obligations which can, under certain circumstances, justify non-compliance with contractual employment obligations? Was I right to insist that we treat all such cases the same way? Was the manner of treatment we had evolved the correct way of handling them? Can a consistent stance of any kind on unauthorised disposal be maintained by archival authorities? In any case, what role (if any) do archives authorities have in support of accountability of governments for recordkeeping?

---

2   The position was advertised and an attempt made to fill it while I was overseas on long service leave. I lodged an appeal, not against the selection but against the process. A competent review authority found the departmental process for filling the position so procedurally flawed that the department was ordered to cancel their selection and re-interview. They did, but it made no difference to the final outcome.

When an archive's authority is established and functions under arrangements which forbid the destruction of records without the necessary permissions, what is the archivist to do when confronted with evidence (or, at least, allegations) that those arrangements are being violated? Especially when no one else is doing anything about it? Even when the archivist's mandate to enforce the arrangements is far from clear and explicit?

There are two possible approaches to this archival task. One, expressed in relation to the utility of the new international Standard on Records Management in bringing government departments into line, is referred to as "thwacking." This approach emphasises regulation, monitoring, compliance, and the threat of penalties. The other approach, which I would call insinuation or service-delivery, suggests that archivists should work through cooperation, by being helpful, forging alliances, conducting campaigns of persuasion, and education. This approach prefers to catch flies with honey.

These are alternative implementation strategies for achieving the same goal, not alternative goals. They can be picked up and laid aside as convenient. They should be treated as objects of choice as to strategy and purpose. Which to use and when depends on the role and function the archivist is mandated to do. Sometimes it is necessary to insinuate, and sometimes it is necessary to "thwack."

THE FIRST LESSON DEALS WITH THE ROLE OF PROTECTORS OF THE PUBLIC RECORD

There is surprisingly little role analysis in our literature concerning the archivist and the protection of the public record. Let us consider for a moment what is involved.

1. There must be a public record.
2. The record has to be useable.
3. The record has to be protected and preserved from concealment or distortion.

In some Australian jurisdictions, as in Victoria, the archives statute contains an obligation to "make and keep" full and accurate records of public business. On paper, this means that public servants and politicians who cannot produce a full and accurate record of their dealings in public business are guilty of a statutory breach. Leaving aside the efficacy of that way of going about it, it is clear that if record-keeping is to underpin accountable practices, there must be some obligation to keep full and accurate records of public business.

Where such obligations are imposed, especially when their enunciation or enforcement is entrusted to a body such as the archives authority, it is common (at least in Australia) for departments and agencies to regard this as an unwelcome intrusion, as red tape, and as a bureaucratic obligation extraneous to their core business. The purpose of recordkeeping obligations, within the public sector or any other corporate enterprise, is largely outside the scope of this paper. However, I will allude to two things which put the matter in another light.

First, a recordkeeping obligation which bears upon a department, agency, or business unit—while it may seem to be extraneous to the business purposes of the department, agency, or business unit—may be an essential requirement for the enterprise of which it is part. Units have no trouble submitting to enterprise-wide requirements for adequate financial and human resource management requirements, but for some reason they have difficulty seeing recordkeeping the same way.

Second, while external regulation can always be legitimately seen as an imposition and an obstacle, it can also be a benefit. By subscribing to recordkeeping requirements, a department, agency, or business unit can give quality assurances which can underpin business confidence. So, in describing the possible role of the regulator below, it is worth emphasising that it is not necessarily a game of cops and robbers.

If recordkeeping obligations are not met—deliberately or through carelessness or lack of support—it loosens the ties of accountability. In the last Australian election, the Government won support by taking a "hard line" on asylum seekers trying to reach Australia by boat. During the campaign, the Government bolstered its demonisation of these boat people by claiming, with the aid of pictures, that asylum seekers were throwing their children into the sea in a vain attempt to prevent the Australian navy from turning them back. It was a lie. It was known to be a lie almost from the moment the claim was made. But the public did not find this out until after the election. A Parliamentary

Inquiry was unable to establish conclusively who, if anyone, in the Government knew it was lie and how it was possible for the lie to remain uncorrected for the whole of the campaign. This was partly due to the fact that inadequate records were made and kept.

In both Britain and Australia, we have seen how difficult it was to reconstruct, after the event, the story of how untruth concerning the existence and threat of chemical, biological, and nuclear weapons in Iraq came to form the policy basis for war. Again, the lack of a comprehensive, accurate, reliable, and useable public record is partly to blame. In both countries, the role of ministerial advisers has come into question. They are unelected, unaccountable, and outside the traditional recordkeeping framework. They wield great vicarious influence in their minister's name and seem to be used to separate ministers from that responsibility which comes from being the recipient of knowledge or unwelcome (but fair and impartial) advice.

It is not enough to oblige our public officials to make and keep full and accurate records—that obligation must be enforced in some way. In Australia, even where the obligation is given a statutory basis, it is not enforced. If it is to be enforced, it becomes necessary to ask the question: How? My answer is entirely technical. I do not dwell on the politics of enforcement, but on the methods. What are the possible roles and functions which enforce good recordkeeping in support of accountability? In my chapter of a recently published book,[3] I have identified at least ten. These can fit fairly easily under the two approaches already referred to (insinuation and "thwacking"), with the addition of a third: auditing.

Under the heading of insinuation, we can include the following:
- setting standards; articulating professional wisdom or experience
- advising, recommending, educating
- assisting; participating in a course of action; carrying out a decision
- providing services and the assurance of quality and meeting professional standards
- enabling by proving tools (e.g., metadata frameworks)

---

3   Sue McKemmish, Michael Piggott, Barbara Reed, and Frank Upward, eds., *Archives— Recordkeeping in Society.* Topics in Australasian Library and Information Studies, No. 24 (Wagga Wagga, New South Wales: Charles Sturt University Centre for Information Studies, 2005), ch. 11 "Recordkeeping and Accountability."

Under the heading of "thwacking," we can include :
- issuing instructions or edicts; allowing or forbidding action (e.g., disposal)
- monitoring behaviour and collecting reports on performance
- policing; detecting wrong-doing
- enforcing requirements and intervening to alter behaviour

The audit function must be separated because it is fundamental that audit must not be done by the same person or body responsible for setting standards or enforcing compliance. The recordkeeper's performance in those roles is being audited too.

These are the possible roles of the recordkeeper in protecting the public record. Some of them do not belong together. It follows that two or more entities must be involved. The auditor and the standard-setter, for example, must always be different entities. It would be possible, but very difficult, for one entity to maintain roles in offering advice and assistance while simultaneously monitoring and reporting.

Clarity around the role is one thing. Mandating it and avoiding the temptation, when the going gets tough, of slipping out of an assigned role and adopting another or of simply failing to meet one's responsibilities is another. Let us assume for a moment, what is manifestly not the case, that the role of the recordkeeper in protecting the public record is clear and unambiguously assigned. My second story raises another question: Can the recordkeeper be trusted to carry out such a mandate?

The Heiner Affair

The Second Story Begins in Queensland (Australia) in 1989

For many years, the State of Queensland was politically corrupt. Following embarrassing disclosures and a Royal Commission conducted by Tony Fitzgerald, QC, the incumbent Government was staggering towards its first electoral defeat in decades. In 1989, during the lead-up to the election, an opposition candidate leaked accusations of mismanagement and abuse in a State institution for the incarceration of teenagers. Years later, another Royal Commission exposed endemic corruption and abuse (physical, sexual, and psycho-logical) in such institutions throughout Queensland, but this was not publicly known at the time.

The beleaguered Government set up an inquiry under a retired magistrate, Noel Heiner. We now know that Heiner was beginning to uncover accusations concerning the kind of abuse that was later exposed as endemic throughout the State's institutions. We now know of at least one incident of pack rape that was not properly reported or dealt with. Even now, new abuses of children in care within the Queensland system—the abuse of foster children, for example—are coming to light. Despite the Royal Commission, there has still not been closure or justice. The reason for this, it is suggested, is a climate of neglect and cover-up, involving successive governments, the abiding bureaucracy, and the unions.

In December 1989, a new Government was elected. The Opposition came to power and the candidate who raised the allegations during the campaign was now minister in charge of the institution Heiner was investigating. Something happened and the new Government stopped Heiner's investigation and ordered his records destroyed. The decision to destroy the records went all the way to Cabinet.

By this time, the head of the institution Heiner had been investigating had taken legal advice. His lawyers were alleging lack of proper process and threatening legal action. Its Crown Solicitor advised the Government that there was no legal obstacle to destruction of the documents up to the moment proceedings were filed in court. Those of you who followed the Enron Case in 2002, culminating in a conviction against the firm of Arthur Andersen, will recall that they acted on exactly similar advice with regard to records of their dealings with Enron—and were punished for it.

The Crown Solicitor's advice to the Queensland Government stated, however, that there was another obstacle to destruction. Heiner's records were public records, and, therefore, the consent of the State Archivist was necessary. The circumstances of the destruction were subsequently investigated several times: by two Senate Committees and by a team of two lawyers empowered by a subsequent Queensland Government to look into it. Although we still do not have all the facts, there is a wealth of documentary and testamentary material about it.

We know that the Queensland Cabinet was aware that an intending litigant wanted the records. We know that the Archivist was asked to approve the destruction and that she inspected the records and agreed to their destruction the same day. We know that for months afterward, the Queensland authorities refused to reveal that the records had been destroyed and stonewalled the lawyers who were seeking to access them in preparation for their case.

Almost everything else about the Heiner Case is subject to dispute and ill-tempered disagreement. Since I have written about this in several places,[4] you can refer to those writings if you want to explore the matter further. You should be aware that my view of the case is not universally accepted among my professional colleagues. Others have a different story to tell and, accordingly, draw different lessons from it.

In the intervening period, the Heiner Case has entered the textbooks, not just for its recordkeeping aspects (they are, in fact, almost marginal to everyone but us) but also in books and articles about the law, whistleblowing, and the politics of accountability. It is still current. As recently as May 2003, the Queensland Government and Opposition were exchanging accusations and explanations about it across the floor of State Parliament.

One of those affected by the Heiner Case was Kevin Lindeberg, a union official acting on behalf of the head of the institution under investigation. Kevin was fired by his union for persisting in support of his union member when everyone else wanted the matter suppressed. His dissatisfaction with the treatment of the case by the Queensland's Criminal Justice Commission (QCJC) led to its being investigated in the Australian Senate—twice. It was Kevin Lindeberg who first drew my attention to the case in the early 1990s.

My story of what followed is this: Having read the record, I decided that the professional obligations to defend the public record from political pressure had not been met by the Archivist. She had been asked to approve the destruction, had inspected the records, and given her consent all on the same day. She had participated in the government's refusal to acknowledge the fact of the destruction to the prospective litigant and his lawyers for months after that. In particular,

---

4   My analysis of the Heiner Affair can be found on the Caldeson Consultancy website, http://www.caldeson.com.

I was drawn to comments by an official of the QCJC before one of the Senate Inquiries to the effect that it was not the role of the State Archivist to consider whether records were wanted in prospective legal proceedings. She had no role to consider the interests of potential litigants in her appraisal; she was concerned solely with whether or not the records had enduring "historical" value.

I drew the attention of the Council of the Australian Society of Archivists (ASA) to this statement and the surrounding facts and said they must act to refute these words. At the time, it didn't occur to me that they would not act. I assumed the story was so complex that they had not yet appreciated its significance. I was in my fallow period so I decided to help them by providing a precis. They did nothing. Why they did nothing and the circumstances surrounding their inaction are still matters of rancorous dispute between me and many of my colleagues in Australia. The matter was fought out bitterly for the next decade on the aus-archivists list-serv[5] and elsewhere. The archive of that list-serv debate is still available in cyberspace for those with the endurance to follow it—and a strong digestive system.

After some years, ASA issued a statement refuting the words of the QCJC about the role of the Archivist and blaming the Queensland Government for not fully informing her of the facts. To this day, we still don't know what the Archivist knew. She has never said, and no one has ever investigated it. Whatever the case, some of us felt that this statement by the ASA was inadequate. It blamed an unsatisfactory appraisal outcome on everyone except the person who conducted it. It failed to explain how archivists could escape the blame when appraisals go wrong. It seemed to me, and to some others, self-serving and counterproductive. If we were unable to face up to the implications of a failure to protect the public record when we were involved, how could we credibly comment on such failures by others? The problem was compounded when the Council of Federal and State Archivists (COFSTA) issued a public motion of congratulations and support for their Queensland colleague because it was concluded, following one of the investigations, that there was no basis for proceeding against her for a breach under the Libraries and Archives Act of Queensland.

---

5   http://www.asap.unimelb.edu.au/asa/aus-archivists/maillist.htm.

I, for one, felt that the appraisal—regardless of who knew what and having regard for the Archivist's professional obligations and not just her legal ones—was bad and that professionally we had an obligation to say so. My consistent criticism of the appraisal, ever since I had first drawn it to ASA's attention, was what I call its "ad hoc" nature. There were no rules in place against which either the procedure or the outcome could be benchmarked. There was nothing in place which indicated how records of terminated inquiries should be dealt with. Because there was no prior statement of what the outcome should be for records of this kind, the Archivist's judgment in the particular case could not be tested against what could reasonably be argued was a predictable outcome. It could not be defended on the basis that it was similar to all such outcomes for similar material.

Finally, in 1999, that is what the ASA Council did say, in a second statement, following protracted and furious debates on the Australian list-serv. They said the Heiner appraisal violated the standards of good appraisal and that it was wrong to go about appraisals in an ad hoc way. They began to articulate some professional standards by which the next dodgy appraisal decision by an archivist could be judged.

We know, from what happened next, that they consulted the Council of Federal and State Archivists before issuing their condemnation. Some changes were made. We do not know what. These changes were not enough to satisfy the government archivists. They issued their own statement repudiating key parts of the ASA statement, in particular trying to disavow the condemnation of ad hoc appraisal.

In short, the government archivists of Australia
* banded together to support and defend their colleague (as I suppose they would want and expect to be supported in similar circumstances)
* congratulated her when she escaped censure
* opposed the profession's condemnation of her appraisal
* repudiated the statement of principle by which her ad hoc approach to appraisal was condemned by the profession.

In due course, the Heiner Affair reached the agenda of an ICA Committee dealing, inter alia, with recordkeeping practice. When this happened, the ICA Secretariat intervened to have it removed from the agenda and instructed that it was a matter for Australia and should not be considered by ICA.

THE SECOND LESSON: HOW PROTECTORS OF THE PUBLIC RECORD SHOULD BEHAVE

In exercising any or all of the roles and functions identified, the archivist's own performance becomes an issue. If you are going to be an agent of accountability, it behoves you occasionally to act like one. Are they capable of it?

We have dealt with the regulation or monitoring of the behaviour of others by the recordkeeper in the roles and functions articulated above. In those roles, the archivist operates in the left-hand column of an accountability model. See figure 1.

FIGURE 1

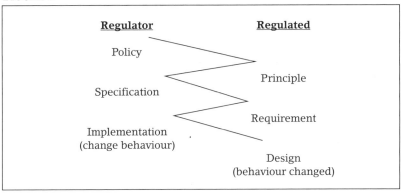

Let us now move the recordkeeper over to the right-hand column. The question is: Who or what regulates the recordkeeper in the discharge of the obligation to protect the archival record? It is a question as old as Plato: Who guards the guardian?

The question has two aspects. First, is it possible for relatively low-level bureaucrats to uphold a role as agents of accountability within a bureaucratic structure which makes them subservient to bureaucratic and political direction? It is, after all, the politically motivated actions of politicians and other bureaucrats which the archivist would have to control in some way.

Let us not look for isolated acts of courage to do the right thing. Let us look for a systemic solution, a set of functional requirements with which recordkeepers themselves must and do comply. Let us try to specify the standards which they must meet, benchmarks we can use to evaluate their performance, the hallmarks of a good appraisal (or any other aspect of our work) so that we too can be made accountable.

Part of the answer, it has been suggested, lies in a second aspect of the matter: according to the government archivist, some degree of independence or autonomy; providing for the archivist to answer to a loyalty or responsibility outside the chain of bureaucratic command or the requirements of an employment contract. This might be to a professional standard, to an external review process, to the legislature, or to some other constituent mechanism which frees the archivist (to some degree or other) from the ordinary chain of command when exercising the role of agent of accountability.

Such arrangements cannot be the whole answer. Even when there is a formal "independence," government watch-dogs are susceptible to subtle pressures to compromise their integrity. Their organisational budgets and personal career prospects lie in the hands of those whose political interests such a role calls upon them to defy. The literature on what is sometimes called the "regulatory capture" of watch-dogs within governments is a growing one. Such capture can be venal or can be simply the demoralisation of good men and women through exhaustion. Many and varied are the ways politicians and the bureaucracy find to wear the watch-dog down. Sometimes, especially when under pressure to perform, the watch-dog, knowing the lengths the system will go to in fighting a particular issue, will simply decide that life is too short and that more good can be done taking on issues with a chance of success.

What I want to deal with, however, is a more basic question. Let us suppose that the archivist has a clearly mandated and clearly articulated role—and the capacity to exercise it. My question is: how can we trust them to do it and, if they do it, how would we know? My question is about benchmarking the performance of the archivist as an agent of accountability.

The significance of the debate about Heiner is not who was right and who was wrong—although that is an important question in its own right. The significance is that the debate went on for years and is still going on, without any way of telling who was right against criteria which had been clearly articulated and consistently applied. All of the opinions expressed (including mine) amounted to little more, ethically, than a personal preference for chocolate ice cream.

I'm not saying there should have been bedrock certainties, immutable laws which covered all possibilities. Benchmarking is not like that. Setting out the benchmarks initiates debate over their application in particular cases. When necessary, they can be modified in the light of experience and with the benefit of hindsight. What the debate over Heiner demonstrated, for me at any rate, was not the inadequacy of our benchmarks but the fact that we didn't have any.

No one was able to say the Heiner appraisal was wrong because it didn't conform to the agreed-upon standard for a good appraisal in this or that respect. If that had been possible, those who disagreed could have argued that my interpretation of the standard was incorrect, that my understanding of the facts was flawed, or that my application of the standard to the known facts was faulty. Finally, there could have been recourse to an argument that the case illustrated that the standard itself was inadequate and should be varied in the light of our experience. None of this was possible. Instead, participants in the debate were, in effect, indicating what they considered good appraisal, in order to apply that opinion to a defence or attack of what happened. But even that dignifies the debate. In May 2003, I made these points to an ASA meeting in Sydney. One of the State Archivists responded by saying (yet again) that the central issue in Heiner was not about any rule concerning what constitutes a good appraisal or establishes when it is bad. He said the issues in Heiner were whether or not the Queensland Cabinet knew the records were wanted for legal proceedings[6] and whether or not the Archivist was told.

In other words, an evaluation of the Heiner appraisal does not depend on our being able to test it empirically against the measures of what a good appraisal should be; it depends on an evaluation of the state

---

6   It is an established fact that they did know.

of mind of the participants. This begs the question. I won't say the state of mind of the participants is irrelevant, but neither is it central. If there were benchmarking about what constitutes a good appraisal, it would matter less what the participants were thinking. We can instead measure their actions, their behaviour, against the criteria which set out what should be done, how it should be done, and what the outcome should be.

With this argument, I felt, my opponent was making my case for me. By saying the state of mind of the participants was the key issue, he was highlighting the absence of standards against which actions, methods, and outcomes could be empirically measured. In the common law system, *mens rea* is an essential ingredient of crime, but so is certainty. You can't be convicted of an offence that hasn't been defined (unless, of course, you're being confined at Guantanamo Bay). He was saying (whether or not he realised it) that because we had no other way of establishing what was, and what was not, acceptable behaviour, we were driven to inquire only into what the participants were thinking at the time. You benchmark by asking what people did, not what they thought. But benchmarking is not just about running a ruler over peoples' actions. It is not simply about measuring the methodology, procedures, and techniques which were used. In some ultimate and fundamental way, it must also be about principle.

The ASA's 1999 statement condemning ad hoc appraisal, calling itself a policy on appraisal, has stayed on the public record for three years. Earlier this year, the current ASA Council issued for comment a document calling itself a draft Appraisal Policy. That document, and my subsequent response to it, can be found on the archive of the *aus-archivists* list. I am highly critical of this draft Appraisal Policy. My reason tracks directly back to the Heiner case. In all the years in which this case was being hotly debated, the fundamental problem, I now see, was that we were arguing about what was, and what was not, the standard for an adequate appraisal. The problem was that there was no satisfactory and credible standard or benchmark against which the actions of the Queensland State Archivist could be judged. And the same can be said, I believe, for any and all aspects of the potential role recordkeepers might have in protecting the public record.

E-mails flew thick and fast, public pronouncements were made, personal endorsements were given, positions were taken, attacked, and repudiated by people (myself included) who were not actually able to demonstrate, by reference to some standards or benchmarks, which view of the matter was correct. The point here is not that such benchmarks could have resolved the debate—there remains plenty of room for disagreement between those who are examining the same set of facts against undisputed benchmarks. The elimination of dispute is not the point. What has been lacking is not just agreement, but a credible basis upon which disagreements could be debated. What was lacking was a point of reference from which expectations of the behaviour of archivists could be derived and against which their actual performance could be measured.

We know that other agents of accountability have such benchmarks and that they do not eliminate disagreement and dispute. Court judgments are appealed and overruled. Audits are shown to have overlooked irregular practices and to have been adapted to obscure flaws in financial management. Ombudsmen and corruption watch-dogs fail to get it right. To a greater or lesser extent, however, the systems within which such agents of accountability operate are self-correcting because these failures can be examined in the light of prevailing benchmarks and the system within which they operate is, to a greater or lesser extent, set up to identify and remedy perceived errors.

Post Enron, the rules about how accountants operate and their relationship with their clients have been adjusted. In a recent tobacco case in Australia, the rules about the way lawyers relate to their clients were changed after another instance of records destruction on legal advice in advance of formal proceedings. It is not that benchmarks prevent untoward behaviour, but rather that they provide a basis for measurement and corrective action.

Above all, such benchmarks provide a statement by which outcomes, not just procedural rules, can be judged. What matters, ultimately, in the Heiner appraisal, is not simply whether or not the Queensland Archivist followed the provisions of the State's Libraries and Archives Act. What matters, ultimately, is: Did she get it right? Professionally, did she do a good job?

My condemnation of the ASA's draft Appraisal Policy was that it did not help to answer that question. The document was almost entirely procedural, explaining how you go about appraising records.

What it needed to say, in my view, is what kind of outcome an appraisal had to achieve in order for it to be a good appraisal: It had to condemn ad hoc appraisal. It had to provide certainty, consistency, and reliability by specifying that, in similar circumstances, the same kind of records would be appraised in the same way with the same result. It had to provide a basis for examining and testing the actions of the recordkeeper and for demonstrating that they were wrong if they did not adhere to the principles outlined in the policy. It had to be possible to use it to determine if their appraisal decision was not what a reasonable person could expect in light of the Policy Statement.

We know how to do this. What we try to teach others about the articulation and implementation of standards is the same for us (or ought to be). My complaint about the Heiner appraisal—that it was ad hoc—would have been void, in part, if the Queensland Archivist had had pre-determined rules about how to treat categories of material so that some degree of consistency and predictability was achieved. But that would be doing no more than replacing ad hoc appraisal with disposal schedules. Ultimately, disposal schedules are no more satisfactory because they are still validated by the archives institution itself. They are not referenced to any externally promulgated standard of performance and outcome. That, however, is what accountability means.

To be an effective accountability tool, an appraisal policy must not stop at requiring that appraisal outcomes be consistent and predictable. Those criteria would be satisfied by schedules. The policy must define what is needed to test whether the archivist's decision in particular cases (however that decision is expressed) is good or bad. This is what archivists, and anyone faced with new accountability requirements, find so threatening. The autonomy they now enjoy to keep or dispose of records entirely within their own discretion would be eliminated.[7]

There lies the paradox. If archivists are to be considered for the kind of autonomy that is the hallmark of any profession, their individual

---

7 Submitting appraisals for external comment is no answer for several reasons. First, mechanisms to elicit effective external scrutiny do not exist and will not until we create parallel contextual frameworks within which others can apply appraisal criteria appropriate to them rather than the organisational concerns within which traditional appraisals are carried out. Second, no external commentator has a mandate to validate appraisal outcomes. Third, such methodologies simply spread the arbitrariness in the absence of articulated standards and benchmarks by which appraisals must be judged. Peer review, however, provided it was done externally, could be acceptable if it were properly managed.

judgment must be circumscribed by standards which remove the freedom to make professional judgments unfettered by any requirement to
meet stated outcomes and achieve prescribed benchmarks. That
means, in order to be trusted with autonomy, archival judgment must
first be professionally constrained.

This will be neither a simple nor an easy thing. But the model of
how to do it lies before us in the lessons we teach others about the
implementation of recordkeeping standards. First, the principles (the
functional requirements) must be articulated. These fundamental purposes are abiding. Underneath the principles, appropriate statements
of requirements and practice must be developed. See figure 2.

FIGURE 2

Theoretical Model	Actual Application
Implementing Functional Requirements	*Napoleon's Plans for 1812*
• Principle: What do you want to do?	• Conquer Russia
• Requirement: How you must do it.	• Capture Smolensk
• Implementation: Have you done it?	• Get out of bed

Implementation can take a variety of forms, so long as they meet the
same functional requirement. See figure 3.

FIGURE 3

My purpose is to reach the Indies:
• I propose to sail to the Cape of Good Hope, then turn
  east (Vasco da Gama)
• I propose to sail west (Christopher Columbus)
• We don't propose to sail anywhere (Wright Brothers)

There still remains a question of whether, even if we were given
such a mandate for developing such standards, clearly and unequivo-
cally, we would be able, allowed, or willing, given the political circum-

stances in which we find ourselves, to carry it out. My point here is much more modest. Without the necessary policy statements which can be used to benchmark our actions in protection of the public record, not just appraisal, but any of the recordkeeping requirements necessary for the creation and preservation of a full, accurate, and useable record, how would we (or anyone else) know?

I very much fear that there is an element within the recordkeeping profession which wants to prevent the emergence of such standards. Fearing, not without justice, that they would not be able (or permitted) to sustain them, they prefer not to have benchmarks in place against which their failures can be measured. Be that as it may, while we lack the benchmarks against which particular appraisals, and the work of particular appraisers, can be judged by others against something like objective standards which give predictability to the task, any claim we might make to act as protectors of the public record must remain hollow.

I am optimistic that it can be done, less so that the will exists to do it. Therefore, if we want to protect the archival record from political pressure, the first step is to wake up and get out of bed.

II

ARCHIVES, POLITICS, AND JUSTICE

Verne Harris

I want to add my voice to the many others who have praised the organizers of the conference, Political Pressure and the Archival Record, held in July 2003, at the University of Liverpool. Much has been said about the number of attendees and, in particular, the notable absences. That says something about the politics of archives—as does the fact that among the keynote speakers, there was only one woman and not a single person who was not white. Politics always is unavoidable. Although I wrote an overly long and complex paper for that conference, I would like to pull out two strands of the argument here. First, I want to argue that the archive *is* politics—not that it is political, but that it is politics. And second, I want to make the case for an approach to archival work defined by the phrase "archives for justice."

This text captures the content of my short address in speaking to a full-length paper prepared for the conference. The paper's title was "The Archive Is Politics: Truths, Powers, Records, and Contestation in South Africa." Two years have passed since I made the presentation, and much of my analysis in relation to South African specificities is outdated. Wherever appropriate I have added footnotes to suggest shifts which have taken place in the interim, but in some cases it has been necessary to revise the text.

Let me begin with a verse from a Bob Dylan song.

We live in a political world
Turning and a'thrashing about,
As soon as you're awake, you're trained to take
What looks like the easy way out.
                                        —Bob Dylan[1]

For at least two decades, it has been relatively commonplace for archivists explicitly to talk and write about the politics of archives and of recordmaking. Until quite recently, the discourse has been dominated by voices speaking to the harsh realities of recordmaking by and within what can be called oppressive regimes. These voices tended to adopt uncritically two fundamental assumptions about "the political." The first is that politics tends to pull professional practitioners away from principle, away from the ethical, away from the legitimate. Politics, in other words, is a bad thing when intruding into the recordmaking domain. The second assumption is that the political is something "outside" archives. The archivist, going about a legitimate activity, an activity duly mandated and prescribed, is intruded upon by a power outside the bounds of that activity. These assumptions resonate in the conference title.

The 1990s saw the emergence of influential new streams within the discourse which offered more nuanced accounts and critiques of the politics of recordmaking. These streams have challenged the notion of politics in archives as symptomatic of dysfunction in recordmaking and in society. They have shown that both the assumptions I've just outlined, while clearly connected to the realities we all experience, exclude dimensions which are critical to an adequate problematisation of the political. They have shown these assumptions to be offering us, in the words of Bob Dylan, what looks like the easy way out. On the one hand, politics need not be bad. There are uses of it, deployments of it, which are constructive rather than oppressive and which are in the service of, rather than against, the principled, the ethical, and the legitimate.

On the other hand, political pressure never only comes from "outside." It is always also at work from "inside," from within the processes

---

1   Bob Dylan, lyrics from "Political World," *Oh Mercy* (CBS Records, 1989).

of recordmaking. Recordmakers, including archivists, are, from the beginning and always, political players. We live in a political world, and in that world we are active participants in the dynamics of power relations. This is an argument which has been made from different perspectives and in different disciplines by numerous commentators. I wish to make a more difficult argument, namely, that politics is archival; that the archive is the very possibility of politics.

Scholars and commentators from many disciplines and many countries, working with a range of theoretical and epistemological frameworks, have unfolded how the exercise of political power hinges on control of information. My own favourite is Noam Chomsky,[2] whose searing critiques of democracy, in the United States especially, demonstrate how elites depend on sophisticated information systems, media control, surveillance, privileged research and development, dense documentation of process, censorship, propaganda, and so forth to maintain their positions.[3] But it is Jacques Derrida and Michel Foucault who reach most deeply in exposing the logic, even the law, underlying these phenomena. In the words of Derrida: "[T]here is no political power without control of the archive, if not of memory."[4] And Foucault, coming from a different direction but nailing the same law: "The archive is first the law of what can be said."[5] And *when it* can be said, *how*, and *by whom*. Both of them insist on the archive as a construction, one which issues from and expresses relations of power. Listen to Derrida elaborating this insistence in relation to media apparatuses:

> Who today would think his time and who, above all, would speak about it . . . without first paying some attention to a public space and therefore to a political present which is constantly transformed, in its structure and its content, by the teletechnology of what is so confusedly called information or communication?[6]

---

2 After this conference, I would place Tom Blanton of the National Security Archive a very close second. Tom Blanton, Director of the U.S.-based National Security Archive, delivered a presentation called "From the Stasi files to the White House e-mail: Freedom of information and its challenge to power."

3 See, for instance, Peter Mitchell and John Schoeffel, eds., *Understanding Power: The Indispensable Chomsky* (New York: The New Press, 2002).

4 Jacques Derrida, *Archive Fever* (Chicago: University of Chicago Press, 1996), 4.

5 Michel Foucault, *The Archaeology of Knowledge and the Discourse in Language* (New York: Pantheon, 1992), 129.

6 Derrida in Jacques Derrida and Bernard Stiegler, *Echographies of Television* (Cambridge: Polity Press, 2002), 3.

The confusion in this naming of "information" and "communication" stems from an underestimation—sometimes an ignoring—of what Derrida calls "fictional fashioning":

> No matter how singular, irreducible, stubborn, distressing or tragic the "reality" to which it refers, "actuality" comes to us by way of a fictional fashioning.[7]

(Those of you who watch TV "reality" programmes or CNN coverage of the war in Iraq know exactly what Derrida is talking about.) "Information" is always fashioned, always constructed. Derrida clears away the confusion by deploying the term—the concept—"archive."

In its Derridean deployment, "the archive" is the law determining meanings and significances—the law, if you like, determining contexts. Here, beneath the surface whirl and clatter of information is where the instruments of power are forged, instruments which in their most fundamental of operations create and destroy, promote and discourage, co-opt and discredit, *contexts*. I need not stress, nor resort to citation in order to demonstrate, that archivists—from dyed in the wool Jenkinsonians to Schellenbergians, from so-called postmodernists to records continuum advocates—have conceptualised what they do around their special expertise in context. But it is the politician—more precisely, the archon—who is the purveyor of context. The archon, then, is the archetypal archivist.

If this is a law informing even the most established of democracies, then how do we measure democracy? To this question, Derrida responds decisively, and not surprisingly, in archival terms:

> [E]ffective democratisation can always be measured by this essential criterion: the participation in and the access to the archive, its constitution, and its interpretation.[8]

If power is exercised through the construction of archive, then the locus of participation in the exercise of power is precisely the processes of the archive's construction. And that implies contestation, for society is always an assemblage of competing interests and perspectives. As the British intellectual Richard Hoggart has reminded us: "A well-running

---

7   Ibid.
8   Derrida, *Archive Fever*, 4.

democracy will constantly quarrel with itself, publicly, about the right things and in the right way."[9] The time for activism, in other words, is never past. When we give up on activism, we give up on democracy.

Even in democracies, of course, there are limits—there must be limits—to contestation. These are pointed to by Hoggart with the notion of quarrelling "in the right way." Here he suggests the space for contract—social contract. Activists need to be wary of the penchant of those who hold power in democracies to hold up *contract* as a substitute for *contest*. Sometimes the powerful even go so far as to suggest that contestation unravels the contract. These, I want to suggest, are sub-terfuges, strategies for entrenching power. It is to confuse law, and right, with justice. It is, in Bob Dylan's terms, a being trained to take what looks like the easy way out. Contracts emerge out of contestation. And the very notion of contract assumes potential contest, puts in place frameworks and mechanisms for managing contestation appropriately. Indeed, ensuring that the contract is respected, adapted to accommo-date new realities and new needs, and kept open to the call of justice, hinges on our capacity to foster contestation within and around it, so that the contestants—and at times they might be bitter foes—are at the same time *partners* in a noble endeavour, the endeavour to bring justice. Those who can be at once partners and foes are precisely those who are not seeking the easy way out.

My organisation, the South African History Archive (SAHA),[10] is explicitly and deliberately a contestant in this terrain. In the 1980s, we framed our work as a counter to the dominant narratives of the Apartheid regime. Through most of the 1990s, we were partners in the building of new narratives as South Africa navigated a transition to democracy. Today we are contesting that democracy—the boundaries, the reach, the dynamics, the meaning, and the shaping stories of that democracy. In doing so, we are aware that we are accountable to a range of people, processes, structures, and ideals. We believe that, in the end and in the beginning, our most important accounting is to the call of justice. And we are striving to build an archival praxis which gives expression to the idea of "archives for justice."

---

9   Quoted in Christopher Merrett, "A Tale of Two Paradoxes: Media Censorship in South Africa, Pre-Liberation and Post-Apartheid," *Critical Arts* 15, 1–2 (2001), 64.

10 I was director of SAHA from May 2001 to May 2004.

Why "archives for justice" rather than "archives for truth," "archives for memory," or "archives for accountability"? I can name four imperatives. First, I believe—and I'm expressing a belief rather than offering an analysis—that the call of justice is the most important of all. It comes from beyond records and archives. It comes through the fabric of injustice which is our experience of life. It sounds, for example, through the obscenity of possession being predicated on the dispossession of others; through the obscenity of a global system which mouths human rights while trading in human suffering; through the obscenity of truth commissions prioritising political accommodation and sacrificing accountability; through the obscenity of my having to sacrifice every other suffering child when I focus on my own child's need. I offer no blueprint for identifying the call of justice. Following Derrida, I don't believe that justice, ultimately, can be knowable. Like democracy, it must always be coming. But the obscenities demand that we work for its coming.

A second imperative. The structural pull in all recordmaking is towards the replication of existing relations of power, with the attendant exclusions, "privilegings," and marginalisations. We cannot avoid complicity. But we can work against the pull; and for me it is a moral imperative to do so.

Third imperative. Those who have power—the elites—use "the archive" as an instrument of power. If justice is not to be forgotten in the process, if "use" is not to become untrammelled "abuse," then we are obliged at the very least to trouble such use.

These three imperatives could be called universal, or transcendent. They apply irrespective of particular circumstances. But of course there will always be specificities of time and place shaping them. And every configuration of specificities can be seen as constituting a fourth imperative. Take my own case as an example. I live in a country where almost 40% of the adult population is illiterate; where the unemployment rate is between 30% and 40%; where an estimated 600 people die every day from AIDS-related diseases; where a third of women are raped at least once in their lives; where since 1994 the standard of living for black people has fallen while that of whites has risen. I could go on. My point is that in South Africa today the call of justice is an insistent one. It is less easy for me to ignore that call than it is for someone working as an archivist in Liverpool.

And what about the narrower world of archives in South Africa? How insistent is the call of justice there? Today, the dominant discourse in South African archives suggests that the time for activism is past. Activism was necessary in extreme conditions, so the argument runs, but now, with the coming of democracy, archivists can resume traditional mantles and focus on service delivery.[11] South African society has been "normalised," and archives should follow suit—that is, offer a professional and impartial service outside the buffetings of "politics." Let me offer a brief view into the consequences of this so-called normalisation for South Africa's premier archival institution, the National Archives. These are, I would argue, the consequences of an attempt to take what looks like the easy way out.

The period immediately after 1994, stretching to at least 1998, was a heady one for what became the National Archives in 1997. New blood came into the organisation, all functions and structures were interrogated in terms of developing government-wide legislative and policy frameworks, and the doors were opened to the transformation discourse in archives which had flourished in the period 1990 to 1994. Most important, discussion, debate, and consultation were encouraged at all levels. Change was the order of the day, and there was tangible hope of fundamental democratisation of processes. In 1996, the National Archives of South Africa Act was passed after a long gestation period involving broad-based consultations with stakeholders. It provided a blueprint for the transformation of South Africa's national archival system, including the extension of energies concentrated in the National Archives to nascent provincial archives services.

From the perspective of today, this period seems like a false dawn. The period since then has been characterised by what I call the re-bureaucratisation of the National Archives.[12] Obviously a wide-ranging critique would be required to sustain such an argument. Here, I offer just seven little windows into the phenomenon:

1. In the year 2000, the National Archives management issued a muzzling order to professional staff. From then on all public

---

11 The best example of an overt articulation of this position is the National Archivist's paper at the conference, "Conflict or Contest? Faultlines in the Nexus Between Holding Records and Using Them," University of the Witwatersrand, July 2002.

12 It should be noted that more recently there have been welcome signs of the National Archives re-engaging the transformation energies of the 1990s.

statements by staff, including conference papers and articles in scholarly journals, were to be authorised in writing by the National Archivist.

2. In 2001, the National Archives of South Africa Act was amended without consultation with stakeholders outside of the state.[13] Indeed, over two years later very few interested parties are even aware of the changes.

3. The changes themselves are worrisome. One of them brings the National Archives more tightly under the control of the bureaucracy. Another dispenses with the watchdog National Archives Commission and replaces it with a purely advisory body. This constitutes a fundamental remodelling of the delicate balance between the National Archives, Parliament, and the Commission as envisaged in the 1996 Act.[14]

4. There are a growing number of cases of records more than 20 years old, therefore available without restriction in terms of the Archives Act, being closed in terms of the Promotion of Access to Information Act (2000)—an ironic, and arguably illegitimate, development.[15]

5. Work on developing an access policy in relation to the archive of the Truth and Reconciliation Commission (TRC) began in 1999. This has still not been finalised,[16] and we do not know how open this archive is going to be—this archive which surely should be the most open of all South African archives. Those who have attempted to access records in this archive—in the custody of the National Archives but under joint management with the Department of Justice—have found the process to be complex, frustrating and often futile. And then there is the case of the missing 34 boxes of "sensitive" TRC records. SAHA had to go to the High Court merely to determine the whereabouts of

---

13 In terms of the Cultural Laws Amendment Act of 2001.

14 For an outline of the intentions of the drafters of the 1996 National Archives of South Africa Act in relation to the management and oversight of the National Archives, see Verne Harris, "Transforming Discourse and Legislation: A Perspective on South Africa's New National Archives Act," *ACARM* (Association of Commonwealth Archivists and Records Mangers) *Newsletter* 18 (1996) and *Archives News* 39, 2 (1996).

15 Ultimately the problem here is one of uncertainty about how the two pieces of legislation articulate with one another. A legislative intervention is required to clarify the position.

16 During 2004 considerable progress was made with the policy formulation, but much remains to be done.

these records. We now know that they are with the Ministry for Intelligence, and we are pursuing court action in order to ensure public access to them.[17]

6. There is strong evidence of lack of capacity within the National Archives in dealing with access requests. Procedural flaws and long delays have characterised responses to all SAHA's requests to the National Archives. The average response time in the period 2001–2002 was eight months, whereas the Access Act prescribes a period of 30 days.[18]

7. We see no evidence of serious attempts by the National Archives to locate, audit, and secure the scattered and extremely vulnerable records of the former Bantustan governments and of the Apartheid-era security establishment. Indeed, in at least one case, the former Transkei archives, the National Archives has been paralysed in face of a reckless disregard for the preservation of a priceless and irreplaceable resource. For nearly three years, these archives have been left in a storeroom in the backyard of the Nelson Mandela Museum in Umtata, partially exposed to the elements and at severe risk of damage or loss.[19]

Re-bureaucratisation, I am suggesting, is directly linked to the dominant discourse in archives. Let me point out the flaws in this discourse. First, South African society is far from "normalized." The imprints of Apartheid remain resilient. Second, democracy is always coming. Its values and goals must always be fought for. Third, the transformation of national recordmaking and archival systems has only just begun. Fourth, it is impossible for recordmakers to be impartial, to insulate themselves from politics. Impartiality is a chimera turning recordmakers into the pawns of those who have power. Any attempt to be impartial constitutes a choice, whether conscious or not, to replicate if not to reinforce prevailing relations of power. To return to the words of Bob Dylan, it is a choice to take what looks like the

---

17 A subsequent out of court settlement secured the transfer of the 34 boxes to the National Archives and the placing of a majority of documents in the public domain.

18 It should be noted that in 2004 SAHA reported a strong turnaround in National Archives performance levels in relation to access requests.

19 Subsequent interventions by the National Archives and the Nelson Mandela Museum have seen a significant improvement in the storage facilities, but much remains to be done before the former Transkei archives can be regarded as "safe."

easy way out. And last, in archives as in society, democracy lives and breathes through contestation. The space for contestation is the holy place where justice happens, if it happens. If archivists eschew this space, then they turn their backs on higher callings and condemn themselves to being merely bureaucrats and functionaries.

I refuse to turn my back on the higher callings, and I encourage everyone in archives to make the same refusal. In heeding the callings, we might lose security, status, material well-being, and big pensions, but we are guaranteed the thrill, and the enchantment, of dancing *with* destiny. And we are guaranteed the self-respect which comes from a refusal to seek the easy way out.

Governments under Pressure? Threats and Responses

12

"ANY TANGIBLE THING": THE USA PATRIOT ACT AND ITS IMPACT ON HIGHER EDUCATION ADMINISTRATION

Jackie R. Esposito

> Freedom is not some arbitrary right that is bestowed upon us because of the virtuous nature of our national character. It is a right we must protect and defend in both times of promise and peril if we are to remain in the future what we are in the present—a free and honorable people.
>
> —Abraham Lincoln

The purpose of this essay is to review the social policy implications for higher education administrators when responding to legal requests submitted by law enforcement agencies specifically related to the USA Patriot Act (Uniting and Strengthening America by Providing Appropriate Tools Required to Intercept and Obstruct Terrorism), Public Law 107-56 (hereinafter referred to as the Patriot Act). Sweeping provisions in the Patriot Act compromise privacy because they override "probable cause" requirements in the implementation of law enforcement searches.

Significance of the Problem

The Patriot Act was introduced eight days after the terrorist attacks of 11 September 2001 to provide federal authorities with expanded tools to "intercept and obstruct terrorism." Signed into law on 26 October 2001, the Patriot Act contains "a plethora of legislative changes which significantly increased the surveillance and investigative powers of law enforcement agencies."[1] The Act amends and expands existing federal laws to allow law enforcement agencies freedom to search and seize information, for and about "potential" terrorists. Among the legislative changes, specifically relative to higher education administrators are: Family Educational Rights and Privacy Act (FERPA), Electronic Communications Privacy Act (ECPA), and Foreign Intelligence Surveillance Act (FISA). The change implications in these three areas alone have been considerable.

FERPA

The amendment to FERPA allows educational institutions "to disclose without the consent or knowledge of the student, any records containing information about student transactions."[2] This amendment refers specifically to personally identifiable information contained within a student's educational records as it relates to investigations for terrorist crimes or the perception thereof. These requests for information, previously submitted under warrant or subpoena, can now be requested *ex parte*. "An *ex parte* order is an order issued by a court without notice to an adverse party."[3] The new law allows higher education institutions immunity from prosecution for unauthorized information release as well as recordkeeping responsibilities for the request. The Family Compliance Office, Department of Education, argued that the emergency provisions of the existing FERPA legislation would sufficiently respond to these requests, but Section 507 of the Patriot Act was written to bypass notice to student requirements.[4]

---

1   Charles Doyle, *Libraries and the USA Patriot Act*, Congressional Research Service, Report for Congress, 23 February 2003, 5.
2   Office of General Counsel, Catholic University of America, http://counsel.cua.edu/ Fedlaw/Patriot.cfm (accessed 23 June 2005).
3   Ibid.
4   Family Compliance Office, Department of Education, www.ed.gov/policy/gen/guid/ fpco/index.html (accessed 23 June 2005).

For academic administrators the implications of the language changes increase the type and formats of student records now subject to law enforcement review. The Patriot Act refers to business records as "'any tangible thing' that reflects an activity by a person who may be perceived to be a terrorist."[5] The inherent conflict with the nature of FERPA legislation, which was written to protect the confidentiality of student educational records, has created response problems at a number of universities. The National Center for Education Statistics, in its 1997 report *Guidelines for Education Agencies,* recommends responding to law enforcement requests on a case-by-case basis utilizing legal counsel.[6] With the significance of the legal amendments within the Patriot Act, this procedure would appear to be the best practice for higher education administrators.

ECPA

Originally passed in 1986, this legislation extended the wiretap provisions of the Crime Control Act to computers and the Internet. Ideally, the legislation would be utilized to maintain and increase privacy of communication in electronic media. The Patriot Act amendments (Sections 210 and 216) "expand the scope of subpoena to cover all forms of electronic communication." This revision extends to voice mail, e-mail, websites, Internet chat rooms, and so forth. Section 222 of the Patriot Act recommends the restructuring of information technology infrastructures to allow "federal authorities to install technological tools to capture information across platforms." While the amendments do provide some mechanism for entities to recover "reasonable compensation expenses," it does not detail a process for requesting those reimbursements.

This is a significant change for colleges and universities since the request for content from electronic media is no longer limited to reasonable cause, "it now comes under both a national search strategy and 'any tangible issue.'"[7] This particular provision could potentially cause the most trouble and inconvenience for a higher education administra-

---

5　Electronic Privacy Information Center, USA Patriot Act, www.epic.org/privacy/terrorism/usapatriot/ (accessed 19 May 2005).

6　*Guidelines for Education Agencies: Protecting the Privacy of Student Records* (Washington, D.C.: National Center for Education Statistics, 1997), 73.

7　Tracy Mitrano, Office of Information Technology, Cornell University, www.cit.cornell.edu/oit/PatriotAct/ (accessed 19 May 2005).

tor, since information technology is pervasive and decentralized on most campuses.

FISA

Section 416 of the Patriot Act amends the business record sections of FISA, "so that in a foreign intelligence or international terrorism investigation federal authorities may obtain a FISA order for access to any tangible item no matter who holds it."[8] This requirement has led to the development of the Student and Exchange Visitor Information System (SEVIS). SEVIS regulations were implemented on 10 May 2002 by the U.S. Attorney General's office. The law "increases the reporting obligations of all schools and institutions which receive international students." It requires adding information about international students into a national database and imposes "the mandatory penalty of either termination of the institution's approval to receive such students, or suspension of such approval for a period of at least one year."[9]

Dean Eva Pell, Penn State University, reported:

> [W]hile the enrollment of PhD students has increased, that of MS students has declined ... A major concern is the declining enrollment of students from abroad, in general ... indicating that the attractiveness of the U.S. as a place for graduate studies is declining . . . some [academic] programs have had traditionally a large fraction of international students ... these trends represent a significant challenge for them.[10]

The long-term impact of these changes in legislation has yet to be measured, but the initial results of compliance and additional visa reviews has certainly been sobering.

---

8 Doyle, *Libraries and the USA Patriot Act*, 1.
9 Student and Exchange Visitor Information System, www.sevis.net.
10 Penn State University, report of the Vice President for Research and Dean of the Graduate School, "Graduate Enrollments and Research Activities," Graduate Council Meeting Minutes, 19 November 2003.

Conceptual/Theoretical Framework

> They that can give up liberty to obtain a little temporary safety
> deserve neither liberty nor safety.
>
> —Benjamin Franklin

There are three major conceptual frameworks for higher education administrators to review when developing strategies for dealing with the implications of the Patriot Act. Amitai Etzioni in his seminal article, "Administrative and Professional Authority," establishes criteria for creating and using knowledge and information without undermining the organization. He states that:

> [K]nowledge is produced, applied, preserved, or communicated in organizations especially established for these purposes . . . "Pure" professional organizations [universities among them] are primarily devoted to the creation and application of knowledge; their professionals are usually protected in their work by the guarantee of privileged communication.

Utilizing these criteria as a signpost for response to requests for information allows administrators to structure their response mechanism into standard operating policies and procedures. Etzioni continues:

> [W]hen the hierarchy of authority is in inverse relation to the hierarchy of goals and means, there is considerable danger that the goals will be subverted. [11]

Administrators need not let this happen when responding to specific requests for information under the provisions of the Patriot Act.

Kim S. Cameron in his article, "Organizational Adaptation and Higher Education," further delineates the conceptual policy framework for Patriot Act requests.

> "Organizational adaptation" refers to modifications and alterations in the organization or its components in order to adjust to changes in the external environment. Its purpose is to restore equilibrium to an imbalanced condition.

---

11 Amitai Etzioni, "Administrative and Professional Authority," *Modern Organizations* (Englewood Cliffs, N.J.: Prentice Hall, 1964), 142.

Administrators should not allow the changes described in Patriot Act legislation to alter their standard response scenario. Cameron further argues:

> The population ecology approach suggests that adaptation is meaningful only if viewed from the population level of analysis . . . many constraints and inertias [are] inhibiting managerial action.[12]

If these inhibitors, including law enforcement agents, create a climate where the response mechanism strays from the standard operating procedure, the higher education community is in danger of losing their structure to an external motivator. Cameron recommends that:

> [U]nique organizational features develop in order to overcome certain general problems encountered by all organizations . . . the strategic choice approach . . . found that organizations adapted very successfully to an extremely turbulent and hostile environment by implementing three types of strategies in sequence: "domain defense" strategies (designed to enhance the legitimacy of the organization and buffer it from environmental encroachment), "domain offense" strategies (designed to expand in current areas of expertise and exploit weaknesses in the environment), and "domain creation" strategies (designed to minimize risk by diversifying into safer or less turbulent areas of the environment).[13]

William G. Tierney recommends creating and training administrative teams to respond to external forces.

> Administrative teams composed of president and "cabinet" became the decision makers for colleges and universities. They set goals, generated plans to achieve them, and decided which route was preferable in order to reach their market.

This strategy moves the decision-point responsibilities away from public service staff to the appropriate response venue. This adaptive strategy, according to Tierney, identified administrators as

> struggling to adapt to the demands of the external environment. . . . The importance of information that would help decision makers read the market accurately took on increased significance.[14]

---

12 Kim S. Cameron, "Organizational Adaptation and Higher Education," *Journal of Higher Education* 55 (April/May 1989), 234.

13 Ibid., 235.

14 William Tierney, "Critical Leadership and Decision Making in a Postmodern World," *Building Communities of Difference* (Westport, Conn.: Bergin & Garvey, 1993), 23.

Tierney advocates that certain external influences be dealt with through channels created by the team for just such a purpose. This mechanism is critical in standardizing responses to Patriot Act requests.

Data Sources

There are several websites that have established themselves as compilers of data and information on the responses to Patriot Act requests as well as management strategies. These resources are critical since publications have not kept pace with changes or implementation of federal guidelines. Among the best of these sites are the Electronic Privacy Information Center (EPIC); Catholic University of America, Office of General Counsel; Cornell University Office of Information Technology; and Congressional Research Service, American Law Division. In addition, individual websites have been established to deal with specific Patriot Act requirements and amendments. Significant among these sites is the SEVIS implementation website. Individual units within the higher education community have also begun responding to the Patriot Act implications. Primary among professional organizations which have taken a stance on the impact of the Patriot Act is the American Library Association. The American Civil Liberties Union and First Amendment speech advocates have also established themselves as resource experts.

Recommended Administrative Action Items

What can you as a higher education administrator do to respond to the requirements of the Patriot Act amendments? First and foremost, the higher education community should respond with a single voice. Colleges and universities do want to work together to address crime and terrorism, but they also want to maintain free speech and inquiry. These dual goals should not be at cross purposes any more now than they might have been prior to the enactment of the Patriot Act.

Second, "import the sensibility of constitutional protections and due process into revised policies and procedures."[15] Obviously, new

---

15 Tracy Mitrano, www.cit.cornell.edu/oit/PatriotAct/ (accessed 19 May 2005).

policies and procedures need to be written to respond to changes such as SEVIS. Revisions to existing policies and procedures will also need to be created to reflect changes in FERPA and, especially, ECPA. These changes should not violate the mission and goals of the university under any circumstance. Nor should they completely eliminate expectations of privacy from individuals.

Third, to accommodate ECPA requests, an open search structure will need to be developed for centralized administrative systems, such as student and financial databases. These systems should be created with specific search protocols requiring the authorization of a search from the legal counsel's office and at no other juncture in the transaction of the record. This does not address individually managed databases in academic or administrative units, but guidelines can be written to provide best practice advice for these areas.

Fourth, these amendments require aggressive and proactive training. Training has to be developed on two levels. Initially, all members of the academic and administrative leadership teams need to be informed of all legislative changes as well as revisions in internal policies and procedures. Next, a training protocol needs to be established for public service staff response teams. Practically speaking, law enforcement agents are more likely to address staff than the academic or administrative leaders. These frontline employees need to be sanguine that their response is to forward the request up the chain of command and not handle the request directly themselves.

Finally, each of these internal changes needs to be widely publicized so that "good faith" responses are standardized among all employees and supported by academic and administrative leadership. Good channels of communication are critical in responding to Patriot Act requests.

Value of Records

The impact of the Patriot Act in higher education is similar to that in many businesses and government agencies. It is based upon the dependence on and access to records and recordkeeping systems.

Records are the most faithful witnesses to the detail of information gathering, decision making, and prosecution of events than are the participants themselves. Therefore, no one should be surprised to recognize that records are integral to the "War on Terrorism" which began on September 11, 2001.[16]

In perspective, the war on terrorism is represented by a series of legislative actions and policies established to account for those suspected of perpetrating terrorist acts in or on the United States. Records policies, whether focused on international students like SEVIS, or on actions like those encapsulated in ECPA, have become part and parcel of the Bush Administration's focus on terrorism. Since records represent "evidence of thoughts, plans, and actions," government control of information and its generating sources become a more critical issue during times of war. Managing and making records and information available to law enforcement agencies, logically, becomes a "battleground" during the war.[17]

The Patriot Act as implemented by the U.S. Justice Department has created serious records issues for every form of business. Those most keenly felt within the higher education community directly impact the mission and goal of education within a free society.

Conclusion

Other provisions of the Patriot Act also affect higher education administration, including the Expansion of Biological Weapons Statute, Nationwide Application of Surveillance Orders and Search Warrants, Multi-Point Roving Wiretap Authority, and Authority to Conduct Secret Searches, to name a few. Administrators should follow a simple protocol for handling the implications of these requests—all requests, with or without a subpoena or warrant. That is, all requests, no matter who initiates them, must be handled directly by the University Counsel's Office. All requests, and their compliance, should be thoroughly and completely documented. These documents should

---

16 David Gracy, "Jihad Is, by Definition, Surrounded by Difficulties: Records and the War on Terrorism" (lecture delivered at the University of Texas at Austin, 11 April 2003).

17 Ibid., 9.

be maintained in the Counsel's office for no less than seven years after the date of the request after which they should be transferred to the University Archives for permanent retention. Access to the quantifiable data information should be made public twenty years after the request has been made. Personally identifiable information should not be made available during the lifetime of the individual under review.

13

THE BUSH ADMINISTRATION AND "INFORMATION LOCKDOWN"

Thomas James Connors

Writing in a *Nation* magazine commentary in November 2001, political journalist Bruce Shapiro used the term "information lockdown" to describe the George W. Bush administration's approach to public access to government information. Shapiro specifically cited the unwillingness of Justice Department investigators to release the names and circumstances of individuals being held as terrorists after the September 11, 2001, attacks; Attorney General John Ashcroft's memorandum of 12 October 2001, authorizing federal agencies to deny Freedom of Information Act (FOIA) requests; and the removal of specific information from government agency websites.[1]

Even prior to the appearance of Shapiro's article, a number of scholars, civil libertarians, historians, information professionals, and others had been monitoring the Bush administration's information policy and logging new instances of information lockdown. Here, I will chronicle some of the ongoing instances of information lockdown, put the whole lockdown mentality into a larger policy context that

---

1 Bruce Shapiro, "Information Lockdown," *The Nation*, 12 November 2001, http://www.thenation.com/.

includes personal information harvesting and propagating disinformation, and discuss responses to information lockdown and ways that information professionals who find this trend alarming can join with others to oppose it.

First, it might be good to clarify what I mean by "information." There is a distinction to be made between records, documents, and information. We generally think of records as containing evidence of some activity. Documents may or may not be records. And both records and documents contain and communicate information. For present purposes, I use information as an overarching term for what may be contained in government records, government documents, and government agency websites. (We can think of information as content and records/documents as carriers.)

Probably the most glaring example of the Bush administration's penchant for secrecy is the issuance of Executive Order 13233 to "further implement the Presidential Records Act of 1978." When Bush signed this executive order in November 2001, it caused a major stir among historians, archivists, journalists, and others interested in unfettered access to presidential records. The order effectively removes the power to grant access to presidential records from the Archivist of the United States and hands it to the Executive Office of the President. Researchers seeking access to presidential records can be turned down by a sitting president, a former president, or the heirs of a former president. The order invokes executive privilege as its justification and stipulates that a party seeking to overcome the alleged constitutionally based privileges that apply to presidential records must establish at least a "demonstrated, specific need" for particular records. (The first body of records to come under the access stipulations of the Presidential Records Act of 1978 were those of President Ronald Reagan and his Vice President George H.W. Bush.) This executive order has been challenged in court and a u.s. House of Representatives bill has been drafted to rescind it.[2]

Another example of adamant administration secrecy is Vice President Dick Cheney's refusal to provide information to the General

---

2   Full text of Executive Order 13233 can be found on the website of the Federation of American Scientists, http://www.fas.org/sgp/news/2001/11/eo-pra.html (accessed 19 May 2005).

Accounting Office (the non-partisan investigative arm of the u.s. Congress) on who advised his National Energy Policy Task Force which met in 2001. This too was taken to court where a Bush-appointed judge ruled in favor of Cheney. Cheney made no bones about the reason for withholding the requested information: He and Bush want to return to the Executive Branch power prerogatives that they and other conservatives feel were lost in the aftermath of the publication of the Pentagon Papers, and the Watergate, cia, and fbi scandals of the 1970s, specifically the right to keep Executive Branch operational information secret. (There are also those who feel that Cheney's reluctance to release energy task force records might have something to do with his former association with Halliburton, the energy company of which Cheney served as ceo prior to joining the Bush presidential campaign, and with Enron, the failed Texas energy conglomerate.)[3]

Removal of information from federal agency websites has continued since Bruce Shapiro reported on that activity. While the removal of website information deemed helpful to terrorists can be justified in principle, it is important to look at what information is being removed in fact. One government researcher told me that he wanted to correlate information on clean water availability to low income populations. While he could gather data on low income populations through census records, when he looked for water availability data, which had been on the Environmental Protection Agency website, he found that it had been removed out of fear of its being used by terrorists seeking to poison American water systems. The researcher's use of the data was a legitimate one, but in the name of domestic security, such use was sacrificed.[4]

Another instance of website editing has nothing to do with terrorism and everything to do with partisan politics. According to the American Educational Research Association, the u.s.. Department of Education has pulled website information on abortion, contraception, and risky behavior among adolescents. This is in compliance with a

---

3   This issue was covered extensively in major American newspapers. For example, see Adam Clymer, "Judge Says Cheney Needn't Give Energy Policy Records to Agency," *New York Times,* 10 December 2002, A1.

4   Private conversation, 20 April 2003, in Washington, D.C.

memo from the Secretary of Education that orders removal of information that runs counter to administration "policies, philosophies and goals."[5]

Classification, declassification, and reclassification of government information is another area of administration interest. In 1995, President Bill Clinton signed EO 12958 that ordered declassification of documents relating to national security and foreign relations after twenty-five years of closure. The idea was to err on the side of openness: If a classifier felt significant doubt about a document's need to be classified, the instruction was to declassify. An amendment to this order, signed on 25 March 2003, has turned this around. Now there is a presumption of classification for foreign government information; expanded authority to reclassify declassified information; new authority for the CIA to reject declassification rulings from an interagency panel; and elimination of the instruction not to classify where there is significant doubt of the need.[6]

There are many other instances of information lockdown. These deal mainly with FOIA exemptions and release of federal budget information.[7] Two recent instances in particular should be mentioned however. In June 2003, a federal appeals court ruled that the Bush administration could continue to conceal the identities of hundreds of people detained after the September 11 attacks. This overturned a court decision handed down in August 2002 that ordered the government to release that information. Also in June 2003, the Justice Department refused to release a report on its handling of the case against nuclear scientist Wen Ho Lee who was indicted in December 1999 on 59 felony counts alleging that he mishandled nuclear weapons information. (Lee was held in solitary confinement for nine months before being released in September 2000.)

---

5   American Educational Research Association, "ACTION ALERT: ED Web Information Disappearing," http://www.aera.net/communications/news/federal.htm.

6   "A New Executive Order," *Secrecy News*, Volume 2003, 25, 26, March 2003, 1. For the full text of Further Amendment to Executive Order 12958, as amended, Classified National Security Information, see http://www.fas.org/sgp/bush/eoamend.html (accessed 21 June 2005).

7   In March 2003, the National Security Archive released the findings of an audit it conducted of thirty-three government agencies on how they had responded to Attorney General John Ashcroft's memo of 12 October 2001, which essentially promised Justice Department support to agencies in denying FOIA requests. The audit found that thirteen agencies had taken active steps to implement the memo, the rest of those surveyed were aware of the memo but had not significantly changed their FOIA response practice.

Let me summarize: The main thrust of Bush's policy on access to government information has been to deny or delay responding to FOIA requests, rebuff legitimate legislative branch requests for information, deny or delay access to presidential records, close automatic access to classified information twenty-five years old or older, and remove certain types of information from government agency websites. This push toward ever greater control of information access is seen by many as a threat to the democratic political process and to open government.[8] It could be argued however that American government secrecy has been the name of the game since the outbreak of the Cold War. Each administration has surpassed its predecessor in clamping down on availability of certain information. The Clinton administration was the exception (at least in terms of FOIA and declassification—Clinton sided with his predecessor in the PROFS case, which argued that White House e-mail correspondence was not official government record).[9] And in general Republican administrations tend to be more control-minded than Democratic administrations. (FOIA became law during Lyndon Johnson's administration and the 1974 amendment that gave it teeth was passed over President Gerald Ford's veto.) So George W. Bush, it could be said, is just being true to partisan form.

The full character of the information policy I have here outlined cannot be appreciated without looking at two other information policy strands emanating from the Bush administration. The first has to do with gathering information on individuals. The Foreign Intelligence Surveillance Act of 1978 (FISA) set up a court of review to consider super-secret government wiretap and search requests. Federal agents need to go to this court to obtain permission to gather information on suspected terrorists. In 2001, 934 wiretap applications were granted. This number jumped to 1,228 in 2002. FISA critics argue that the Act's powers are broad and vague, and the secrecy of FISA court proceedings

---

8   As pointed out by Steven Aftergood, Director of the Federation of American Scientists' Project on Government Secrecy, "The boundaries of public access to information determine the boundaries of the democratic process." Quoted from Joe Fitzgerald and Antonia Badway, "Government Secrecy in the Age of Information," *Biodefense Quarterly*, Volume 5 (Summer 2003), no. 1, 1.

9   A lawsuit filed by Scott Armstrong in 1995, *Armstrong v. Executive Office of the President*, became familiarly known as the "PROFS case" after the e-mail system used by the National Security Council. Armstrong sought access to NSA e-mail correspondence under the Freedom of Information Act.

makes FISA powers susceptible to abuse. Moreover, FISA powers extend well beyond spies and terrorists. They can be used in connection with ordinary criminal investigations involving U.S. citizens who live in this country and who may be charged with offenses such as narcotics violations or breaches of an employer's confidentiality.[10]

In 2002, the Defense Advanced Research Projects Agency (DARPA), a unit of the Department of Defense (DOD), proposed establishing a Total Information Awareness (TIA) office. This office would gather information on individuals, mined from records of financial transactions, travel arrangements, library use, bookstore purchases, video rentals, and so forth—in other words, everyday information. The justification for this was to identify terrorists before they strike. In February 2003, a bi-partisan Senate funding provision essentially shut down the TIA project until May 2003 when DARPA was required to submit a detailed report on the program's costs, goals, and impact on civil liberties. On 20 May 2003, DARPA presented its 109-page *Report to Congress Regarding the Terrorism Information Awareness Program*.[11]

The report changes the name of the program from Total Information Awareness to Terrorism Information Awareness. The executive summary notes that:

> This name created in some minds the impression that TIA was a system to be used for developing dossiers on U.S. citizens. That is not DOD's intent in pursuing this program. Rather, DOD's purpose in pursuing these efforts is to protect U.S. citizens by detecting and defeating foreign terrorist threats before an attack. To make this objective absolutely clear, DARPA has changed the program name to Terrorism Information Awareness.

The report assures Congress that TIA contemplates deployment of its search tools consistent with current laws governing privacy. No new statutory laws are recommended.[12] The report is now being reviewed in Congress and by numerous watchdog organizations such as the

---

10 "FISA Surveillance at an All Time High," *Secrecy News*, Volume 2003, no. 37 (May 1, 2003), 1. See also the Electronic Frontier Foundation's "Foreign Intelligence Surveillance Act Frequently Asked Questions (and Answers)," http://www.eff.org/Censorship/Terrorism_militias/fisa_faq.html (accessed 17 June 2005).

11 John Schwartz, "Planned Databank on Citizens Spurs Opposition in Congress," *New York Times*, 16 January 2003, A14.

12 For the full text of the DARPA report, visit http://foi.missouri.edu/totalinfoaware/reporttocongress.html (accessed 21 June 2005).

American Civil Liberties Union and the Electronic Privacy Information Center.

In May 2003, in the course of presenting an intelligence authorization bill, Senate Republicans, at the behest of the White House, included a proposal for granting the CIA and Pentagon the power to issue "national security letters"—essentially administrative subpoenas—requiring Internet providers, credit card companies, libraries, and other organizations to produce records on individual transactions. The FBI has in the past issued national security letters. Allowing the CIA and the military such powers broadens the role of those entities in domestic intelligence affairs. The provision was stricken from the authorization bill when Democrats objected.[13]

The second strand—and maybe strand is too strong a word, so let's call it a potential or incipient strand—has to do with feeding disinformation to foreign governments, journalists, and media sources. A Pentagon Office of Strategic Influence was proposed in early 2002 and was intended to influence public opinion and policymakers overseas. "Information warfare" was to be a component of the work of this office. Information warfare entails spreading inaccurate or misleading information. When word of this hit the newspapers in February 2002, George W. Bush expressed alarm, and Defense Secretary Donald Rumsfeld announced that the proposal for the new office would not go forward. (This brings to mind the so-called documentary evidence on Iraq's obtaining uranium from Niger to be used in production of nuclear weapons. The documents have been shown to be forgeries. They were nevertheless cited in administration arguments for going to war against Iraq. This also brings to mind France's contention that news reports that the French government aided Iraqi officials to escape as U.S. troops advanced on Baghdad in May 2003 was a deliberate disinformation campaign.)[14]

---

13 Eric Lichtblau and James Risen, "Broad Domestic Role Asked for CIA and the Pentagon," *New York Times,* 2 May 2003, A17.

14 Eric Schmitt, "Rumsfeld Says He May Drop New Office of Influence," *New York Times,* 25 February 2002, A13, and "Bush Seals Fate of Office of Influence in Pentagon," *New York Times,* 26 February 2002, A11. For French allegations of disinformation, see "Letter from Jean-David Levitte, Ambassador of France to the U.S., to the Congressmen, Administration Officials and Media Representatives," Washington, 15 May 2003, http://www.info-france-usa.org/news/statmnts/2003/levitte_us051503.asp (accessed 21 June 2005). On this, see Karen DeYoung, "U.S. Denies Campaign against France," *Washington Post,* 16 May 2003, A23.

You could say that the larger Bush information policy is two-pronged, with a third prong waiting in the wings: (1) limit public access to government information while (2) increasing the government's ability to gather information on private individuals, plus (3) contemplating the creation and dissemination of false information to cover your actions. Information lockdown is just one part of the overall Bush administration information policy equation.

What has been the response to this trend toward information closure and control? In particular, how have scholars, journalists, information professionals and others responded? Immediately following Bush's signing EO 13233, a group of historians, archivists, and civil liberties advocates met in Washington to discuss the order and what to do about it. The result of the meeting was a lawsuit filed by Public Citizen[15] and several individual researchers who had been denied access to records of the Reagan presidency. The lawsuit asks a federal court to order the National Archives to allow public access to presidential records and to disregard Bush's executive order because it violates federal law.

By February 2002, both parties involved in the lawsuit (Public Citizen and the U.S. government) had submitted requests for summary judgment based on their filings. As of June 2003, the assigned judge had not made any judgment. (This was mainly due to her involvement in two other high-profile cases, one of which had to do with campaign finance review.) While the Society of American Archivists (SAA) was not a signatory to the lawsuit—and I mention this because of my involvement with that organization and because what I am saying here, I am saying on my own—SAA did speak out in opposition to the executive order. In an article published in the *Washington Post*, SAA president Steven L. Hensen asked the question, "How can a democratic people have confidence in elected officials who hide the record of their actions from public view?" He went on to state that:

> Access to the vital historical records of this nation should not be governed by executive will; this is exactly the situation that the existing law was created to prevent. Furthermore, for such access to be curtailed or nullified by an executive process not subject to public or legislative review or scrutiny violates the principles upon which our nation was founded . . . [President] Bush should demonstrate the

---

15 Public Citizen is a national nonprofit consumer advocacy organization that represents American consumer interests in Congress, the executive branch and the courts. For background information on Public Citizen's presidential records lawsuit, visit http://www.citizen.org/litigation/briefs/FOIAGovtSec/PresRecords/index.cfm (accessed 21 June 2005).

values and openness of our government and of his administration by canceling this order . . . It shouldn't have to take legal proceedings, congressional action or public pressure for [the president] to come to the understanding that the president's papers are not in fact the president's papers, but rather the records of the people's presidency.[16]

This opinion piece, which ran on the front page of the *Washington Post's* Sunday Outlook section, was something of a new step for SAA in the direction of issue advocacy. SAA continues to remain alert to policy issues in which it has a professional stake and will continue to speak out publicly on such issues.

As mentioned earlier, the U.S. Department of Education removed website information that was deemed counter to administration policies, philosophies, and goals. In early 2003, the American Library Association, the American Educational Research Association, and fourteen other national organizations signed a letter to Education Secretary Roderick Paige requesting all Department of Education web materials retain the current level of accessibility and asking for the inclusion of representatives from the relevant professions in revamping the website. (Among the American information professions, the American Library Association is really a leader in monitoring freedom of information, copyright, access to government information, and privacy issues.)

A number of professional organizations and civil liberties groups maintain timely information on government secrecy on their websites. They include:

- Federation of American Scientists at http://www.fas.org/.
- OMB Watch at http://www.ombwatch.org/.
- Center for Public Integrity at http://www.publicintegrity.org/dtaweb/home.asp.
- Electronic Frontier Foundation at http://www.eff.org/.
- Friends Committee on National Legislation at http://www.fcnl.org/.
- Freedom Forum at http://www.freedomforum.org/.
- Electronic Privacy Information Center at http://www.epic.org/.

---

16 Steven L. Hensen, "The President's Papers are the People's Business," *Washington Post,* 16 December 2001, B1.

- American Civil Liberties Union at http:www.aclu.org/.
- Freedom of Information Center at http://foi.missouri.edu/polinfoprop/govtwilllaunch.htm.
- Center for Democracy and Technology at http://www.cdt.org/.
- Center for National Security Studies at http://www.cnss.org/.
- National Security Archive at http://www.gwu.edu/~nsarchiv/.

A number of public symposia and seminars have been held to discuss the Bush administration's information policies. While not all of these have presented opposing views to those policies, they show that access to government information is a topic of interest among certain academic and professional constituencies. Examples of such meetings are:

- FLICC Forum 2002: The topic was "Homeland Security: Impact of Policy Changes on Government Information Access," held in March 2002. (FLICC is a group of librarians and information specialists from U.S. government agencies.)
- A symposium at the University of Maryland was held in May 2002 titled "Public Records and the Public Trust: President Bush's Executive Order 13233 and its Implications for Government Information Policy." (This was organized by the University of Maryland's student chapter of SAA.)
- A symposium on "Information and the War on Terrorism" was held at the University of Texas at Austin in April 2003.
- In May 2003, the Maxwell Campbell Public Affairs Institute, Syracuse University, and the Open Society Institute co-sponsored a symposium on "National Security and Open Government: Striking the Right Balance." This was held in Washington, DC, at the Brookings Institution.
- A "Government Symposium on Information Sharing and Homeland Security" was held in Philadelphia in early July 2003. Attendees came from federal, state, and local government agencies and the intelligence and law enforcement communities.

The legislative arena is of course the obvious setting for challenges to the policies in question, and several legislative efforts can be cited here:

EO 13233 Rescission

House of Representatives bill HR1493 "to revoke an Executive Order relating to procedures for the consideration of claims of constitutionally based privilege against disclosure of Presidential records" was introduced on 27 March 2003, by Doug Ose (R-California) with support from Henry Waxman (D-California) and several other congressmen. The bill has been referred to the House Committee on Government Reform.

Restore Freedom of Information Act

Senate bill s609 was introduced in the u.s. Senate on 12 March 2003, by Senator Patrick Leahy (D-Vermont). Its aim is to amend the Homeland Security Act of 2002 so that freedom of information exemptions cannot be used to keep information on industrial infrastructure vulnerabilities from the proper government oversight bodies. HR2526, the House version of the Senate bill, was introduced in June by Representative Barney Frank (D-Massachusetts).

Human Rights Information Act

This bill was reintroduced in June 2003 by Representative Tom Lantos (D-California) and a number of co-sponsors to expedite the declassification of records related to human rights violations abroad. It seeks to assign responsibility to the Interagency Security Classification Appeals Panel for overseeing the process.[17]

Opposition to the Domestic Security Enhancement Act

Also called Patriot Act II, a draft of this bill was presented to the public in February 2003 by the Center for Public Integrity. It seeks to expand federal law enforcement and surveillance powers; reduce or eliminate judicial oversight over certain surveillance; empower the government to remove American citizenship from persons who belong

---

17 The Interagency Security Classification Appeals Panel (ISCAP) was established by executive order 12958 to perform three primary functions:
  - to rule on appeals from government employees who challenged agency classification policies
  - to approve, deny, or amend agency exemptions from automatic declassification requirements
  - to rule on appeals from members of the public who have filed requests for mandatory declassification.

  (Source: Federation of American Scientists website, www.fas.org)

to certain political groups; and decrease FOIA access to certain information, among other provisions. Opposition to the bill has been building since the release of the draft last February.

While public statements against information lockdown, support for legislative efforts to restore openness, and symposia and teach-ins geared to educating a broader segment of the population on the issue are necessary responses to the information policy I have described, they remain reactive responses to something that appears to be a deliberate and thorough political move to limit what U.S. citizens can know about their government's plans and activities.

The political crux of the matter has to do with where one stands on the question of openness versus secrecy in government information policy. Important questions to ask are: In a democracy, how much government secrecy is necessary? At what point does openness backfire? How can accountability be measured and how can it be enforced? What is the pragmatic relationship between open access to government information and democracy itself? I would emphasize here that, though political, this is at heart a non-partisan issue. There are Democrats who support greater secrecy and Republicans who are for greater openness.

Let me conclude with a few observations on how open access to government information might relate to democracy, at least in "historical roots" terms. In the United States, when arguing our "Right to Know," we hark back to oft-repeated quotations by Thomas Jefferson and James Madison. For example, in his first inaugural address in 1801, Thomas Jefferson declared:

> The diffusion of information and the arraignment of all abuses at the bar of public reason, I deem [one of] the essential principles of our government, and consequently [one of] those which ought to shape its administration.[18]

James Madison wrote in 1822 that:

> A popular Government without popular information or the means of securing it, is but a Prologue to a Farce or a Tragedy or perhaps both. Knowledge will forever govern ignorance, and a people who

---

18 Thomas Jefferson, "1st inaugural address, 1801," ME 3:322 in *Thomas Jefferson on Politics and Government*, http://etext.lib.virginia.edu/jefferson/quotations/ (accessed 21 June 2005).

mean to be their own Governors must arm themselves with the power [that] knowledge gives.[19]

These are both very stirring statements on how information relates to democracy. Yet the following statement by Thomas Jefferson would certainly please Mr. Bush and Mr. Cheney:

> It is essential for the public interest that I should receive all the information possible respecting either matters or persons connected with the public. To induce people to give this information, they must feel assured that when deposited with me it is secret and sacred. Honest men might justifiably withhold information, if they expected the communication would be made public, and commit them to war with their neighbors and friends.[20]

While we cite the broad slogans of the founding fathers, we have not delved deeply enough into the theoretical and historical underpinnings of the idea of the "Right to Know"—which is nowhere enshrined in our founding documents. Rather, it is implied in our constitutional right to petition government. The right to petition allows citizens to approach government to seek redress on government waste, corruption, and misconduct; information sharing among the appropriate government bodies is part of this redress.[21]

The literature on executive privilege, government secrecy, and freedom of information gets at this in a broad legal sense but not so much in historical or political philosophical depth.[22] I think those of us who oppose information lockdown and its correlates of personal information harvesting and public disinformation need to come together in a forum to research, discuss, write about, and popularize serious studies of the whys and wherefores of accountability in democratic governance

---

19 Quoted from the home page of The James Madison Project at
    http://www.jamesmadisonproject.org/ (accessed 21 June 2005).
20 Thomas Jefferson, "Thomas Jefferson to John Smith, 1807," ME 11:203 in *Thomas Jefferson on Politics and Government,* http://etext.lib.virginia.edu/jefferson/quotations/ (accessed 21 June 2005).
21 Adam Newton, "Petition Overview" at http://www.firstamendmentcenter.org/petition/overview.aspx (accessed 21 June 2005).
22 Some examples of this literature are:
    • Mark J. Rozell, *Executive Privilege: Presidential Power, Secrecy, and Accountability* (Lawrence: University of Kansas Press, 2002).
    • Harold Relyea, et al., "The Presidency and Information Policy," *Center for the Study of the Presidency, Proceedings,* Volume IV, Number I (1981).
    • Philip H. Melanson, *Secrecy Wars: National Security, Privacy and the Public's Right to Know* (Washington, D.C.: Brassey's, 2001).

and how information openness supports that. We need to continue to push public relations, legislative, and educational agendas, but alongside this, we need a think-tank apparatus to make the case as, one would suppose, the party of closure and control has done on its side.

To do this I propose establishing an Institute for Information and Democracy. Or better, the Information and Democracy Foundation. Or at the very least—and this may be doable—an Information and Democracy Study Group to begin exploring the political, philosophical, legislative, and economic ramifications of Jefferson's, Madison's, and others' thoughts on the subject over time. This is not to eschew activism aimed at the restoration of openness; it is, along with activism, to achieve some scholarly concentration, collaboration, coordination, and intellectual depth on the many issues relating to open access to government information and the proper role of secrecy.

At the same time, this proposal may suggest a slippery slope of ideology and partisanship. An argument against such a study endeavor might be that we are information professionals. Let others immerse themselves in politics—we should remain above the fray.

To this I would say that it is finally up to those who recognize the threat to begin the work of countering that threat. Those who have a stake in this—personal, professional, or general—need to join the discussion in a meaningful and sustained way. If we leave it to the politicos, we run the risk of seeing our profession, not to mention our broader cultural environment, manipulated for narrow partisan ends.

In the end, democracy is a fragile proposition. It requires the ongoing care and attention of the citizenry to make it work. And though the definitions and practices of democracy may vary from culture to culture, the need of the citizenry to have access to the information that allows it to judge how the democratic process is working remains constant. Information lockdown in a democracy seeks to limit popular participation in the processes of democratic governance. Taken to its logical conclusion, information lockdown, along with the correlates I have mentioned, without critical and political rebuttal, could result in the end of democracy itself. As archivists, as members of the larger information profession, and as citizens of democratic societies, we have a definite stake in working to restore and expand open access to government information as a means of protecting our fragile democracies.

14

"BUT WHO WATCHES THE WATCHERS?" SECURITY INTELLIGENCE RECORDS IN NEW ZEALAND: A CASE STUDY

Rachel Lilburn

Introduction

Does a democracy need secrecy and, if so, why and for how long? Unfortunately, New Zealand's security intelligence agencies compare poorly with similar agencies worldwide which have been far more proactive about opening their records for inspection. An assessment of the state of disposal of, and access to, security intelligence records in New Zealand is presented here; cases, past and present, are used to illustrate the issues faced by our country's public archival institution, Archives New Zealand, as well as by archivists and records managers; and possible actions needed to redress these issues are discussed.[1]

The cases and issues presented illuminate the role of a public archives in supporting government and historical accountability not only through disposition processes, but also through the negotiation of

1   The unqualified support given by Archives New Zealand staff to this paper, as directed by the Chief Archivist, is hereby acknowledged. I am also grateful for the considerable assistance of Dr. Anne-Marie Brady, Lecturer, Political Studies, Canterbury University, who provided copies of her extensive correspondence with the New Zealand Security Intelligence Service (NZSIS), the Ombudsman, and Prime Minister, Rt. Hon. Helen Clark for access to SIS records.

appropriate storage and access arrangements, with resources to ensure that inadequate arrangement and description or storage are not impediments to transfer. Strong legislation underpins the accountability role, which often can be enacted only through the dedication and activism of the recordkeeping professional bodies to ensuring this is the case. Finally, the political support and will given by our elected representatives to archives legislation and more open government are essential.

Under present public archives legislation, the Archives Act 1957 Section (15), no records created or maintained by a government office may be destroyed or disposed of without the approval of the Chief Archivist, head of our public archives institution, Archives New Zealand.[2] The security intelligence-related agencies fall within the definition of a government office. It is a fact that the records of very few internal and external security-monitoring agencies have been subject to formal appraisal and transferred to Archives New Zealand. Nor have these agencies been magnanimous in allowing access to their records, while under their management, through the Official Information Act 1982 (OIA) or the Privacy Act 1993.[3]

Meanwhile, our government has enacted and drafted more security-related legislation under the guise of needing to protect the country against terrorist threats, in the wake of 9/11, notably the Terrorism Suppression Act 2002, the Telecommunications (Interception Capability) Bill and the Counter-Terrorism Bill. If freedom of official information is a cornerstone of democracy, then the balance between a possible need for greater national security and this fundamental freedom is perceived by some to be jeopardized, "with snooping into people's private lives the norm."[4]

---

2   Archives Act 1957, Section 15 (1). Public archives not to be destroyed or disposed of without authority of Chief Archivist—1. No person shall destroy or otherwise dispose of, or authorise the destruction or other disposal of, any public archives of any kind whatsoever that are in his possession or under his control, except with the consent of the Chief Archivist given in accordance with the provisions of this Act.

3   A principle of the OIA is that information should be made available unless there is a good reason for withholding it. The Privacy Act protects information about living individuals. An excellent summary of the provisions of both acts and a comparison with other countries can be found in the document by Paul Bellamy, Access to Official Information, Background Paper No. 27, Parliamentary Library, May 2003. This paper is available from http://www.clerk.parliament.govt.nz/Content/ResearchPapers/BP27_OfficialInformation.pdf (accessed 14 June 2005).

4   The Green Party, for example, believes this and other legislative amendments amount to an attack on our privacy and civil liberties. See http://www.greens.org.nz/campaigns/sis/ (accessed 9 April 2003).

New Zealand—Background

New Zealand, Aotearoa—or the land of the long white cloud, as it is known by its indigenous people, the Maori—is composed of three islands in the Pacific Ocean, 40 million sheep, 4 million people, and is at least 2000 miles by sea from any other country. New Zealand was settled by Maori from East Polynesia around 800 C.E. and discovered again by Captain Cook in 1789. European migration began in the late 1700s, with the population expanding to such a point that by 1840 the British government saw fit to sign a treaty (Treaty of Waitangi) with the indigenous inhabitants to establish a basis for relations between the races, which endures as a living document even today.

Although initially run by a bicameral government, New Zealand now has a single unitary government, elected on a multi-member proportional basis and controlled by the Labour Party, with a female Prime Minister, a female Governor-General, and a female Attorney-General. One might deduce, first, that the country would be subject to few, if any, security threats. The last incident was the bombing of the Greenpeace ship, the Rainbow Warrior, by French secret agents in 1985 (ironic, given the French government's lack of support for the Iraq war). Second, a Labour government may be predicted to be left-wing and liberal in its views, especially one led by a Prime Minister who has infuriated U.S. President George Bush on several occasions with her anti-Iraq war statements, and thus who may be expected to encourage a more open access policy to records involving matters of national security.[5]

Not so. Well-known local activist, author, and specialist on security related activities, Nicky Hager, states that

> New Zealand, like many similar countries, is in the midst of a period of very "right wing" politics . . . although the tide is beginning to turn . . . [and] although there are some decent and socially-concerned people at the highest levels of government, this government clearly feels constrained from making more than quite minor changes to the far-right policies introduced since 1984.[6]

---

5 Jane Clifton, "It's Only Words," NZ *Listener* 189, no. 3291 (June 2003), 16–17.
6 Nicky Hager, "Seeking the Truth: The Power and Politics of Using Archives and Records," *Archifacts* (October 2001), 14–15.

Hager discerns a trend, even in a free country such as New Zealand, towards secrecy-based and public-relations driven government. He is well-qualified to make that judgment, having personally used the Official Information Act hundreds of times over the period in question, and recently failing in an attempt to obtain records about the two new surveillance laws mentioned in the introduction.[7] In particular, he cites intelligence agencies as being at the extreme end of the spectrum, withholding virtually all their papers on often-flimsy grounds.[8] While it is not possible to discuss in detail what public documentation is available from these agencies in the form of annual reports and so on, there is evidence to conclude that it is also heavily censored from the public, and even from monitoring agencies established to oversee security intelligence policy and planning. Hager also alleges that even Prime Ministers over time have only been informed on an unwritten "need to know" basis.[9]

New Zealand Security Intelligence Agencies

The security intelligence sector in New Zealand, looking after the welfare of four million people, is currently made up of the following agencies:

- The New Zealand Security Intelligence Service (NZSIS), responsible for domestic security
- The Government Communications Security Bureau (GCSB), responsible for signals intelligence and advice on electronic security and technology
- The Center for Critical Infrastructure Protection (CCIP), responsible for providing advice and support to protect New Zealand's critical infrastructure from cyber-threats
- The External Advice Bureau (EAB), responsible for researching

---

7 Ibid., 18–19.
8 Ibid., 21.
9 See Nicky Hager's chapter, "Who Watches the Watchers? Overseeing the Intelligence Agencies," in his book, *Secret Power: New Zealand's Role in the International Spy Network* (Nelson: Craig Potton, 1996).

and assessing overseas developments with possible impact on New Zealand interests
- The Directorate of Defence Intelligence and Security (DDIS), responsible for the New Zealand Defence Force's intelligence and security

The Prime Minister is currently the Minister in charge of these agencies. Her policy advisory body is the Domestic and External Security Secretariat (DESS). Oversight of the activities of these intelligence community agencies is also carried out by a committee of senior officials—the Officials Committee for Domestic and External Security Coordination (ODESC).

Limited Access to Security Intelligence Records

Limited access to security intelligence records is now a major bone of contention for politicians, journalists, and, increasingly, for historians, activists, and archivists who are disturbed not only by the unavailability of records of events that occurred over fifty years ago, about people long since dead, but also by their possible destruction without referral to the Chief Archivist.[10]

Two cases are pertinent to the issue of security intelligence agency activity with public records: the first occurred in 1974 (the so-called Nash case) and the second in 2002.

THE 2002 CASE

In late 2002, 31 political scientists and historians had become sufficiently infuriated by lack of access to SIS archives that an open letter on the matter was sent to the Prime Minister, as head of security intelligence activities. The letter urged the Prime Minister to instigate a

---

10 In a phone conversation with Dr. Anne-Marie Brady, 8 April 2003, she mentioned that a colleague, writing on the New Zealand Communist Party, had been told by the NZSIS that the 1951 Waterfront Lockout papers had been destroyed. She thus stated this in her interview with Linda Clark on National Radio's *Nine to Noon* show on 13 November 2002, whereupon Brady tells me that the NZSIS faxed Clark to say that this was not the case.

review of access to the archives of the SIS, stating that the "archival policies of much of the former Soviet bloc are currently more open and unrestricted than those of New Zealand." The letter went on to say that "in the interest of scholarly research into New Zealand's foreign and defence policy and its place in the world and in the interest of a more open and democratic society . . . we ask the New Zealand government to bring the SIS in line with its international counterparts."[11]

The letter, organised by Dr. Anne-Marie Brady, Lecturer in Political Science at Canterbury University, was the culmination of many frustrating years of trying to obtain access to files on China-New Zealand relations in the 1940s, 1950s and 1960s: for example, for her biography of Rewi Alley, a New Zealander who spent many decades in China working on philanthropic activities and, hence, a suspected communist in the New Zealand government's eyes.[12]

Inspection of her correspondence with the SIS, dating back eight years, reveals a uncompromising interpretation and application of the Official Information Act (OIA) legislation; for example, the SIS would neither confirm nor deny the existence of information on Alley or other matters, as allowed under Section 10 of the OIA, and continued to cite reasons of national security under Sections 6(a) and (b) for withholding access. Brady's appeals to the Ombudsman and the Prime Minister proved futile.

At the same time, Brady was being given the full cooperation in her other research on New Zealand-China relations in the 1950s by the Ministry of Foreign Affairs and Trade (MFAT), which was systematically declassifying documents to enable their use. Yet the current Director of the NZSIS, Richard Woods, stated in a letter to Brady that, "To date no Service records have been released to the public. . . . The only records held by the NZSIS that have been released to the public pre-date the formation of the Service. A very limited amount of this material . . . has been made available to academics."[13]

Copies of the open letter were sent to the national daily newspapers, and stories duly appeared in *The Press* and *The Dominion Post*. A

---

11 "Open Letter to the Prime Minister and Minister of State Security, the Honourable Helen Clark, on Opening the SIS Archives to Scholarly Research," November 2002.

12 Anne-Marie Brady, *Friend of China: The Myth of Rewi Alley* (London: RoutledgeCurzon, 2003).

13 Letter to Dr. Anne-Marie Brady from E.R. Woods, Director of Security, 24 January 2002.

five-minute interview by the host of the National Radio network show, *Nine to Noon,* was conducted with Brady on 13 November 2002.[14] The Prime Minister's reported reply to the allegations was that "Contrary to the assertion in the open letter, releases by other security and intelligence agencies are quite selective and significant areas of information are withheld . . . in Australia, Britain and Canada." Furthermore the Prime Minister said, "The New Zealand SIS does not withhold information without good reason."[15]

Archives New Zealand did not respond publicly to Brady's public call for better accessibility to security intelligence archives and the need for investigation of allegations that the Security Intelligence Service in particular had destroyed certain records. However, at the Archives New Zealand Consultation Group meeting on 11 December 2002, when I queried as to why this was so, the Chief Archivist responded that the institution "was working actively with the SIS and that such work was not necessarily known to users or the media [and that] . . . the Prime Minister led the public response." Unwritten public service rules suggested it would be inappropriate for the Chief Archivist to comment further. The Chief Archivist was also out of the country at the time. Another senior member of the profession, Stuart Strachan, Hocken Librarian, also present at the meeting commented that "by not responding to negative news like the destruction of documents, it appears the organization is indifferent or lacks authority or standing" to which the Chief Archivist replied that such "agencies are often dealt with through direct contact, as it is not always appropriate to go through the media."[16]

Further investigation has revealed, however, that progress has been made with security intelligence records, in spite of Archives New Zealand actions with regard to making a public comment. In stark contrast, the "Nash case," almost thirty years earlier, highlighted major

---

14 Tara Ross, "Call for Access to Archives," *The Press,* 12 November 2002, 4.

15 Michelle Quirke, "Researchers Denied Access to SIS Archives," *The Dominion Post,* 19 November 2002, 2.

16 "Minutes, Archives New Zealand Consultation Group Meeting, Wellington" (11 December 2002), 4, photocopied. Stuart Strachan was made an Honorary Life Member of the Archives and Records Association of New Zealand in 1988, was in charge of appraisal services during his stint at National Archives, is a regular contributor to public debate, and is considered a senior and most influential member of the profession.

problems in the leadership and administration of New Zealand public archives. It was, in fact, one of the roots of change which finally bore fruit in the year 2000 with the granting of independent departmental status to National Archives.[17]

THE "NASH CASE"

In the 1970s, National Archives, as it was then known, was a fledgling but undernourished institution, with a small staff and a Chief Archivist who reported to a public servant three times removed from the Minister of Internal Affairs, and thus with no political clout or influence.

Sir Walter Nash had been Prime Minister of New Zealand. Upon his death, his papers, occupying a double garage in a Wellington suburb, were eventually removed to National Archives, whereupon they were used to write his biography by eminent historian, Sir Keith Sinclair, despite minimal arrangement and description and therefore control of access to the content of the papers.[18] Prior to final publication in November 1976 the SIS demanded that three passages be deleted from the book (printed but as yet unbound) as they were based on documents owned by the SIS and found among Nash's papers.[19]

Publishers refused and the passages were not deleted, but by 1 April 1976 SIS records originating from the Nash papers had already been removed to the registry of the SIS.

The then Prime Minister, Rt. Hon. R. D. Muldoon, in response to a question in the House preferred the word "returned" for "removed," stating, "What did happen was that certain reports of a highly classified nature were returned to the SIS, as the originating department, for safe custody."[20] The action was defended on the grounds of protocol; that is, that all SIS documents be returned to them once read by the Prime Minister and that Nash had, therefore, wrongly retained these records. When further queried as to the nature and extent of the "removal" the

---

17 This occurred under the Archives Culture and Heritage Reform Act 2000.

18 They were nearly 14 tons in weight and filled 213 metres of shelving, according to the article, "The Nash Estate," *Archifacts* n.s., no. 1 (February 1977), 2; the book by Keith Sinclair was titled *Walter Nash* (Auckland: Auckland University Press and Oxford University Press, 1976).

19 "Auckland Writer Censored by SIS," *The Week,* Issue 12, 10 September 1976, 1.

20 *New Zealand Parliamentary Debates,* vol. 413, August 23–September 21, 1977, 2592–3.

Acting Prime Minister further denied that the SIS removed papers and stated that it did not ask for permission to search the collection. Instead "the Chief Archivist did, however, deliver to the . . . Service 32 papers which had originally emanated from the Service."[21]

The removal actions were also supported by a legal opinion from Crown Law. When, in 1994, I requested, under the Official Information Act, a copy of the opinion, dated 19 August 1976, my request was turned down on the basis that the information "is of a category that should be withheld under Section 9(2)(h) of the Act on the grounds that the withholding of information is necessary to maintain legal professional privilege." The Solicitor-General went on to say that he had also borne in mind the security considerations arising from the opinion and that public interest considerations did not outweigh either criteria.[22]

The case received considerable publicity (and undoubtedly boosted book sales). Perhaps the SIS did have some justification for removal of the papers. An important issue raised by the case was the question of ministerial documents in private political papers and their ultimate ownership. Perceptions that the Chief Archivist and the institution she headed, the National Archives, had been bullied into returning these papers and that the confidence of potential depositors would be seriously undermined by the incident were highlighted in the public debate. In his *Listener* editorial, Vincent O'Sullivan also raised the vexed question of historical accountability if the SIS were allowed to remove the Nash documents.[23]

Concern was expressed by the then President of the Archives and Records Association of New Zealand, Thomas Wilsted, about the inadequate accommodation for the institution, one of the reasons given for the necessity for the removal, and the lack of staff to process the collection which could have identified this material and made it secure from inappropriate access. Wilsted called for the urgent instigation of a declassification procedure in order that security intelligence agencies need not defer deposit. He flagged this question as the one on

---

21 *New Zealand Parliamentary Debates,* vol. 413, August 23–September 21, 1977, 2945.
22 Letter from Solicitor-General, J. J. McGrath, to Rachel Lilburn, "Crown Law Opinion on Nash Papers: Request Pursuant to the Official Information Act 1982," 25 February 1994, ref: PVT122/56.
23 Vincent O'Sullivan, "Underneath the Archives," *New Zealand Listener,* 17 December 1977.

which most of the discussion should hinge, and it is a question that remains, to this day, unanswered.[24]

Minutes of a private meeting held by National Archives staff on 2 November 1977 record dismay about lack of documentation as to what was removed, not being privy to the Crown Law opinion, and about conflicting statements made by the Chief Archivist to staff, her lack of a public response and so on. It was the "final straw" in a series of incidents that had occurred at National Archives in those years and had considerably weakened staff morale.[25]

Probably unbeknown to staff (as its existence was surprisingly not noted in the aforementioned minutes) was a disposal schedule for SIS records, signed by the Chief Archivist and the Head of the Service in 1974, three years before the Nash case, which would appear to give the SIS the right to destroy all vetting files, as well as classified and non-classified material from New Zealand government agencies, overseas sources, and personal files. The job file for the schedule has absolutely no paperwork as to how the schedule came about.[26]

In 1977, the Archives and Records Association of New Zealand invited Dr. Wilfred Smith, Dominion Archivist of Canada, to visit New Zealand to write a report containing recommendations for future archival development and legislation. This invitation was a response, in part, to the perception of lack of leadership by the national public archives institution.

Recent Developments

Progress towards greater regulation of the disposal of some security intelligence archives has been made, due to the relatively new independent status accorded to Archives New Zealand, and a commitment by the new Chief Archivist and staff to redressing the problem. The new Head of Appraisal Services, for example, was disturbed to read the

---

24 Thomas Wilsted, "Underneath the Archives," *New Zealand Listener*, 17 December 1977.

25 "Minutes of a Meeting held 2 November 1977, at . . . Wellington. Purpose: To Document Some of the Inefficiencies & Malpractices Found to be Occurring or Having Occurred at National Archives in Recent Years," photocopied, 8 pages.

26 See Archives New Zealand file, NA 2/66/2 Records Disposal: New Zealand Security Intelligence Service—Schedules, 1974–2001 (Restricted File).

following comment in the publication, *Security in New Zealand Today:* "[T]he Service is authorized by the Government's Chief Archivist to regularly purge its files of personal information which is assessed as being no longer of security significance."[27] The Chief Archivist wrote to the director of the SIS in 2001 suggesting that the terms of the schedule drawn up in 1974 were outdated and should no longer be used. It was a moot point as to whether the schedule was revocable, as it did not contain an expiration date. Archives New Zealand offered to develop, in consultation with the Service, a new schedule. The NZSIS agreed to cease destruction of all records at this point.[28]

A new schedule for the vetting records has been developed and is about to be put into operation, pending approval. Interestingly, the retention rate recommended is very low: one linear metre, "reflecting the routine administrative nature of the records appraised," while 210 linear metres are recommended for destruction.[29] Classes recommended for retention include: information on people vetted who have made an historically important contribution to New Zealand; precedent-setting cases; and cases which resulted in appeals or reviews of a decision. The retention period is left to the judgment of the SIS, as is the determination of historically significant people; the latter is a responsibility for which the Service expressed an interest.

The Chief Archivist has also held meetings with the heads of the big security agencies (in her opinion possible largely because of Archives New Zealand's improved status), and says there is a lot of support "for the development of retention and disposal schedules that are in the public domain,"[30] including the Government Communications Security Bureau (GCSB). It is stated elsewhere that Archives New Zealand hopes that these initial discussions "will facilitate further projects in the security sector."[31]

---

27 The New Zealand Security Intelligence Service, *Security in New Zealand Today* (Wellington: NZSIS, 1997), 18.

28 Conversation with Eamonn Bolger, Head of Appraisal Services, 30 May 2003. Appraisal of public records is a contestable service in New Zealand. Therefore, it is possible that the SIS could have conducted its own appraisal, although the report and recommendations would remain subject to the Chief Archivist's approval. The implications of this scenario are all too obvious. See also Draft NZSIS Appraisal Report, Job No. 2003/0625.

29 Draft NZSIS Appraisal Report, Job No. 2003/0625.

30 E-mail to Rachel Lilburn from Dianne Macaskill, Chief Archivist, 29 May 2003.

31 Appraisal Report, DESS, Job No. OP 2001/46, 2.

These actions have resulted in the appraisal and scheduling of various registered and unregistered filing systems of the Domestic and External Security Secretariat, Department of Prime Minister and Cabinet (DESS). Approximately half of the records are recommended for retention.[32] Furthermore, it has been reported that the SIS is developing an archives policy. In a recent newspaper feature article, the "SIS director Richard Woods [says he] doesn't want to comment on the proposal till it has been announced by Prime Minister Helen Clark, but it is likely to be finalized this year."[33]

According to a letter from the Prime Minister received by Dr. Brady, the policy "envisages that information on people and organizations will be eligible for release fifty years after the death of the person and, in the case of subject files, fifty years after the creation of the document." But the Rt. Hon. Helen Clark also admits that there will be provisos for longer withholding periods if significant security or privacy concerns remain or, under Section (18) (f) of the OIA, there would be substantial collation of documents or research required. "The Service must necessarily balance various priorities. It is unrealistic [she says] to expect the Service to release all records as soon as they become eligible."[34]

Ongoing Issues

A number of issues and questions, some old and some new, are raised by the previous comments about the state of security intelligence records. They include:

- legislative coverage,
- transfer of custody and storage arrangements,
- appraisal protocols, and
- access concerns.

In Brady's open letter to the Prime Minister, she notes the existence of a Ministerial Certificate under Section 8 (2) (c) of the Archives Act,

---

32 Ibid., 21.
33 Diana McCurdy, "They're Keeping Our Secrets," *Dominion Post*, 23 May 2003, B5.
34 Letter to Dr. Anne-Marie Brady, from Prime Minister Rt. Hon. Helen Clark, 2 December 2002.

exempting deposit of SIS records on the grounds of national security, which did not require the approval of, or discussion with, the Chief Archivist. This expires in 2005. Politicians, particularly from the Green Party, lost no time in using the opportunity to ask written questions in the House of Representatives about the nature of this exemption and others that may have been given to security agencies. It was discovered that the GCSB also has an exemption, issued in January 2002 by the responsible Minister, for a period of 25 years and for an unspecified number of cryptologic records in GCSB's custody or control. (See appendix 1.)

Under the proposed Public Records Bill, about to be drafted by the Parliamentary Counsel Office, the current provision for varying coverage of the legislation (or "varying agencies or records out of transfer") by the mechanism of Order in Council will continue, with some changes. The decision to defer deposit on national security grounds will be removed, nor can the decision be made unilaterally by the Minister. There has to be significant consultation and public scrutiny. Also, security intelligence agencies will not be able to be removed wholly from the operation of the act by Order in Council. The one provision that the varying-out mechanism will not allow is the disposal provision: that is, the need to obtain the Chief Archivist's approval to dispose of records. It appears, too, that the Chief Archivist will be able to specify how these records continue to be cared for and managed.[35]

On the matter of transfer of custody, appraisal reports for the SIS and the Domestic and External Security Secretariat (DESS) note that, while schedules now exist, they do not specify transfer of custody. Therefore, access will continue to be administered by these agencies within the terms of the Official Information Act and the Privacy Act. However, Archives New Zealand also flags, in the aforementioned appraisal reports, the probable need for formal negotiations in the future over the complicated issue of physical transfer of highly classified material and what form secure storage should take. Archives New Zealand has a secure stack (with swipe-card access) in which it stores

---

35 According to the Frequently Asked Questions website for the Proposed Public Records Bill, the Order in Council process involves: developing policy, consulting within government, and obtaining approval from the Cabinet Legislation Committee, Cabinet, and, finally, the Executive Council, before the Order is signed by the Governor-General. See http://www.archives.govt.nz/archivesnz/press_releases/proposed_public_records_bill_frame.html (accessed 3 April 2003).

some sensitive defence records, but it would require significant upgrading to meet requirements for the storage of highly classified material.[36]

Protocols for working with security agencies have been identified as a necessity by Archives New Zealand; for example, the security clearance level required of the appraisal archivist should be "Top Secret." (With the September 11 tragedy, ironically, there is a significant backlog of archivists to be vetted by the SIS.) To complicate matters, initial discussion and the development of a draft document by staff while engaged in the SIS appraisal has revealed that these agencies view themselves as having distinct and different roles, and as handling different intelligence information.[37]

A major area of debate has been whether the appraisal reports for these agencies should be restricted or open documents, due to the possible inclusion of classified material in, for example, the archivists' notes about file contents. Archives New Zealand intends to make its appraisal reports electronically accessible to the public eventually, through the GLADIS System (Government Locator and Archival Descriptive Information System). The institution's preference is for as much openness as possible.

Archives New Zealand has also commented on the problem of lack of systematic declassification of security intelligence records. It is noted in the DESS report, for example, that "apart from the Ministry of Foreign Affairs and Trade (MFAT), [that] there is little evidence of systematic records declassification within the security intelligence community, despite several agencies holding records from the Second World War. This has led to increasing pressure on space, and almost certain unauthorized records destructions."[38]

Summary and Conclusions

The now independent Archives New Zealand has shown that it is neither prepared to be intimidated by the security establishment nor lacks

---

36 Greg Goulding, Archives New Zealand Security Officer/Head of Policy and Planning bases this judgment on the national *Protective Security Manual*, which provides rigorous specifications for such material (itself a classified document).

37 Conversation with Eamonn Bolger, Head of Appraisal Services, 30 May 2003. Approval to give me access to the SIS Draft Appraisal Report was given by the Service Director himself.

38 Appraisal Report, DESS, Job No. OP 2001/46, 3.

the will now to act decisively on occasion—for example, to stop possible illegal disposal of their records. However, it must be equipped with legislative powers adequate to deal with security intelligence archives: their disposal, custody, transfer, management, and access. As has been discovered during the course of the use of the Official Information Act, legislation alone could be an insufficient safeguard against a security intelligence culture in New Zealand that has demonstrated an unwillingness to cooperate with the concept of open government. "When push comes to shove, a considerable amount of moral persuasion is also required by the Ombudsman," says one journalist.[39]

The observations of a former New Zealand Chief Archivist, Ray Grover, provide other perspectives on the difficulties that public archives may have in achieving their goals with security intelligence records. First, archivists must seize opportunities, he says; "choose the strategy for the time and area, the tactics and the weaponry for the ground, and keep ahead on intelligence."[40] Success with security intelligence archives may come more easily if Archives New Zealand follows this approach and is prepared to build networks and alliances, as it appears to want to do. Security intelligence agencies may, in fact, be forced to consider transfer of records to the institution due solely to lack of space! Second, Grover reminds us that public archives institutions should remember that restrictions placed on records—whether they be placed by bureaucracies or archivists, breed resentment among our supporters, the users. "It also qualifies our role in an open society" and, sooner or later, public archives in a market economy will find themselves paying the price.[41] Third, public archives must balance the need to be accountable to funders and supporters with vision: "A vision that will keep in view the values we hold and the fundamental role we play in an open and civilized society. A vision that will lead us to persevere through the compromises and knockbacks."[42]

The battles over improving access to security intelligence archives are far from over—and the possible transfer of records now scheduled

39 Deputy editor of the *Evening Post*, Karl du Fresne, makes this observation in his paper, "The Right to Know: A Media Viewpoint," *Archifacts* (October 1996), 189.
40 Ray Grover, "The Realpolitik of Archives," *Archifacts* (October 1996), 102.
41 Ibid., 103.
42 Ibid., 106.

for retention into Archives New Zealand is probably still a "twinkle in their eye." Change will not occur without political pressure, commitment, and will, such as has been exhibited by the Green Party. Their interest in security intelligence records could be crucial to the final state of the Public Records Act on the "varied out of transfer" provisions or for the resourcing of improved secure storage. Resources must be forthcoming for a declassification process to commence as soon as possible and on an on-going basis. Given the comments of the prime minister, it would seem that this is still a matter for discussion.

Change will not occur without a concerted effort by, and coalition of, archives and records professional bodies and individuals, political scientists, historians, and activists who want to use these records. By not engaging in the debate, archivists and records managers will be tacitly supporting the status quo and those in power who choose to mislead the public, believing that a democracy survives on never-ending secrecy. Let us remind ourselves again that archivists and record-keepers are not impartial custodians, but are the active documenters of society and shapers of social memory.

Ultimately, the societal risks of recordkeeping accountability failures, as McKemmish points out, will result in the inability of societal watchdogs to call to account governments and individuals.[43] Nowhere is this more important than with the records of security intelligence agencies, which have significant power to ruin the lives of innocent people.[44]

---

43 Sue McKemmish, "The Smoking Gun: Recordkeeping and Accountabilty," *Archifacts* (April 1999), 1–15.

44 See the article by Richard Hill on access versus privacy, "'Secrets and Lies' in Official Files," *Archifacts* (October 1996), 95–207.

Appendix 1.

Keith Locke, MP, Written Question No. 16639, 19 December 2002 to the minister responsible for Archives New Zealand.

Relevant section of the Archives Act 1957

8. Deposit of public archives in National Archives—

  2. Notwithstanding anything in subsection (1) of this section,–
    a. Where the Chief Archivist is satisfied that the deposit in the National Archives of any particular public archive of the age of 25 years or over would unduly prejudice the effective administration of any Government office, he shall defer the deposit of that archive for such period as may be agreed upon between the Chief Archivist and the administrative head of the Government office affected:
    b. Where any public archive is required by any enactment to be kept secret or confidential, or where the administrative head of the Government office having the possession or control of any public archive satisfies the Chief Archivist that by reason of its secret or confidential nature it would not be in the public interest immediately to deposit that archive in the National Archives, the Chief Archivist shall from time to time defer the deposit of that public archive for such period as may be agreed upon between that administrative head and the Chief Archivist:
    c. Where the Minister in charge of any Government office certifies that in his opinion any specified public archive or specified class of public archives in the custody or control of that Government office contains information the release of which may adversely affect the national security of New Zealand or relations between the Government of New Zealand and the Government of any other country, the deposit in the National Archives of that public archive or of public archives of that class shall be deferred for such period or shall be made subject to such conditions as to access or otherwise as that Minister from time to time directs:

d. Where the deposit of any public archives in the National Archives is deferred as aforesaid, the Chief Archivist may prescribe any conditions he thinks fit to ensure the safe preservation of any such archives during the time they are kept in a Government office.

3. Any public archives deposited under subsection (1) of this section may be deposited unconditionally or, if the administrative head of the Government office making the deposit so requires, shall be deposited subject to such conditions as to access and otherwise as may be agreed upon from time to time by the Chief Archivist and the administrative head of that office.

4. Where the administrative head of any Government office and the Chief Archivist are unable to agree as to whether or not the deposit of any public archives in the National Archives should be deferred or as to the period for which that deposit should be deferred or as to the conditions as to access and otherwise on which any public archives should be so deposited, that question shall be determined by the joint decision of the Minister and the Minister in charge of that Government office, and the decision of those Ministers shall be final.

15

BEWARE OF THE LEOPARD? POLICE ARCHIVES IN GREAT BRITAIN

Chris Williams & Clive Emsley

Before 1999, the London metropolitan police reported directly to the Home Office and were thus covered by the Public Records Acts. British police outside London did not, and are not covered. Thus, the documentary evidence they have left is poor. This has been one factor leading to a distorted historiography of the British police which has focussed too closely on developments in the capital.[1] Without adequate records from the provinces, this distortion is likely to endure. Provincial forces have played a key role in many headline political events, such as the General Strike and the 1974 and 1984–1985 miners' strikes. Their records are also a way in to the social history of all manner of issues.[2] Here we will look at the way the vast majority of British police forces currently organise their ongoing production of historical records.

There are approximately 50 provincial police forces. Most are the product of a process of amalgamation from smaller forces: at their peak in the 1880s, there were over 200. The most significant contractions

---

1 C. Emsley, "The Archives of the English and Welsh Police Forces: A Survey," in L.A. Knafla and S.W.S. Binney, eds., *Law, Society and the State: Essays in Modern Legal History* (Toronto: University of Toronto Press, 1995), 465–476.

2 Emsley, "Archives," 468–469.

took place between 30 and 40 years ago. This loss of institutional continuity has led to a loss of the records of many smaller forces. It has
also created forces with more than one local record office in their area.
For example, the West Mercia force covers Herefordshire,
Worcestershire, and Shropshire. Provincial police are not national, but
neither are they legally part of local government, and thus not subject
to the archive provisions of the 1972 Local Government Act.[3] This is a
consequence of their constitutional development in the twentieth century, which saw them, with the support of the Home Office, effectively
break free from accountability as part of local government, without
central government acknowledging that they were in large part now
under its control.[4]

The police have a vested interest in secrecy for several reasons,
some highly justifiable. Legally, they need to avoid contempt of court
for *sub judice* proceedings, and to keep within the provisions of the
1996 Criminal Procedure and Investigations Act.[5] Operationally, there
is an imperative to maintain security, which can sometimes literally be
a life and death issue, for example in the case of payments to inform-
ers. Above and beyond this, police have a strong symbolic attachment
to control of information about the way they work, especially information about the way a job is done in practice rather than in theory.
Malcolm Young, an anthropologist who was also a detective superintendent, wrote that for a police force, academic study can be a threat:

> The fear is always that the outside will be presented with the chance
> to gain knowledge and power at the expense of the institution;
> although this is often only obliquely implied.[6]

It is worth noting that Young was referring mainly to his experience in the police service in the 1970s and 1980s. Like many other
organisations, police forces are keen to talk about a new spirit of openness to scrutiny.[7] Some individuals in these forces may sincerely believe

---

3 Local Government Act, 1972 (c.70).
4 C. Emsley, *The English Police, a Social and Political History* (London: Longman, 1996), 162–165.
5 Criminal Procedure and Investigations Act, 1996 (c.25).
6 M. Young, *An Inside Job: Policing and Police Culture in Britain* (Oxford: Clarendon Press,
   1991), 35.
7 For example, ACPO guidelines on media relations state that: "As a publicly accountable
   body, the Police Service is committed to openness and accessibility"; ACPO Guidelines,
   December 2000. Metropolitan Police Commissioner Paul Condon pledged "to encourage
   openness, understanding, and trust" in 1998; "Building an Anti-Racist Metropolitan Police
   Service," MPS press release, 1998.

this, but this does not alter the fact that few organisations welcome outside critical scrutiny, and fewer are more dependent on a culture of insider knowledge than are the police.[8] Furthermore, the British police derive much of their legitimacy from an appeal to their history, featuring the democratic heritage of the office of citizen-constable, combined with the contradictory legacy of Peel's disciplined but unarmed force.[9]

This is a follow-up to a survey of provincial police archives by Ian Bridgeman and Clive Emsley in 1989 that led to the publication of a catalogue of the archives of the Police Forces of England and Wales. In it, the authors concluded that police archives "have often been neglected and vast amounts of material has been destroyed or taken to decorate someone's book shelf." The foreword to the survey was written by Lord Knights, ex-chief constable and then president of the Police History Society. He called for police forces to adopt "a coherent archive policy dealing with the criteria for selective weeding and the support system necessary for police records as a whole."[10]

In 1992, the Police History Society produced and distributed a pamphlet for police forces on the best way to set up a records management policy.[11] Action was taken by a few forces who founded museums and appointed archivists, but while some new documentation has come to light in the years after the 1989 survey, some of the catalogued documents have subsequently disappeared.[12] Some museums have also gone: for example, the document holdings of Cambridgeshire's closed museum went to the county record office, but the artefacts went somewhere else.

---

8   H. Beynon, "Regulating Research: Politics and Decision Making in Industrial Organisations," in A. Bryman, ed., *Doing Research in Organizations* (London: Routledge, 1988), 23; Young, *Inside Job*, 29.

9   Sir Robert Mark called his memoirs "In the Office of Constable." R. Mark, *In the Office of Constable* (London: Collins, 1978). The most explicit historical hagiographies of the British police were written by Charles Reith. C. Reith, *British Police and the Democratic Ideal* (London: Oxford University Press, 1943). Many more recent and popular historians have taken up his themes, for example, D. Ascoli, *The Queen's Peace: The Origins and Development of the Metropolitan Police, 1829–1979* (London: Hamish Hamilton, 1979).

10 I. Bridgeman and C. Emsley, *A Guide to the Archives of the Police Forces of England and Wales* (Cambridge: Police History Society, 1989).

11 L.A.Waters, *Towards a Record Management Policy for Provincial Police Forces in England and Wales* (Cambridge: Police History Society, 1992).

12 Emsley, "Archives," 468.

This brings us to the title, which is a quote from Douglas Adams's *Hitchhiker's Guide to the Galaxy:*

"But the plans were on display . . ."

"On display? I eventually had to go down to the cellar to find them."

"That's the display department."

"With a torch."

"Ah, well the lights had probably gone."

"So had the stairs."

"But look, you found the notice, didn't you?"

"Yes," said Arthur, "yes I did. It was on display in the bottom of a locked filing cabinet stuck in a disused lavatory with a sign on the door saying Beware of the Leopard."[13]

The present survey was intended to test whether or not Lord Knights's plea had been noted and acted upon in the intervening 13 years. Its methodology was highly crude. In late March 2003, a circular letter was sent out to the chief officers and chairs of police authorities of all the provincial forces in Britain outside London. See table 1 for the response rate to our enquiry.

TABLE 1.

Response Rate to Survey

	Total Sent	Responses Received	% Return
Great Britain	49	29	59
England	37	21	57
Wales	4	2	50
Scotland	8	6	75

We asked:

1. What is your force's policy for archiving its records for future research access?

---

13 Douglas Adams, *The Hitchhiker's Guide to the Galaxy* (London: Pan, 1980), 12.

2. What is your force's policy for controlling access to these records?
3. Do you have any contact with the local record office?
4. Is there an officer or staff member in your force with specific responsibility for archive policy?
5. Do you consider that the implementation of the 2000 Freedom of Information Act and the recommendations of the government's "e-envoy" regarding the archiving of electronic information will change the way your force deals with these issues?

We might assume that the forces who did not respond would include all of those who place little priority on access to their records by historians—but we would be wrong. The non-respondents included at least one force which we know has a very restrictive policy, but also at least one other that has an active museum and a good archive policy.

Several forces referred us to the Association of Chief Police Officers (ACPO) which is coordinating a project to develop procedures for police forces to implement Freedom of Information legislation.[14] ACPO has written a draft set of procedures which they published last month—but this is currently an internal consultation document (as of July 2003) for circulation among police forces only.[15] A similar process is going on in Scotland in order to comply with the 2002 Freedom of Information (Scotland) Act, but the Scottish branch of ACPO has yet to arrive at a final draft.[16]

The answers we got showed that the five questions were more ambiguous than we had hoped. For example, many forces had very different views of what constituted an "archiving policy": some saw it as pertaining only to "old" records, some saw it pertaining only to those records still in regular use, and others saw it as an ongoing process involving the selection and retention of records. In order to reach conclusions about those issues that interested us, we needed to analyse the responses further, to get an idea of the key issues the responses revealed. In some cases the responses were explicitly stated, in others they only became apparent from the answers given concerning to our original questions.[17] See table 2.

---

14 Freedom of Information Act 2000 (c. 36).
15 Personal communication, 11 June 2003, from Superintendent David Chinchen.
16 Freedom of Information (Scotland) Act, 2002 (asp. 13).
17 Number of responses was 28 because no final return was received from one force due to a failure to respond to their request for clarification.

TABLE 2.

Interpretative Summary of Answers Regarding Key Issues

	No.	% of Responses
Does the force appear to only be thinking about the use of records for operational reasons?	10	36%
Was there any contact with a record office?	13	46%
Is there an internal force museum of any kind?	6	21%
Does there appear to be provision for ongoing archiving of material as it becomes useless for operational purposes?	10	36%
Is there an appreciation of the wide variety of material that will be of interest to future historians?	3	10%
Has the force realised that the preservation of electronic records involves a whole new series of challenges?	1	4%

Just over a third of the forces that responded appeared to consider records only in terms of management and operational material, and thus chose to interpret the question about "future research access" as referring essentially to sociological, rather than historical research. Records were there to be kept for a few years—generally between three and twenty-five, depending on the status of the document. Just under half had had some kind of contact with a local record office for the purposes of records deposit. This does not necessarily mean that all was well; one force claimed that:

> Our local Record Office are [sic]occasionally contacted to see if they are interested in any documents due for disposal. This is a rare occurrence. I spoke to the local office and they pointed out that much of what is of interest to them is in the public domain anyway.[18]

Six forces had their own museums or museum collections, or were in contact with local museums, but all but one of these were also in contact with record offices. Most museums operated on a small scale, although at least one of the forces that responded employs a full-time curator and consequently has a policy that appears very good indeed. Others have an active voluntary curator or an interested group of retired police officers who appear to do this job properly.[19]

---

18 Force 5.
19 Forces 8 and 16.

An overt resistance to research was present in some responses. On the issue of policy, one force wrote that:

> We are in the process of adapting the Cabinet Office Rules in respect of Protective Security. These impart a need to know principle. We do not necessarily interpret "research" as a "need to know."[20]

Some responses also demonstrated an overwillingness to close "sensitive" documents—though to be fair, these came from forces that had at least preserved and archived documents and had worked out a policy of access to them.[21] Nevertheless, this approach produces the possibly misleading impression (common also in the case of secret or embarrassing central government activities and their attendant records) that things can only get better. When the anodyne and laudatory is available instantly, the organisational machinations appear after 30 years, and the skeletons fall from the cupboard after 75 or more; the image as recorded by historians for the public is one of ever more benign activity by government agencies. This may or may not be true.

The most important finding is probably the question of ongoing archiving. Only about a third had archive policies with provisions for weeding out and preservation of items of historical interest, for indefinite retention. Although four forces had donated "historical" material to record offices and thus were obviously aware that they possessed material of historical significance, they did not have a procedure for dealing with the material they were generating.[22] A further complicating factor for a decent archive policy was the semi-autonomous nature of many departments within police forces. Four forces stated that it was departments, rather than the force as a whole, who "owned" documents and could control access and disposal policies.[23] It is worrisome that one of these forces appears to be leading the ACPO project to develop model guidelines for records management.

If we want to write any but the most narrowly administrative history of the British police, we need to look beyond minutes of meetings or sources designed for immediate public consumption. Instead, this

---

20 Force 1.
21 Forces 7 and 8.
22 Forces 1, 2, 14, and 27.
23 Forces 4, 5, 10, and 22.

history has to be worked out from other sources, such as notebooks, refused charge sheets, station incident books, and internal investigations. This is all the more true when using police records to examine other social issues historically: the treatment of prostitution, white-collar crime, and traffic policing are just a few that spring to mind. For example, the Old Bailey Sessions Papers, now online, are a wonderful source for the study of eighteenth-century social history.[24] From our responses, three forces appear to have understood that that "boring" documents need to be archived too.[25] One force answered the question of whether or not they had an archive policy by saying:

> The Force does not have Policy for archiving its records for *future research access*. However records and files, for example the Chief Constable's Annual Report and those files relating to incidents which may be of an historical interest are kept indefinitely.

And it answered the question about access requirements thus:

> Many records such as the Annual Report are already in the public domain. Any application to see other files is judged on its own merit. Public interest and security would be primary considerations.[26]

We can wonder what this force will collectively decide is of historical interest. Given that they are so keen on the annual report, the omens are worrisome: police annual reports are glossy and Panglossian publications, designed to show the force in the best light possible.

The final interesting issue is whether these forces appreciate the forthcoming problems for permanent storage that might be caused by the increased use of electronic access? Twenty-seven did not list that concern in their expected impacts of the move towards e-government. The exception was one Scottish force whose archivist also noted that the different provisions of the Scottish and English/Welsh Freedom of Information Acts mean that certain categories of United Kingdom-wide information might be open on one side of the border but not the other.[27]

Almost all police forces appreciate the likely impact of the

24 http://www.oldbaileyonline.org/.
25 Forces 7, 20, and 28.
26 Force 23.
27 Force 28.

Freedom of Information Acts, and it is this that is driving them to adopt a unified records management strategy for the first time. This strategy will of necessity incorporate some degree of public access. However, given the real need for security, the demands of confidentiality, and attitudes displayed in the survey responses—notably the absolute priority often given to operational use of information—there is a chance that the guidelines might make things worse. What we need to do, therefore, is make sure that when the guidelines are finalised, a role for the preservation of all kinds of records—sensitive or not—for future historians is written in. Long delays in access might even be preferable if the alternative was the status quo, which in too many cases is complete destruction. We need a levelling-up to the practices of the best forces, rather than a levelling-down to those of the worst.

In conclusion, we have heard enough encouraging noises in the responses of these forces to feel that the British provincial police service as a whole deserves the question mark in the title, "Beware of the Leopard?" Most police records continue to be consigned to a locked filing cabinet, or destroyed outright with no thought for the needs of posterity, but in a few forces a more enlightened attitude prevails. For most of the forces, however, there is a lot more that needs to be done, and the policy changes currently in progress are not obviously taking into account the need to preserve a cross-section of records so they can be studied by future generations. Until this happens, the provincial police of Britain will continue to be overshadowed in the historical record by the metropolitan police and by the intelligence services.

At War: Records and
International Conflict

16

FROM SOLFERINO TO SARAJEVO: ARMED CONFLICT, INTERNATIONAL LAW, AND ARCHIVES

George Mackenzie

This paper will deal with the most extreme form of political pressure, armed conflict, and its impact on archives. In justification, let me quote Carl von Clausewitz, the Prussian soldier and military theorist. War, von Clausewitz wrote, "is not merely a political act, but also a real political instrument, a continuation of political commerce, a carrying out of the same by other means."[1] Von Clausewitz had a bad press in the early part of the 20th century, partly because he was Prussian and his views were seen as underlying German aggression in two world wars. But his view today seems essentially realistic, given the huge number of conflicts in the past 20 or even 10 years, the current minor wars raging in Africa and South America, and the developments in asymmetric warfare we see today. He wrote his famous treatise *On War* around 1827, though it was not published until after his death in 1831. It remains one of the most quoted works on the subject, and his views are now studied as much in business schools as in military academies across the world.

---

1   Carl von Clausewitz, *On War (Vom Kriege)*, translated by J.J. Graham (London, 1873).

Clausewitz is also, interestingly, a good starting point for the concept of cultural protection in wartime. Patrick Boylan, in his review of the Hague Convention published in 1993, draws attention to Book V, chapter III of *On War*, which stresses the principle of proportionality in conducting war, and how it is essential to restrict military efforts to genuinely military targets, or as Clausewitz puts it himself, "the principle of only applying so much force and aiming at such an object in War as is just sufficient for the attainment of the political object."[2] This is a pragmatic argument, based on self-interest rather than any aesthetic or moral basis, but nonetheless proportionality is a necessary step towards limiting the effects of warfare.

The battle of Solferino, during the Franco-Austrian War, was characterised by great ferocity and carnage, but had the positive result that it led to the foundation of the Red Cross. French and Piedmontese armies, seeking to drive the Austrians out of northern Italy, clashed with their adversaries on 24 June 1859. As in the Crimean war a little earlier, military technology had advanced to a stage where the ability to kill and wound far outstripped the abilities of medical services to deal with the casualties. At Solferino, 40,000 men were killed or wounded in a single day. The Swiss businessman, Henri Dunant, horrified at the way the wounded were left on the battlefield, engaged local people to help give rudimentary first-aid. Both haunted and inspired by what he had seen, Dunant returned to Geneva and wrote a memoir of Solferino,[3] in which he advocated international cooperation between states, in the form of a convention, "inviolate in character, which, once approved and ratified, might serve as the basis for societies for the relief of the wounded." Together with a general and two doctors, he helped found the first international committee for the relief of wounded soldiers, which drew up the first Geneva Convention. Thus was born the Red Cross.[4]

Just as Solferino gave rise to a major international humanitarian effort, highlighting the human tragedy of war, events at Sarajevo some 130 years later stimulated an international effort to draw attention to

2   Quoted in Patrick Boylan, *Review of the Convention for the Protection of Cultural Property in the Event of Armed Conflict* (Paris: UNESCO, 1993. CLT-93/WS/12), 25.

3   British Red Cross Society, *A Memory of Solferino*. Translation of the first edition (1862) by J. Henry Dunant (London, 1862).

4   For a simple history of the Red Cross, see the website of the International Committee of the Red Cross (ICRC), www.icrc.org.

the cultural casualties. This was partly because of the closeness of the events. The conflicts in the Balkans were the more horrifying, at least to a European audience, because they were happening on their continent, and made more immediate to the whole world by the ever-present eye of television. It was also partly because of the nature of the events, and the use of deliberate "ethnic cleansing" against different groups. For archives, this was a particular challenge, since their role as the source documents for citizens' identity was brought into sharp focus.

But it was the attacks on cultural buildings that had the biggest impact on attitudes. The damage to Dubrovnik and Sarajevo, in particular, fired the popular imagination. In Dubrovnik, world-famous historic buildings were shelled, and the UNESCO flag flying above them seemed only to underline the powerlessness of the international community. In Sarajevo, the National Library and Oriental Institute with their priceless contents were destroyed. One positive result was to bring existing international instruments, and their limitations, into closer focus. The idea of revising the 1954 Hague Convention, which had been conceived to deal with a quite different set of military and political circumstances, quickly gained support and led to agreement in 1999 on a new, Second Protocol.

The events of the Balkan wars also stimulated action by the international professional community, and led to the formation of the International Committee of the Blue Shield (ICBS), uniting four non-governmental organisations. The aim of the ICBS is that the Blue Shield symbol will be as recognised and respected for cultural protection as the Red Cross is for humanitarian protection. This is an ambitious aim, but it is both desirable and achievable.

Damage and destruction to archives is not a new phenomenon, and armed conflict is by no means the only agent. It is, however, one of the most destructive. In 1996 UNESCO published a list of archives and libraries damaged or destroyed during the twentieth century. The fact that it was limited to this relatively brief period of time is itself an indication of the enormity of destruction over the centuries, as the introduction acknowledged.[5] The report covered damage from all causes, and the archive section was based on a questionnaire sent to organisa-

---

5   Hans van der Hoeven and Joan van Albada, *Lost Memory—Libraries and Archives Destroyed in the Twentieth Century* (Paris: UNESCO, 1996, CII-96/WS/1), 3.

tions in over 200 countries. It formed part of the Memory of the World programme in UNESCO and was "intended to alert public opinion and sensitise the professional community and local and national authorities to the disappearance of archival and library treasures of inestimable value." It also aimed to use the destruction that had occurred to highlight the need to act to prevent or reduce further damage. Its appearance coincided with the destruction of cultural institutions in Sarajevo, and these traumatic events helped stimulate the work and underline its urgency.

The archives report was based on returns covering about 6,250 institutions in 105 countries, the vast majority of which indicated some losses, particularly in Asia and Europe, but with several in Africa also. The statistics are far from perfect, and the report itself provides a critique of the methodology, but it is clear that armed conflict was one of the biggest causes of damage. In three areas, Asia, Europe, and the Pacific, it was given as the major cause.[6]

Views of cultural property and its protection in armed conflict have developed over several centuries. The classical view of war and property was expressed clearly and succinctly by Xenophon, the Athenian writer, in about 400 B.C.E. in his *Cyropaedia*. He puts the words in the mouth of Persian King Cyrus, speaking to his troops after the capture of Babylon. Having congratulated his men on taking possession of broad and fertile lands, of subjects to till them, and of houses and furnishings, Cyrus stresses that these all now belong absolutely to them, as the conquerors: "for it is a law established for all time among all men that when a city is taken in war, the persons and the property of the inhabitants thereof belong to the captors."[7]

This is in stark contrast to the modern view, expressed in the 1954 Hague Convention on the Protection of Cultural Property in Armed Conflict:

> [D]amage to cultural property belonging to any people whatsoever means damage to the cultural heritage of all mankind. . . . the preservation of the cultural heritage is of great importance for all peoples of the world.[8]

---

6   Ibid., 29

7   Xenophon *Cyropaedia* VII, 72–73. English translation from the Tufts University *Perseus* website: http://www.perseus.tufts.edu/.

8   Hague Convention preamble.

In between these two views lie several centuries of development of international humanitarian law and its eventual extension to cultural property as well as to human beings.[9]

For most of the time, the classical view held good, and in the Middle Ages not just castles, but churches, villages, and even whole towns and cities were laid waste. The idea of protecting sacred, rather than artistic sites slowly emerged, though it had some origins even in classical antiquity—the sacred olive groves of ancient Greece were often spared in war. It was with the Renaissance, and its attention to artistic endeavour, that the idea of protecting cultural property in international law finally emerged. But it was not until the Peace of Westphalia, ending the Thirty Years War in 1648, that the idea of restoring objects, including cultural objects, after a conflict emerged. This was not a big change in itself—indeed, as Kecskemeti has pointed out, the treaty merely formalised the situation *de facto*.[10] In retrospect, however, it appears as the first step along the way to according a new status to property in time of armed conflict.

The Enlightenment led to further development in concepts of property and the protection of it in armed conflict. Perhaps inspired by Rousseau's argument that war is a relation not between men, or citizens, but only between states, the idea followed that public property belonging to the state could be taken or destroyed, if it could serve a military purpose. As Jiri Toman points out, "a measure of protection was thus accorded to public property which did not directly serve military interests."[11] The Swiss legal philosopher Emmerich de Vattel, writing in 1758, argues that in the event of conflict:

> For whatever cause a country is ravaged, we ought to spare those edifices which do honour to human society, and do not contribute to increase the enemy's strength, —such as temples, tombs, public buildings, and all works of remarkable beauty.[12]

---

9   Jiri Toman, *The Protection of Cultural Property in the Event of Armed Conflict* (Dartmouth and UNESCO, 1996) and Patrick Boylan, *Review*, give good accounts on which I have relied in the following sections.

10 Charles Kecskemeti, "Displaced European Archives: Is It Time for a Post-War Settlement?" *American Archivist* 55 (Winter 1992), 132–138.

11 Toman, *Protection of Cultural Property*, 5.

12 Emmerich de Vattel, *The Law of Nations*, New Edition (Philadelphia: 1883) chap. 138, http://www.constitution.org/vattel/vattel_03.htm (accessed 21 June 2005).

De Vattel went on to say that those who did damage such buildings would be "an enemy to mankind." He did, however, believe that military necessity could justify destruction.

There is an interesting contrast in views at the time of the French Revolution and the subsequent Napoleonic Empire. Charles Kecskemeti points out that the ancient regime monarchs believed in archives because they supported their titles to territorial gains, and that this monarchical conception carried through to the Revolution, combined with "the new practice of cultural plundering." The Napoleonic vision of a new Empire to rival the ancient Roman one produced "an extraordinary archival project." Archives from the Vatican, the German Empire in Vienna, and Simancas in Spain were all taken to Paris and were to be housed in a huge new building near the Champ de Mars.[13] The collapse of the Napoleonic first Empire put an end to the scheme.

On the other hand, the British, victorious in the Napoleonic wars, took a different view. Toman quotes a memorandum by Lord Castlereagh that the removal of works of art was "contrary to every principle of justice and to the usages of modern warfare." I do not think this an example of French barbarism contrasted with British civilisation, but rather a reflection of the French revolutionary ideals which accorded great value to the cultural objects but felt an intellectual superiority over the old regimes elsewhere which gave France a right to take possession of *objets d'art*.

The development of concepts protecting cultural property which has no military value during war is paralleled in other cultures. Toman points out that, "The protection of property is in fact universal in nature. . . . we find striking examples in all cultures, all religions and all political systems." In pre-colonial Africa, places of a religious nature, of culture and art, were protected. In Japan as early as 1339, the emperor forbade the destruction of sacred property. In Islamic law and tradition, there is a clear imperative to distinguish between civilian and military objects.

It is worth noting, however, the comments made by Australia in a 1995 report to UNESCO on the implementation of the 1954 Hague Convention. They raised issues of how cultural property was defined,

---

13 Kecskemeti, *Displaced European Archives*, 134.

in relation to their aboriginal peoples, given the fact that their culture was not adequately protected because the definitions used in the Convention are based on Western concepts.[14] To some extent, this is covered by the requirement in the 1949 Geneva Conventions for states to respect the religious and cultural beliefs of civilian populations. Recent work by UNESCO on intangible cultural heritage may also help to redress the bias towards physical cultural property.

The general concepts of protection were not codified until the nineteenth century, when international humanitarian law (IHL) as we know it today began to emerge. IHL is also known as the laws of war and its aim is to limit human suffering in armed conflict. IHL itself developed over a long period in response to the experiences of war. Each major conflict stimulated changes, as the international community recognised the problems and agreed on measures to avoid them in the future. The role of the Red Cross in humanitarian work was applied more widely, to prisoners of war as a result of the 1914–1918 conflict and to civilians as a result of the Second World War. In 1929, the Red Crescent was added as a symbol alongside the Red Cross. Today, the cornerstone of international humanitarian law and the starting point for the work of the Red Cross remain the Geneva Conventions of 1949.

In addition to treaties and conventions, there is customary international humanitarian law, which is not written but is accepted by a significant number of states as proper behaviour. It need not be unanimous, and contrary behaviour by some states may in some cases strengthen the case for customary law.

The protection of cultural property in armed conflict follows directly on from developments in IHL. It is seen primarily as part of the necessary protection of civilians and non-combatants. It first appears in 1907, in the Hague Convention of that year. However, the first and one of the most significant steps was taken by the United States in 1863, at the time it was engaged in the bitter Civil War. The "Instructions for the Government of Armies of the United States in the Field," were prepared by a military lawyer, Francis Lieber,

---

14 Jan Hladik, "Reporting System under the 1954 Convention for the Protection of Cultural Property in the Event of Armed Conflict," *International Review of the Red Cross* 840 (2000): 1001–1016; available on the ICRC website, www.icrc.org.

approved by President Abraham Lincoln and published as General Order 100 in April 1863. Lieber's Code is the first instrument which specifically and explicitly protects cultural property in wartime. Sections 34 to 36 cover civilian property. Property of churches, hospitals, establishments of a charitable character, establishments of education or foundations for the promotion of knowledge, observatories, and museums of fine arts are all to be protected, and classical works of art, libraries, and scientific collections are all to be secured against avoidable injury. Interestingly, the code that states that what is worthy of protection is "not to be considered public property."

As the Code prohibits seizure or destruction of private property in general, this seems to put cultural property into a new category, and to create a distinction that would not fit comfortably, for example, with the modern concept of inalienability of public records displaced by war. Like all the later initiatives to protect cultural property in wartime, the Lieber Code was a reaction to the nature of contemporary warfare, in this case the Civil War in the United States. This traumatic experience may have helped shape the early commitment of the u.s. government to humanitarian law and to cultural property protection.

The exclusively u.s. Code was taken up in two international initiatives, the Brussels Declaration of 1874 and the Oxford Code of 1880. Neither was ratified as an international treaty, but they were later adopted by what was to be the first Hague conference in 1889. The u.s. commitment continued with its joint sponsorship, along with Russia, of the larger and more influential 1907 conference at the Hague which adopted a series of conventions that went further than the Code.[15] However, the continuing importance of the Lieber Code should not be underestimated. Much of it is still valid today, and I understand it is quoted and used in teaching u.s. military commanders and their legal advisers.

At the 1907 conference, the convention agreed to prohibit attacks on undefended civilian targets. It required all necessary steps be taken to spare "buildings dedicated to religion, art, science or charitable purposes." It also for the first time imposed a duty on the defenders of besieged targets "to indicate the presence of such buildings or places by

---

15 Boylan, 25–26.

distinctive and visible signs, which shall be notified to the enemy beforehand."[16] This was how things stood at the outbreak of the First World War. The agreements did little or nothing to stop the huge destruction of cultural sites and property in Europe during the 1914–1918 conflict. Boylan points out that the soul-searching after the conflict focussed on two aspects. First was the concept of military necessity, which had been used by both attacking and defending forces to override the regulations. The second was the way in which military technologies, including the use of chemical agents and aerial bombing, took matters beyond the scope of the agreed-upon rules.

There were also attempts to get agreement on rules for aerial warfare at a further Hague conference in 1923, but these were not ratified. The next major development in international humanitarian law came in the Americas, not Europe, and once again the United States was the effective driving force. Nicholas Roerich, a Russian artist who had established a museum of his works in the United States, drew up a pact for safeguarding cultural institutions. Although discussed at a conference in Bruges in 1931, it was only signed into international use on 15 April 1935, Pan America Day, by 21 American states in the Treaty of Washington. Partly because of its simplicity, the pact was quickly passed and put into force by the u.s. government, and it is still technically in force throughout most of the American continent. The pact specified that "historic monuments, scientific, artistic, educational and cultural institutions" and their personnel were to be considered neutral, and respected by belligerents. Institutions were to be identified by a distinctive mark, a red circle with a triple red sphere in the middle, on a white background. Boylan points out, however, that "despite the high ideals and explicit commitments of the Pact, most Parties to it did little or nothing to implement its provisions at the practical level."[17]

The Spanish Civil War again showed the inadequacy of current protection measures. There was widespread destruction of cultural property and further developments in the use of aerial bombing by the Nationalist forces. The League of Nations and the International Museums Office commissioned an expert report which led to a

---

16 Regulations annexed to the *Fourth Hague Convention on the Laws and Customs of War on Land* (1907), quoted by Boylan.

17 Boylan, 30.

Preliminary Draft International Convention for the Protection of Historic Buildings and Works of Art in Time of War, which was very influential in the later 1954 Hague Convention.[18] The draft convention introduced new principles, including the organisation of protection in time of peace, the education of military forces, and addition of protection to military regulations and manuals, an undertaking to punish looting or depredations, and the idea of introducing refuges to which works of art could be moved in times of danger. Furthermore, as Toman points out, it introduced the notion that "monuments and works of art were not protected as the national heritage but as the universal heritage to be safeguarded for the benefit of mankind as a whole." The draft remained just that with the outbreak of the Second World War.

What happened during the Second World War was, according to Toman, "an absolute shock" since even the limited provisions of the 1907 Convention were scarcely applied and there was wholesale destruction of cultural property, together with major plundering of works of art by occupying German forces. At the outbreak of the war, u.s. President Franklin D. Roosevelt contacted all the potential belligerents, Germany, France, Poland, and the United Kingdom, demanding explicit assurances that they would not mount air attacks on civilian populations or unarmed towns. All responded positively, and Boylan points out that these "rules of engagement" were generally observed for the first 30 months of the war. A change came, he argues, in March 1943, when the British set out to destroy the town of Lübeck with experimental fire-bombing, and the Germans responded by attacking the English cities of Exeter, Norwich, York, and Canterbury, in what were known as the "Baedeker Raids." The British tactic was strongly criticised by the United States.[19]

Elsewhere, the Allied campaign did take important steps to avoid damage. One of the most explicit was u.s. General Dwight D. Eisenhower's message to commanders on the eve of the 1944 Normandy landings:

> Shortly we will be fighting our way across the Continent of Europe in battles designed to preserve our civilization. Inevitably, in the path of our advance will be found historic monuments and cultural centres

18 Toman, *Protection of Cultural Property,* 18–19.
19 Boylan, 34–36.

which symbolise to the world all that we are fighting to preserve. It is the responsibility of every commander to protect and respect these symbols whenever possible.[20]

Eisenhower was acutely aware of the dangers, having issued a similar appeal during the Italian campaign in 1943, and having heard the criticism that was voiced when the medieval monastery of Monte Cassino was attacked in order to dislodge a well-dug-in German force.

The Allies also set up a special corps of monuments, fine arts and archives officers, staffed by civilian experts, who were attached to the u.s., British, and Free French forces. Although small in number, they were significant in minimising direct damage, by identifying sites of special cultural importance to be protected. Many sites were listed before the Normandy landings. The corps was also able to supervise the protection of buildings and collections during and after the invasion, and once hostilities were over, to advise on the restitution of cultural property that had been displaced by looting or other illegal activity.[21]

The end of the Second World War brought further reflection, in the light of experience, on how the laws of war should be strengthened. The charter of the United Nations outlawed war, and the Genocide Convention of 9 December 1948 extended not just to international armed conflict, but also to civil wars, to internal armed conflict, and to peacetime. Even more important, in Geneva in 1949 existing humanitarian measures were revised and expanded into four conventions, concerning protection of land forces, naval forces, prisoners of war, and civilians. The Geneva Conventions are now adopted by virtually all states and would in any case be considered as binding customary law. They contain provision for international efforts to seek out and prosecute those thought to have committed grave breaches. The Fourth Geneva Convention is particularly important because, for the first time, it extended international humanitarian law to the protection of civilians. It does not contain specific provisions on protection of cultural property, but it does extend the 1907 Hague Convention principles prohibiting the targeting of civilian property and non-combatant populations. Boylan points to the provision under which protected

20 Quoted in J.J. Rorimer, *Survival: The Salvage and Protection of Art in War* (New York: Abelard Press, 1950).
21 Boylan, 37.

persons are entitled, in all circumstances, to respect not only for their persons, but also for their religious and cultural practices.[22]

It was against this background of major review and revision of international humanitarian law that the 1954 Hague Convention, the first to specifically deal with cultural property, emerged. There were actually three instruments: the Convention, Regulations for its implementation, and a First Protocol prohibiting the export of cultural property during occupation and providing for its restitution afterwards. By this time, the establishment of UNESCO meant there was also an international organisation with a responsibility for cultural matters, and it was given a supervisory role over the Convention. The Convention provides a definition of cultural property (or biens culturels in French) which includes three elements: moveable and immoveable property itself, premises used for housing it, and centres containing monuments or sites, such as historical cities. It covers occupied territories, putting a responsibility on the occupying power to protect cultural property. It also picks up the element from the pre-war agreement, that military forces should be trained about cultural property and respect for it, and this should be done in peacetime. The 1954 Convention also introduced the concept of special protection, under which states could nominate certain property, fulfilling special criteria including distance from any military site. Jean-Marie Henckaerts points out that the significant thing here is the obligation on the holder, who must not use it for military purposes.[23] The Convention introduced protection also for personnel engaged in protecting cultural property, and the Blue Shield symbol for marking. It also followed the Geneva Conventions in extending protection to internal armed conflicts.

With the benefit of hindsight, we can see that the 1954 Convention has certain drawbacks. There is nothing about developing an understanding or sensitivity in the civilian population. The terms for enforcement of the instruments are vague and could not be used, the regime of special protection did not work well and was virtually never used, and due to the vagueness and lack of examples, the terms were implemented by states in an inconsistent way. At the time of writing this article, 103 states have ratified or acceded to the 1954 Convention, more than half the possible countries that could accept it, but there are regional varia-

---

22 *Geneva Convention Relative to the Protection of Civilian Property in Time of War*, 12 August 1948; Boylan, 139.

23 Jean-Marie Henckaerts, "New Rules for the Protection of Cultural Property in Armed Conflict: The Significance of the Second Protocol to the 1954 Hague Convention for the

tions: Europe and North America have the highest number of states parties, with 86% of countries, and the Arab countries come in second, with 78% being states parties. In Africa, by contrast, the figure is much lower and only 33% of countries are parties.

One of the major gaps in the adoption of the 1954 Convention was, and remains, the absence of the United States, the United Kingdom, and Canada. The Convention (but not the Protocol) was signed by the United States and the United Kingdom in 1954, but they did not go on to ratify it. Boylan has tried to piece together the reasons, based on u.s. documents and on the recollections of W. Hays Park, Chief of the International Law Branch of the u.s. Army Office of the Judge Advocate General. The United States took an active part in the negotiations for the Convention, and some articles in it were drafted on their initiative. The problem arose when the Convention was passed to the u.s. Joint Chiefs of Staff. The principles in it were not exceptional, as they were already in the 1935 Roerich pact which the u.s. and many Latin American nations had adopted. They were also in line with clear and explicit instructions on the protection of cultural property issued in the later stages of the Second World War by Supreme Allied Commander General Eisenhower, who by 1954 was u.s. President. However, air force and navy chiefs of staff were hostile and could not present a unanimous position, so the secretary of state decided no further progress could be made towards ratification. The United Kingdom and Canada appear to have been asked by the u.s. also to refuse to ratify, and they agreed. Boylan says that the reasons for the military opposition were not recorded, but he asserts:

> [T]here seems little doubt that the Convention's attempt to protect 'centres containing large amounts of cultural property' was regarded by the Strategic Air Command in particular as threatening an unacceptable restraint on the use of the high yield nuclear weapons of mass destruction then being introduced.

Boylan mentions an additional worry that u.s. military chiefs may have been concerned about—their ability to target the Kremlin—but, if so, he thinks this was a misreading of the Convention, since use of the buildings as a politico-military centre would have removed the protection afforded and made them a legitimate target.[24]

Protection of Cultural Property in the Event of Armed Conflict," *International Review of the Red Cross* 835 (1999), 593–620, available on the ICRC website at www.icrc.org.
24 Boylan, 104.

Despite their decision not to ratify the Convention, the u.s. and the United Kingdom have supported its principles and implemented many of its obligations in subsequent policy. Boylan points out that: "it has long been recognised by the u.s. military as the applicable international humanitarian law." At the start of the negotiations on the 1999 Protocol, the u.k. delegation announced that its government intended in principle to ratify the 1954 Convention, provided the outcome of the negotiations on the Protocol were satisfactory.[25] And a brochure recently published by the u.k. Foreign and Commonwealth Office points out that the United Kingdom "played a full role in the negotiations" for the Second Protocol "and is considering the ratification of the Convention, together with the new Protocol." It notes, however, that this will require primary legislation and will depend on the availability of parliamentary time. In the meantime, "the u.k. remains fully committed to the protection of cultural property in times of armed conflict in accordance with international law."[26]

The Balkan wars and very public destruction of cultural property gave renewed impetus to revising the 1954 Convention. The Netherlands, which has taken a close interest in the subject since the conference leading to the original treaty took place on its territory, took the initiative again, by commissioning, with unesco, a report on the Convention. The work was entrusted to Patrick Boylan, a u.k. expert with a background in museums but a wide knowledge of other cultural institutions. His report was published by unesco in 1993 and made a series of important recommendations to states parties, to unesco, and to the United Nations. Overall, however, Boylan felt that the Convention was still entirely valid and realistic and that the problem lay with the application of it and the Protocol rather than with defects in either instrument.[27] This was an important conclusion, and it underlines two aspects of the subsequent revision process. First, the new Protocol did not change the Convention, but merely added to it. Second, the measures in the Protocol aimed at making the systems of protection work better, rather than changing them in principle.

---

25 Intervention by Martin Eaton, Deputy Legal Adviser, Foreign and Commonwealth Office, at the British Red Cross conference, "Heritage Under Fire," London, June 2001.

26 "The United Kingdom and International Humanitarian Law," published by the Foreign and Commonwealth Office, September 2001.

27 Boylan, 7.

The revision process occupied most of the rest of the decade.[28] Following on from the Boylan report, three meetings of experts in humanitarian law and cultural protection took place, which culminated in what became known as the Lauswolt document, after the Dutch town where it was drafted. Lauswolt was in effect a new draft treaty based on Boylan's review. In 1997, a revised Lauswolt document was drawn up by 20 government experts, and the UNESCO Secretariat submitted this to the states party to the 1954 Convention. A series of expert meetings were held with representatives from governments, non-governmental organisations, the Red Cross, and UNESCO.

These meetings concluded that there were five main areas in the existing Convention that needed to be tackled. The first concerned the occasions on which the protection provided by the Convention was reduced, the cases where "military necessity" could be invoked. The second concerned precautionary measures that states should take before armed conflict occurred. The third was the regime of special protection, accorded by the Convention to certain particularly valuable cultural objects. Fourth was the question of responsibility of military and other personnel who breached the terms of the Convention, and fifth were a series of institutional questions about how the Convention was operating.

Having thus established the agenda for the negotiations, the government of the Netherlands convened a diplomatic conference, once again in the Hague, which ended with the adoption of the Second Protocol on 26 March 1999. The conference decided that it was not necessary to create a new convention, or to amend the existing one, either of which would have required extensive negotiation and unanimous agreement by all the states party to the 1954 instrument. Instead, the conference decided to follow the model of the Geneva Conventions and Protocols. As a result, the 1954 Convention remained the basic text, and the conference worked on a new Protocol "which would in no way amend the 1954 Convention but would supplement it and would only apply to the States who ratified it." This means that states can only

---

28 For the account of the revision process, I have relied on Toman, and especially on Henckaerts.

become party to the new Protocol if they have already ratified the 1954 Convention.

The first area for revision was military necessity. Article 4 of the 1954 Convention provides for waiving protection "where military necessity imperatively requires such a waiver," but as Boylan pointed out in his review, the lack of a definition of this was a serious weakness. Boylan in fact argued strongly against any inclusion of military necessity or limitations on the protection to be given. It is difficult to see how this could have been done, because it was already in the Convention and there was considerable pressure at the various meetings leading up to the diplomatic conference, but the 1999 Protocol did put further restrictions on military commanders. Henckaerts takes a contrary view and favours the continuing exemption, but notes that

> the concept of military necessity has not limited warfare in any significant way. The Second World War, for example, was fought under the restriction that no property could be destroyed unless there was an imperative military necessity to do so. Yet entire cities were destroyed.

Jan Hladik points out that during the negotiations that led to the 1999 Protocol, military necessity was again hotly debated:

> Two opposing tendencies appeared, both during the plenary debates and in the working group on this matter: the attempt of military participants (both lawyers and operational staff) to broaden the scope of the definition of military necessity, and the attempt of cultural heritage protection experts to narrow the scope of this definition so as to limit potential abuses.[29]

The final text includes two provisions strengthening the military necessity regime, articles 6 and 13. Article 6, Hladik argues, adds two new elements. First, which concerns the attacker, is the waiver of imperative military necessity where cultural property has been transformed into a military objective. The second, which concerns the defender, is the waiver in the case of property used for purposes likely to expose it to destruction or damage when this use is necessary for obtaining military advantage. Article 13 brings in the concept of decision to attack being taken at a certain level, and the obligation to give advance warning.

---

29 Jan Hladik, "The 1954 Convention for the Protection of Cultural Property in the Event of Armed Conflict and the Notion of Military Necessity," *International Review of the Red Cross* 835 (1999), 621–635, www.icrc.org.

These vary: for general protection, decision is at battalion commander level and a warning shall be given "if possible"; for enhanced protection, decision is at divisional level, and a warning shall be given.

The Second Protocol recognised that the special protection system under the Convention had not worked well, and added a new scheme of enhanced protection, which was more clearly defined and easier to comply with. In fact, Henckaerts points out there is no difference in the level of protection. The differences are that the holder of the property is also under an increased obligation, in the case of enhanced protection, never to use it for military purposes. There is also a duty to give advance warning of an attack on cultural property, which parallels a provision in the 1977 Geneva Protocol which Henckaerts says "in some respects approximates the protection of the civilian population as such and goes beyond the protection of other civilian objects." Interestingly, the ICRC proposed at the Hague conference to give cultural property under enhanced protection the same degree of protection as that given to medical units. This was not adopted, but shows that the ICRC is strongly interested in extending IHL to cover cultural property and that it is prepared to press for even wider and stronger protection.

The Second Protocol makes a major advance in clarifying individual criminal responsibility for attacks on cultural property. It lists three which are grave breaches as defined in the Geneva Conventions: attacking cultural property under enhanced protection, using cultural property under enhanced protection for military purposes, and extensive destruction of cultural property under general protection. States have to establish universal criminal jurisdiction over these, meaning that anyone can be charged or extradited for these crimes, whether or not they are nationals of the state charging them and whether or not the violations were committed on the territory of the state. A provision excluding nationals of states not party to the Convention from this criminal jurisdiction was included at the request of the United States, but customary international law might override this.

Two other violations, attacking cultural property under general protection and the theft or destruction of such property, were added at the request of the ICRC, in order to encourage states to recognise these as war crimes and penalise them under domestic law. States are, however, only required to try these under common criminal jurisdiction, rather than the universal jurisdiction for grave breaches.

The Second Protocol applies equally to international and non-international armed conflicts, taking it further than the 1954 Convention and the 1977 Protocol to the Geneva Conventions. This is essential, as most conflicts are now of this kind. And as Henckaerts notes "the International Criminal Court has jurisdiction over war crimes committed against cultural property in both international and non-international armed conflict." The understanding throughout the diplomatic conference, he says, was that the phrase "party to the conflict" includes rebel groups in states party, but not states which are not party to the Convention and Protocol.

For archivists, librarians, and curators of museums and historic sites, one of the most significant parts of the 1999 Protocol was the recognition of the International Committee of the Blue Shield and its four non-governmental organisation members: International Council on Archives (ICA), International Council of Museums (ICOM), International Council on Monuments and Sites (ICOMOS), and International Federation of Library Associations and Institutions (IFLA).

The figures for states parties to the 1999 Protocol are inevitably lower than for the Convention. To date, 44 have signed but only five have found time to enact legislation to ratify or accede to a treaty.

We can see a clear development in international humanitarian law—from the protection of sacred sites in ancient civilisations, affected by new ideas of property and civil society in the eighteenth century, through the codification of the nineteenth century, to the late twentieth-century instruments that are now in force. Development of the law has followed the experience of war, essentially reacting to the last conflict, and perceived failings in the former system. Major conflicts have consistently triggered greater awareness and led to strengthening of rules.

We should not, I think, be worried by the essentially reactive posture the international community has adopted in all this. The basic principles of protection are clear: proportionality of warfare; the protection of certain sites; attacks confined to military objectives; the idea that cultural heritage is universal not just national; that peacetime measures are necessary, including safeguarding property and training military personnel; and enforcement. These have evolved steadily and coherently. We should also be clear that revision is not so much about changing the regime, as making it work properly; this was certainly the case with the 1999 Protocol, as Boylan points out.[30]

We should also recognise, in the past 100 years or so, the prominent role of certain countries—the Netherlands in particular, which hosted a number of the most important conferences on protection of cultural property, and the United States which led a number of initiatives, from the Lieber Code through the 1907 Hague conference to the Geneva Conventions of 1949.

The development of cultural heritage protection has also closely followed development in international humanitarian law, and is now firmly established as part of it. This is an important point, first because it underlines the crucial importance of cultural objects, including archives, to human life and values. It also brings us natural allies, and means that we should be working with colleagues in the Red Cross and Red Crescent on protection issues and on dissemination and education. Making the Blue Shield the cultural equivalent of the Red Cross is a goal worth aiming for.

It is a sad fact that the development of cultural property protection has not stopped or even reduced damage and destruction; if anything, the twentieth-century conflicts have done more damage than ever. Cynics might hear the sound of horses bolting and barn doors closing. However, this emphatically does not make protection worthless or invalidate the work of the international community. It is always going to be extremely difficult to ensure that the law is adhered to in the heat of armed conflict, and there will always be casualties. But the adoption of an internationally recognised code is an essential precursor if we are to have any chance of controlling destruction of cultural property. As the ICRC puts it: "[G]iven that this body of law applies during times of extreme violence, implementing the law will always be a matter of great difficulty. . . . [but] . . . striving for effective compliance is as urgent as ever." It is perhaps similar to the argument about not marking cultural buildings with the Blue Shield because of the risk that they will be tar-

---

30 The problem is essentially one of failure in the application of the Convention and Protocol rather than of inherent defects in the international instruments themselves. Boylan, 7.

geted, as happened on occasion in former Yugoslavia. The Red Cross
has on occasion been attacked, but that is never a reason for not using
it. Cultural property has been attacked in the past and will be again, but
we should all strive to reduce and mitigate attacks.

To deal with the challenges of destruction of cultural property, the
archive profession needs an agenda that is professional, multi-disciplinary, and international. We need it to be professional so that we can
develop and deploy our knowledge of cultural property in general and
in archives in particular. We need to be multi-disciplinary because we
have to reach out, not only to our traditional colleagues in museums
and libraries, but also more widely. We have to engage in dialogue with
government, emergency services, the armed forces, the Red Cross, and
the Red Crescent. And we need to be international because cultural
heritage is a universal rather than national asset, because the threats to
it are international, and because we need to share experiences and
knowledge with colleagues in other countries.

We need to promote understanding of the international conventions among colleagues, our employers and the public. We need to
encourage more countries to ratify the 1954 Convention and Protocols.
We need, at a national level, to increase dialogue with potential partners and stakeholders, including colleagues in other institutions, emergency services, and armed forces. We need to form national Blue
Shield committees to work with these stakeholders and partners. We
need to work at the national and local levels to improve our prepared-
ness for managing disasters, whether man-made or natural.

Responses to disasters and armed conflicts need to be planned, to
avoid duplication, to be ready when the event occurs, and to build credibility of the archives domain. We should exploit the publicity value of
destruction of cultural heritage to focus attention on the importance of
archives and records and the need to protect them, both at home and
abroad. We need to exploit the publicity value of cultural heritage disasters worldwide in order to increase public awareness of the importance of cultural property, of threats to it, from armed conflict and
terrorist attack as well as from civil and natural causes. We need to learn
from colleagues in other countries through the Blue Shield and other
networks. We must never forget that damage to national and international cultural heritage is damage to all of our histories.

17

ARCHIVES IN SERVICE TO THE STATE

Trudy Huskamp Peterson

The Headlines

"Hunt for Hussein's Archives Starts," *Radio Free Europe/Radio Liberty Newsline,* 28 March 2003. "*Nezavisimaya gazeta* speculates that the Russian intelligence stations in Baghdad have been ordered to evacuate the archives of the Iraqi secret services to Russia . . . It is possible that the archives could end up at the embassy, which is protected by extraterritoriality."[1]

"Hunt for the Missing," *New York Times,* 12 April 2003. "Iraqis searched for missing relatives in the military intelligence headquarters in Baghdad yesterday. . . . A man went through documents . . ."[2]

"Files in Basra Detail How Baath Party Kept Tabs on Comrades, 'Traitors,'" *Washington Post,* 17 April 2003. "When

1 RFE/RL Newsline, 28 March 2003, Part III.
2 *New York Times,* 12 April 2003, B2.

> British forces seized Basra . . . these documents and thousands more were left scattered about the looted party compound . . ."[3]
>
> "The Saddam Files," *Newsweek*, 28 April 2003. "Last week, at the Baghdad headquarters of Mukhabarat, the secret police, an Iraqi man went up to photographers from *Newsweek* and the *Los Angeles Times* carrying a bulging, grimy white rice sack. . . . Inside were more than 200 cassette tapes, videos and passports, photographs and negatives, CDs and floppy disks, as well as a fat binder thick with documents addressed to the Director General of the Iraqi Intelligence service."[4]
>
> "Germany Offers Iraq Files Advice," *BBC World/Middle East*, 4 May 2003. "Iraq should secure documents from Saddam Hussein's ousted regime as soon as possible so crimes perpetrated under his leadership can be brought to justice, a leading German official has said."[5]

Citizens combing through intelligence files and handing them over to reporters, reporters picking up party documents, personal papers, and photographs—it happened in Iraq, and before that in Afghanistan, and before that in conflicts around the world. But the real scavengers of documents are not the citizens and the press, important as they are; the real scavengers are the opposing military forces. Some of the most tightly controlled records held by a state are those that were not created by the state itself. Seized, captured, stolen, pilfered—the records from the battlefields are some of the most political archives of all.

Archivists have focused on the legal questions of replevin: how to return or regain (or both) the records armies have seized. Archivists generally have not looked at the law of war to see how if affects what documents are seized in the first place.

---

3   *Washington Post*, 17 April 2003, A1.

4   *Newsweek*, 28 April 2003, 22.

5   *BBC World/Middle East*, 4 May 2003, http://news.bbc.co.uk/2/hi/middle_east/2999517.stm (accessed 9 June 2005).

Most archivists will never be able to influence the decision of an army or a rebel group to seize records. Archivists come into the picture later, sometimes much later. But in every major conflict armies take documents. The depredations of Napoleon, for example, are well known—so well known that, when the world's archivists attempted in 1994 to establish a policy on the replevin of captured records, they set the date after which all seized records should absolutely be returned as the end of the First World War, with one archivist noting, "We can't go back and undo Napoleon!"[6] The Napoleonic army was only the most famous of the acquisitive armies. Korean archivists talk about the 1866 seizure of royal manuscripts by the French Navy; these materials are held in the Bibliotheque Nationale de France.[7] The records of the Kuwaiti Foreign Ministry were seized by Iraq during the 1991 Gulf War and were returned to Kuwait just six months before the current war broke out.[8] The Russian, U.K., and U.S. holdings from World War II seizures are extensive. Every major national archival system at some point has or will have seized materials.

Armies seize documents for a variety of reasons: to gain information on the plans of the opponents (military information); to understand the organization of the opposing government (political information); to protect the records from destruction by the opposing state; to deny the opposition the information in the records; and to obtain documents to make public, thereby exposing the workings of the opposing state. As we shall see, the seizures are indiscriminate. Armies seize every physical type of document, from electronic to audiovisual to paper. And after the seized materials are exploited to the full satisfaction of the military and political authorities, they may find their way to an archives, either in the original format or in a copy format.

I want to look, first, at what kinds of records are seized. Then I will look at what the international laws of war say about seizing property. Finally, I will ponder why records are seized as they are. I will argue

---

6   International Council on Archives, Resolutions, *Proceedings of the XXX International Conference of the Round Table on Archives* (Paris: International Council on Archives, 1998), 135–136.

7   U.S. Presidential Commission on Policy Planning, "The Problem of Korean Archives held in BNF in France," May 2002, copy in possession of the author.

8   See, for example, Mohamed Hasni, "Iraq, in Fresh Overture to Kuwait, Returns National Archives," 18 October 2002, *Middle East Times*, http://www.metimes.com/articles/normal.php?StoryID=20021018-043555-699r (accessed 9 June 2005).

that the laws of war fit awkwardly with the reality of records seizure, and I will suggest that a more modest approach may work better as a protection of property. I will urge recognition of the needs of international tribunals and of the need to preserve documents to protect human rights. And I will suggest that the traditional emphasis on return of government records, government-to-government, obscures the real character of the seized materials.

The Character of Seized Records

The first question is what do armies seize?—from whom and of what physical type. Reviewing the captured records held by the u.s. National Archives for the period from the end of the Second World War to the end of the twentieth century provides a convenient overview of what armies seize, both because the u.s. military has been involved in numerous conflicts during that period and because the records held by the National Archives were described as of 1995. There are, almost surely, captured records that have not yet been turned over to the u.s. National Archives, but the ones that have been transferred provide a sufficient sample for our purposes.

The most important bodies of captured documents that the u.s. National Archives holds are: captured German documents, now mostly on film, with the originals in Germany; captured Polish and Russian documents, which have been returned, also, with film retained; captured Italian and Japanese documents, also on film; captured North Korean documents; film of captured North Vietnamese documents; and paper and microfiche of documents captured in Grenada. Let us look briefly at several of these.

The story of the World War II German, Polish, and Russian documents is familiar to archivists. Basically, the u.s. Army seized both records of the Reich and records that the Reich had seized from others, such as Polish and Russian records. Most of this material was shipped to Washington, D.C., was used by military and civilian intelligence services, and was eventually turned over to the National Archives. The preponderance were government records, but included a little of everything—bits of the records of the Reich's train service, for example; records of the municipal court at Hamburg; records of some official cultural institutions such as the Deutsche Akademie München; Nazi Party records; holdings from at least two archives; private papers of individuals; records of private enterprises; and Eva Braun's diary and photo albums. There was a lot of paper, but also huge battle maps, motion picture reels, sound recordings, and tens of thousands of photographs.[9]

The North Korean situation was different. Here, the seized records include, in the words of the 1995 *Guide to Federal Records in the National Archives of the United States,* "records of North Korean military, governmental, and party organizations," "343 reels of North Korean and Communist Chinese films on the Korean War," and library materials: bulletins, books, periodicals, and newspapers. The 1974 edition of the *Guide* noted that these materials are "mostly in the Russian and Korean languages."[10]

The captured records from Vietnam are different again. The military took papers from soldiers captured or killed on the battlefield; these documents were taken to a collection center called the Combined Document Exploitation Center where they were sorted and those deemed significant were filmed. Although the military told the National Archives that "documents judged to be of little or no intelligence value were passed on to South Vietnamese representatives without further processing," the existing film includes a mélange: battle orders, military communications, love letters, photographs, diaries. "After filming," says the finding aid, "all captured document originals were returned to the Republic of Vietnam"—in other words, captured North Vietnamese documents were given to South Vietnam.[11]

---

9 *Guide to the National Archives of the United States* (Washington, D.C.: U.S. Government Printing Office, 1974). Record Group 242, National Archives Collection of Foreign Records seized 1941–. The description of this record group notes the property issues, stating, "Some of the material in this record group (whether available on microfilm or in its original form) is of private origin. The fact of its seizure does not necessarily divest the original owners of literary property rights in them."

10 *Guide to Federal Records in the National Archives of the United States* (Washington, D.C.: U.S. Government Printing Office, 1995). The description of the Korean holdings is fuller in the 1974 edition.

11 Special List 60, Captured North Vietnamese Documents of the Combined Document Exploitation Center. (Washington, D.C.: National Archives and Records Administration, 1993). These records are part of Record Group 472, Records of the United States Forces in Southeast Asia, 1950–1975.

The Grenada records, seized during military operations on the Caribbean island of Grenada in October 1983, are principally records of government ministries and the Communist party. Like the materials seized in Korea, some of these items seem to be of questionable military or intelligence value, such as projection prints of Soviet feature films, newsreels, and documentaries that were seized from the Soviet Embassy in Grenada.[12] The bulk of the paper records were returned to Grenada.

These, then, are the categories of records: government records, records from governments other than the one in the conflict, records from political parties, holdings from archives, records from cultural institutions, records from local governments (German court records, for example), records of private businesses and organizations, documents from individuals with official connections to combatants, private letters of political figures or their families (Eva Braun), and private letters from ordinary people (love letters of soldiers).

Turning from international conflicts to civil wars and rebellions, are the seized materials different in character? Let us look at three examples.

First, the u.s. Civil War. If the u.s. Civil War of the mid-nineteenth century is any indication, seized records are much the same. They include official records of the Confederacy, records of local and business organizations, and currency taken from killed and captured Confederate soldiers, among others.[13]

Second, the Kurds in northern Iraq. During the Gulf War in 1991, the Kurds seized an estimated eighteen tons of Iraqi records. Now deposited at the University of Colorado, they include the records of the Iraqi secret police in the three northern Kurdish governates of Iraq, records of the Baath party from the region, records of local government offices, and records of regional offices of the central government in Baghdad. Published reports do not indicate that there were personal papers among the seized documents, but it is hard to believe that there were none.[14]

---

12 *Guide* 1995. Record Group 242 and (for films) Record Group 306, Records of the United States Information Agency.

13 *Guide* 1995. Record Group 109, War Department Collection of Confederate Records; and Record Group 365, Treasury Department Collection of Confederate Records.

14 There are many sources of information on the records seized by the Kurds. Samples of the records are on the website of the Iraq Foundation and the Iraq Research and Documentation Project, http://www.fas.harvard.edu/~irdp/ (accessed 9 June 2005); Bruce Montgomery, "The Iraqi Secret Police Files: The Documentary Record of the Anfal Genocide," *Archivaria* 52 (2001): 69; Human Rights Watch press releases on Iraqi records

Third, the 1991 Russian coup attempt. The Russian government seized the records of the coup plotters that attempted to overthrow Mikhail Gorbachev in August 1991. In 1993, I watched the Russian archivists sort the records that had been taken from the Russian White House after the rebellion was crushed. Every type of document was included: official records, printed materials, personal letters, photographs, and stacks of publications.

This is admittedly a very selective sample of two cases with records in the hands of outright conflict winners (the u.s. and Russian governments) and a protected group (the Kurds). Furthermore, in the u.s. and Russian cases, the records stayed in the country, although in the United States they were moved from their place of origin to Washington, D.C. In the case of the Iraqi materials, they were taken completely out of the country. Still, assuming that this very selective sample is representative of the types of materials seized, civil wars and rebellions result in the seizure of at least as many and varied types of records as international conflicts.

Seizure and the Laws of War

Having now determined that the types of documents seized in conflicts cover the full range of archival materials, what are the rules that govern seizure?

International law, like many national systems, has a hierarchy of authority. The highest authorities are international conventions (treaties). Below the conventions are, in descending order, international custom as evidence of a general practice accepted as law, general principles of law recognized by civilized nations, judicial decisions, and the teachings of the most highly qualified specialists.[15] The law of war has been codified in a series of international conventions.[16] Seizure provisions are regulated in the

---

at http://www.hrw.org/press, see especially the release of 10 April 2003 and the paper, "Bureaucracy of Repression: The Iraqi Government in Its Own Words," http://www.hrw.org/reports/1994/iraq/TEXT.htm (accessed 9 June 2005).

15 The International Law of War Association has a Law of War home page with a useful basic tutorial on the law of war, http://www.lawofwar.org. See, for example, 2.2 "The Sources of the Law of War (Statute of the ICJ [International Court of Justice])," www.lawofwar.org/outline/html (accessed 9 June 2005).

16 The Yale University Law School's Avalon Project has all the international conventions on the law of war on its website, http://www.yale.edu/lawweb/avalon/lawofwar/lawwar.htm.

- 1907 Hague IV Convention respecting the Laws and Customs of War on Land (while naval bombardment certainly causes losses of property, including records and personal papers, it does not normally lead to seizure);
- 1907 Hague V Convention on the Rights and Duties of Neutral Powers and Persons in Case of War on Land;
- 1949 Geneva III Convention relative to the Treatment of Prisoners of War; and
- 1949 Geneva IV Convention for the Protection of Civilians in Time of War (for personal property).

In addition, the 1954 Hague Convention for the Protection of Cultural Property in the Event of Armed Conflict governs the treatment of historical archives and manuscripts, among other types of cultural property.

The treaty rules on seizure of documents vary, depending both on the status of the possessor of the document and the use to be made of the documents by the seizing power. The possessors of documents being seized may be military units, governmental offices that are not military, officials of the combatant government, local governments, prisoners of war, medical and educational institutions, cultural institutions, archives, neutral parties, and non-combatant individuals. We will look at the Convention provisions governing each of these.

RECORDS OF THE STATE

The most important treaty regarding seizure of documents is the 1907 Hague IV Convention respecting the Laws and Customs of War on Land. The regulations are set out in the Annex to the Convention. In Article 53 of the Annex, the Convention permits an army of occupation to "take possession of . . . all movable property belonging to the State which may be used for military operations." Battle maps, battle plans, organization charts, orders, architectural drawings of fortifications, engineering documents for weapons systems, plus any other government document that could be used by the military to disrupt the organization of the enemy are included here.

This sweeping permission is somewhat limited by Article 23 of the same Annex, which provides that:

> It is especially forbidden . . . to destroy or seize the enemy's property unless such destruction or seizure be imperatively demanded by the necessities of war.

The critical phrase here is "demanded by the necessities of war." As we all know, in the time of war there are many necessities.

The provisions of the 1907 Convention are echoed in the 1949 Geneva IV Convention for the Protection of Civilians in Time of War, which states in Article 53:

> Any destruction by the Occupying Power of real or personal property belonging individually or collectively to private persons, or to the State, or to other public authorities, or to social or cooperative organizations, is prohibited, except where such destruction is rendered absolutely necessary by military operations.

Interestingly, this 1949 article does not refer to seizure, only to destruction.

In addition to seizing records for use in military operations, combatants may seize records for use by the occupation government. When a territory is occupied, the occupying power needs the records of the former government to enable the new government to function. In the 1907 Hague IV Convention's Annex Article 43, these administrative needs are recognized:

> The authority of the legitimate power having in fact passed into the hands of the occupant, the latter shall take all the measures in his power to restore, and ensure, as far as possible, public order and safety, while respecting, unless absolutely prevented, the laws in force in the country.

It is reasonable to assume from this that the occupying power can use the records of the state as needed to govern the territory occupied. Furthermore, it is reasonable to assume that such records as needed for governance are to be seized for use, not for removal.

RECORDS OF PARTICULAR PUBLIC INSTITUTIONS

The 1907 Hague IV Convention also specifies the protection of the property of certain types of public institutions. Annex Article 56 states:

> The property of municipalities, that of institutions dedicated to religion, charity and education, the arts and sciences, even when State property, shall be treated as private property. All seizure of, destruction or willful damage done to institutions of this character, historic monuments, works of art and science is forbidden.

This provision has two complications: first, how is private property to be treated and, second, what if the property of municipalities is needed for the administration of the municipality? It seems, from the provisions cited above on use by occupying powers, that municipal property can be seized and used for administrative purposes. If it is not needed for administration, the question then is which rules govern the seizure of private property.

RECORDS OF PRIVATE INSTITUTIONS AND PRIVATE PAPERS OF INDIVIDUALS

The 1907 Hague IV Convention treats private property by stating flatly in Article 46:

> Private property cannot be confiscated.

In Article 47 it says adamantly:

> Pillage is formally forbidden.

These blanket provisions have limits, however. In the 1949 Geneva IV Convention's Article 5, the rights of persons believed to be posing a danger to the occupying forces are limited:

> Where in the territory of a Party to the conflict, the latter is satisfied that an individual protected person is definitely suspected of or engaged in activities hostile to the security of the State, such individual person shall not be entitled to claim such rights and privileges under the present Convention as would, if exercised in the favour of such individual person, be prejudicial to the security of such State.
>
> Where in occupied territory an individual protected person is

detained as a spy or saboteur, or as a person under definite suspicion of activity hostile to the security of the Occupying Power, such person shall, in those cases where absolute military security so requires, be regarded as having forfeited rights of communication under the present Convention.

In other words, if the person (or an institution treated as a person in terms of the Convention) is "suspected or engaged in" hostile activities, his private property can be confiscated. That would also apply to the particular public institutions covered by the 1907 Hague IV's Annex Article 56 discussed above.

PAPERS OF PRISONERS OF WAR

The 1949 Geneva III Convention Relative to the Treatment of Prisoners of War says in Article 18:

All effects and articles of personal use, except arms, horses, military equipment and military documents, shall remain in the possession of prisoners of war. . . . At no time should prisoners of war be without identity documents.

The definitional problem here is what constitutes "military documents."

RECORDS OF NEUTRAL PARTIES

The 1907 Hague V Convention covers the rights and duties of neutral powers. Its first article declares that the territory of neutral powers is inviolable. Because the territory occupied by an embassy or consulate is the territory of that State, the property within that embassy or consulate is likewise exempt from seizure.[17]

SUMMARY

- If the occupying power needs state records for military operations, it can seize them.

---

17 However, a staple of war photography is a picture of embassy staff, often in the backyard of the embassy, hastily burning records as troops advance, clearly fearful of seizure. United Nations compounds, too, are often invaded and records are destroyed.

- If the occupying power needs state records for the administration of occupied territory, it can seize them.
- If the records are those of municipalities, religious, charitable, educational, and institutions of arts and sciences, they should be immune from seizure unless the persons employed by the institution are "definitely suspected of or engaged in activities hostile to the security of the State." Records of municipalities, however, are probably liable for seizure for the purpose of administering the municipality.
- If you are a private person or a private business or organization definitely suspected of or engaged in activities hostile to the security of the State, your records and personal papers can be seized.
- If you are a private person or business or organization that is not engaged in hostile activities, your records and papers are immune from seizure.
- If you are a prisoner of war, your "military documents" can be taken from you, but all other personal documents are yours. You are specifically authorized to keep your identity papers.
- If the records are those of a neutral party, they are immune from seizure.

Archives

But what about archives *per se?* The Hague IV Convention of 1907 does not use the word "archives." It is, perhaps, fair to read "archives" into Annex Article 56's "property of municipalities, that of institutions dedicated to religion, charity and education, the arts and sciences, even when State property," but it is not explicit. Furthermore, archives are both cultural and administrative property and fit somewhat awkwardly into a purely cultural definition. The 1954 Hague Convention for the Protection of Cultural Property in the Event of Armed Conflict solved this ambiguity by including in the definition of cultural property to be protected "manuscripts . . . and important collections of books or archives" and buildings such as "depositories of archives." However, its Article 3, item 2, notes that the obligation to protect such property "may be waived only in cases where military necessity imperatively requires such a waiver."

Can we stretch the definition in the 1954 Hague Convention to cover current records and personal papers? Probably not. While we could argue that letters in the possession of a soldier are "manuscripts" and the records of the secret police are "archives," the intent of the 1954 Convention is clearly to protect noncurrent historical materials, particularly those housed in a facility designated as an historical archive.[18]

CIVIL WAR, REBELLION, AND THE LAW OF WAR

The final question is whether these same laws of war can be applied in the cases of civil war and rebellion. The four Geneva Conventions of 1949 extended the principles of international humanitarian law to "non-international armed conflicts" by including in each of the four an identical Article 3 that binds the parties to apply humanitarian principles and says that the parties "should further endeavor to bring into force, by means of special agreements, all or part of the other provisions of the present Convention." The 1954 Geneva Convention on Cultural Property echoed this provision. The seizures of civil war and rebellion are, therefore, covered by the post-war Conventions.

Reality Is What's on the Shelf

A sound archival adage is, "Reality is what's on the shelf." Clearly, the seized records that archivists have on their shelves and what the laws suggest archives would have on their shelves are two different things. Why this disparity? What are the forces that result in armies seizing more records than the laws of war prescribe? What makes armies go beyond the records with military information or those that are needed to administer occupied territories? International laws generally codify the results of experience and the counsels of prudence. I treat your prisoners of war decently because I want you to treat my captured soldiers decently. I leave the property of municipalities alone because as

---

18 There are many publications on the 1954 Convention. See, especially, Patrick J. Boylan, *Review of the Convention for the Protection of Cultural Property in the Event of Armed Conflict* (The Hague Convention of 1954), published by UNESCO, 1993. It has a helpful bibliography and reprints both the Convention and other pertinent international agreements.

an occupying power I will need that property to run the country. Those principles are reasonably clear and easy to explain to soldiers.

Experience and prudence appear different when documents are involved. Experience says that documents are usually simply swept up as the army moves forward. Prudence says that you take any document that might possibly help you or harm the opposing force. International custom is evidence of a general practice accepted as law; seizing every document in sight is an international custom; therefore, is it evidence of a general practice accepted as law? In effect, we have a conflict between the international law as stated in the Conventions and the law derived from custom. What propels this divergence?

As we all know, records and personal papers are very special forms of property. In wartime conditions, their peculiar characteristics are even more distinctive, for a number of reasons:

First, government records, in particular, are highly political. A friend of mine reports that when she asked a museum official why there was no significant outcry over the reported destruction of archives in Iraq, the museum official said simply, "Archives are too political." The impulse of war leadership to obtain the official records of the opposition state in order to understand how it operates is understandable and probably irresistible.

Second—and a new feature of war starting in the late twentieth century—human rights groups may urge the government to protect or seize records to be used in future prosecutions. Human Rights Watch did just that on 10 April 2003, when it sent a letter to u.s. Secretary of State Colin Powell and u.s. Secretary of Defense Donald Rumsfeld, urging coalition forces to "prevent Iraqi government offices from being ransacked because government documents will undoubtedly be key evidence in future war crimes trials." (Human Rights Watch also noted the need for the records to enable Iraqi citizens to assert their human rights.)[19] BBC World/Middle East reported on 4 May 2003 that Marianne Birthler, head of the German federal agency responsible for the Stasi archives, urged the Iraqis to "secure documents from Saddam Hussein's ousted regime as soon as possible so crimes perpetrated under his leadership can be brought to justice," adding that the

---

19 Human Rights Watch press release, 10 April 2003, http://www.hrw.org/press/2003/04/iraq041003.htm (accessed 9 June 2005).

"Americans should aid the Iraqis in the preservation of such documents."[20] While these two demands are for protection, not seizure, the most likely scenario would be to put the records in the custody of the occupation forces, at least until such a time as an Iraqi successor regime is able to assume control of the government and its archives.

Third, records and personal papers as property concepts are unknown to the general public—and equally unknown to soldiers. Many if not most soldiers are unfamiliar with basic recordkeeping operations and cannot easily judge what is a record that should be seized for military needs. Add to that the urgency of wartime activity, the language problems of soldiers unable to read the records they are encountering, and the impulse to sweep up all documents and sort them out later is well near irresistible. The language problem also holds true for the papers taken from prisoners of war, although it is surely within the capability of soldiers to determine that a document is a photograph (mother, lover, child), rather than a military order.

Fourth, during military activity it is extremely difficult for troops to determine which persons are truly non-combatants and which are, in the words of the 1949 Geneva IV Convention, "definitely suspected of or engaged in activities hostile to the security of the State." Consequently, it is likely that soldiers will take from a large number of persons as many papers as they can find.

Fifth, if, in the case of rebellion or civil war, the aim is to separate from the current country—not to occupy and govern but to secede—the practical need for records such as those of municipal governments (other than those of municipalities in the secession territory) does not apply. In other words, there is no need for the rebels to protect these records.

Conclusion

The laws of war as applied to seizure of documents are complex. For a variety of reasons, they are mostly ignored. The Conventions, although carefully developed, do not work well in this area. Armies seize every type of document they encounter, and they are likely to continue to do

20 *BBC World/Middle East,* 4 May 2003, http://news.bbc.co.uk/2/hi/middle_east/2999517.stm (accessed 9 June 2005).

so, irrespective of what the Conventions say.[21] Insisting on adherence to complicated rules and fine distinctions will go nowhere. This reality suggests three tentative conclusions.

1. Simplify the Rules

Archivists should develop a bottom-line position for military units to use in educating troops on the rules regarding seizure of current records and personal papers. The following elements are a start:

- No personal pillage.
- Turn over to military or occupation authorities as soon as possible all documents seized, whether records or personal papers.
- No destruction of seized documents.[22]
- After analysis, return all documents not required for military or intelligence needs, either to the individual, the institution, or the successor state.
- No seizure of records of neutral parties, such as embassies and United Nations establishments.
- No seizure of historical archives and manuscript collections.

Then, in the years after the hostilities cease, seized records should be moved into archival custody and, ultimately, be repatriated.

2. Acknowledge the Pressure to Seize for International Trials or Human Rights Protection

Since 1990, the world has seen the unprecedented development of international tribunals for the former Yugoslavia and Rwanda and the establishment of the International Criminal Court. Throughout this period, the international human rights community has repeatedly insisted that documents are critical to protect-

---

21 For a statement on the seizure of property in Iraq, see statement by Larry L. Lanzillotta, U.S. Principal Deputy Under-Secretary of Defense (Comptroller), before the House Financial Services Committee, Subcommittee on Oversight and Investigations, 14 May 2003, http://www.state.gov/e/eb/rls/rm/2003/20693pf.htm (accessed 9 June 2005).

22 In modern war, the records may be copied very quickly, as in Vietnam with the microfilming project, or now by scanning. This technological change does not affect the basic position that the original records should not be destroyed and should ultimately be returned.

ing the rights of individuals and to developing cases for the international justice machinery. As a result, during war and civil conflict, there is a renewed interest in securing records that would serve these two purposes. This type of seizure does not fit neatly under the provisions of the relevant Conventions.

The question is whether the need to seize records in order to protect human rights or to prosecute criminals trumps the laws of war. The Universal Declaration of Human Rights, adopted in 1948, is authority for seizure to protect the rights of individuals.[23] It prohibits "any State, group or person" from destroying human rights and freedoms; it is logical, then, to assume that actions taken to prevent such destruction—such as by seizing records that would otherwise be destroyed—are permitted.

The case of seizing records that may be needed for future criminal prosecution is different. Were the Kurds, for example, right to seize the documents of the Iraqi government in 1991, thus capturing evidence of the government's abuse of the Kurds? taking those documents out of the country? allowing third parties such as Human Rights Watch to use them, sharing them with the government of a State opposed to Iraq? If the answer is yes, the Kurds acted responsibly. What are the parameters in which such a seizure is legitimate?

If a government violates fundamental moral principles and attempts to keep such violations secret, people of conscience may decide to combat these activities by exposing them in public. One way to do that is to seize the documentation that would prove what the government did or is doing. This is, of course, a very slippery ethical slope, but that is true irrespective of whether the action occurs during a time of war or not; it is simply easier to seize documents when civil life is disrupted as it is during conflict.

The likelihood here is that the international criminal tribunals themselves will develop a body of law on the acceptability of documentary evidence. From that will flow the procedural requirements for admissibility, including the manner in which admissible records can be seized.

---

23 http://www.un.org/Overview/rights.html (accessed 9 June 2005).

3.   Recognizing the Complexity of Seizure Leads to the
     Complexity of Replevin

Archivists have generally discussed replevin in terms of government records being returned to the State or its successor. The art
and antiquities world has painfully learned over the past decade
that the return of property to private persons is necessary.
Archivists must understand that principle, too. While it is simple
to return all property captured from a territory to the government
of that territory and then place the burden on that government to
sort out the ownership, that may not be just. Why should the government receive the replevin of corporate records or private love
letters, for example, property it never had or had access to in the
first place?

Returns to non-government owners will not be simple. If, for
example, the United States had retained letters taken from soldiers
in Vietnam, how would it be best to return them to the writers?
Perhaps it would be possible to work with a non-governmental
organization in the country; perhaps UNESCO could play a role as a
broker, maintaining a list of materials eligible for return.

In the end, the documents of a state are inalienable and remain
subject to replevin without limitation. The international standards
of human rights protect the property interests of private citizens in
their documents. One day, perhaps far in the future, all seized documents, of any type, must go home. And the more we understand
about the conditions of seizure in the first place, the more responsible our temporary custody and eventual replevin will be.

18

SREBRENICA: A BALKAN TRAGEDY AND THE MAKING OF A DUTCH AFFAIR

Agnes E.M. Jonker

Setting the Scene

In 1993, the Dutch decided to send a battalion to the former Yugoslavia.[1] The troops left in 1994 on their peacekeeping mission: 600 lightly armed Dutch infantry forces took position in the Bosnian town of Srebrenica, an area designated as a "safe enclave" by the United Nations. Srebrenica, close to the border with Serbia, was an isolated area controlled by Muslims.

In the summer of 1995, Srebrenica, where tens of thousand civilians had taken refuge from earlier Serb offensives, became the scene of massacres. Dutch troops were powerless against the Bosnian-Serb forces that overran the enclave. On 11 July 1995, more than 7,500 Bosnian Muslim men and boys were missing, presumed dead.

In June 2003, the Dutch Parliament (*de Tweede Kamer*) debated—and this was probably the final parliamentary debate on the subject—the report of a parliamentary committee on the political aspects of the

---

1   A succinct account of events leading up to the conflict can be found at BBC History File, http://news.bbc.co.uk/hi/english/static/map/yugoslavia (accessed 16 June 2005).

decision to send out troops. After years of intensive discussions, only the role of the Minister of Foreign Affairs and the Minister of Defence during the months preceding the decision seemed to be of interest.[2] What, in fact, did they know at the time about NATO air support to the Dutch base, should Serb forces attack? And what about the lines of communication? Were members of government and the parliament well informed by the Minister of Defence on the scope of the Dutch mandate? Once again, reproaches were heard, directed to the minister of the day, Relus ter Beek: his picture of the mission had been too rosily tinted and the information to parliament on the risks of the mission had concealed the truth.

This debate reduced the tragedy of Srebrenica to a topic in terms of the political arena in 2003 where, in the intervening period, the tables have been turned: coalition parties, positions, and names have changed since 1995. The spectacle turned out to be a rather smooth political ending of a Dutch affair—empty benches in Parliament, no public in the strangers' gallery. The Minister of Defence dared to say aloud things unsaid until then, such as: the troops were not to blame. "Feeling of guilt evaporated," wrote a daily newspaper.[3] To the victims in Srebrenica, the massacres and the helpless Dutch battalion will remain a tragedy for many years to come. Srebrenica is Europe's worst single act of mass murder since World War II.

To the beholder, it is hard to imagine that in 2002 Srebrenica was in the middle of public debate in the Netherlands and was a deeply oppressive burden on Dutch Prime Minister Wim Kok. Indeed, the Dutch government resigned in April 2002, one week after the report of the Netherlands Institute for War Documentation (NIOD)— *Srebrenica, a Safe Area*—was published.[4] "The international commu-

2   June 2003. The Dutch government was close to sending troops to southern Iraq; after
    Somalia, Afghanistan, Macedonia, a new peacekeeping mission was in sight.

3   NRC-Handelsblad, 19 June 2003.

4   J.C.H. Blom, P. Romijn, et al., *Srebrenica: een "veilig gebied." Reconstructie, achtergronden en
    analysesvan de val van een Safe Area* (Amsterdam: Boom, 2002) [vol. I-II-III-IV]. English
    version: *Srebrenica—a "Safe" Area—Reconstruction, Background, Consequences and Analyses of
    the Fall of a Safe Area.* See also J.C.H Blom, "Politiek versus historie. NIOD maakt onder-
    scheid moraal en wetenschap," *Academische Boekengids* 36 (Amsterdam: Amsterdam
    University Press, 2002), http://www.academischeboekengids.nl/abg/do.php?a=show_visitor_
    artikel&id=9 (accessed 29 April 2004); Peter Bootsma, *Srebrenica. Het officiële rapport
    samengevat* (Amsterdam: Boom, 2002). The NIOD Srebrenica website is at http://
    www.srebrenica.nl (English and Bosnian/Serbian/Croation versions are available).

nity has failed to protect the people in the UN safe areas [in Bosnia]," Kok said in parliament.[5] The point of departure of this essay is that NIOD-enquiry.

From an archival perspective, the *Srebrenica* report is something other than an answer to questions on what exactly happened before the resolution to send troops was made and what exactly happened in Srebrenica. Since 1995 these two topics—first, the decision and the decision-making and second, the actions or non-actions of the Dutch battalion—have continued to arouse huge, and at times very emotional, public interest.

Before looking at the archival issues, I will outline the birth and aftermath of this enquiry, the NIOD, its sources, and some results of the enquiry. Then I will focus on the archival issues raised by this investigation, the reaction of three public agencies statutorily involved with archival procedures, and some other consequences. My position is that of an outsider; I was in no way involved in the research. Working at the University of Amsterdam, my interest in this subject is that of an archivist.

The Enquiry and the Institute

After the tragedy in July 1995, the Dutch government called for an international enquiry. Why did the Dutch battalion fail to help the civilians in Srebrenica? What went wrong in the chain of command and in the co-ordination of the UN Protection Force (UNPROFOR)? The request for an international enquiry was unsuccessful.[6] However, Dutch society somehow persisted in investigating what happened in Srebrenica; the incomplete and chaotic—and at times even clumsy—

---

5   In no way was the resignation based on the contents of these reports. Kok's attitude may be considered a symbolic step, expressing the inability of the international community—"a fiction," in the words of Ignatieff—to carry through humanitarian intervention. See Michael Ignatieff, *Empire Lite. Nation-building in Bosnia, Kosovo and Afghanistan* (London: Penguin, 2003), 2; and Mark Bovens, *The Quest for Responsibility, Accountability and Citizenship in Complex Organisations* (Cambridge: Cambridge University Press, 1998), ch. 4.

6   Some years later though, in January 1999, the UN General Assembly decided to investigate the fall of Srebrenica (A/RES 53/35): "The Fall of Srebrenica," November 1999 (A/54/549). And by the end of 2003, the government of the Serb-run republic in Bosnia had set up a commission to investigate the atrocities. The commission was given until Spring 2004 to complete its work.

information on the matter, heightened political dispute and general indignation. Rumour had it that things were hushed up by the ministries and by the military; but were they themselves well informed? Did they tell the public all there was to tell? The Dutch were eager to hear the view of an independent outside party on the matter.

Political pressure at the time was the incentive for the Dutch government—the first Kok administration—to propose that the NIOD investigate what had happened. That was in August 1996. At the end of that year, in December 1996, the NIOD agreed: conditions were all settled; academic freedom was guaranteed as well as access to primary sources in the Netherlands; no impediment could stop the researchers from using public records. Part of the deal, as required by NIOD, was that no information on the subject was to be released to the outside world during the project—there would be complete silence until the final results of the research project.

Three ministries—of Foreign Affairs, of Defence, and of Education, Culture and Science—commissioned NIOD to collect and analyse relevant sources from a historical point of view, an investigation in order to reconstruct and analyse accurately what happened before, during, and after the fall of the safe area.[7] No further questions were dictated. It was up to the researchers to design their own project, to define their own topics.[8]

The history of the current moment—a subject and research questions that matter to present-day society, politicians, and the public—is not the kind of work, nor the conditions, which NIOD researchers are used to. NIOD is a research institute as well as an archives. The Institute's task concerns historical research exclusively on World War II in relation to the Netherlands; "Srebrenica" is the first project in the history of NIOD on a subject other than World War II.[9]

7   Blom, Romijn, et al., vol. I, g.
8   Tweede Kamer der Staten-Generaal, vergaderjaar 1996–1997 ('s-Gravenhage: Sdu Uitgevers, 1996), 25 069, nr.1.
9   After NIOD, some kind of investigation was commissioned three more times. See for example, Blom, Romijn, et al., vol. I: 28; Tweede Kamer der Staten-Generaal, vergaderjaar 1999–2000 ('s-Gravenhage: Sdu Uitgevers, 2000), 26 454, nr. 8; and Blom, Romijn, et al., vol. III: 3057 fn. 203. The last one was the parliamentary committee 2002, mentioned above.

What sources?

The research approach of the NIOD is the use and analysis of public records at home and abroad, interviews and questionnaires, documentary evidence, books, newspapers, and audio and video material.

Public Records in the Netherlands. In the Netherlands, researchers were allowed unrestricted access to public records, even to records classified as "top secret" (though reference to these top secret files was subject to restrictions based on national and international law).[10] At the time the investigation started, the researchers found out that the Ministry of Defence and the Royal Army needed considerable time to arrange their records.

Public Records and Other Records Outside the Netherlands. These were used as far as access was allowed. The French government, for example, was not eager to cooperate. It was hard as well to get access to Balkan records, partly because of suspicions about this enquiry. For example,

- the Dutch were to blame for the massacres, says the Bosnian-Serb version;
- the "independence" of the researcher and the autonomy of the Institute are difficult concepts to comprehend in a post-Communist society; the project was considered to be a set-up to plead in favour of the Dutch battalion; and
- to Bosnian-Serbs, the researchers were in league with the International Criminal Tribunal for the former Yugoslavia.

In addition, records of international and non-governmental organizations were consulted, including those of NATO, the UN, and United Nations High Commissioner for Refugees.

Interviews and Questionnaires. At home and abroad, the Dutch government relieved civil servants of compliance with the Official Secret Act: they were allowed to answer all kinds of questions. However, the verbatim accounts of these interviews had to be kept secret. Access to the verbatim accounts of the operational debriefing of

---

10 Such as FOIA (Wet openbaarheid bestuur art. 10 en 11), Wet op de justitiële documentatie, Wet op de inlichtingen- en veiligheidsdiensten.

the Dutch battalion (Dutchbat)—in Zagreb (July 1995) and in Assen (Autumn 1995)—was not allowed. The consent of the individuals concerned was the only key to opening these confidential files.[11] Most of the Bosnian Serb-military, including General Ratko Mladic and war leader Radovan Karadzic, showed no interest in being interviewed.

Results of the NIOD Enquiry

In the end, researchers interviewed more than 900 people, consulted hundreds of archives, and thousands of books and newspaper articles. After five-and-a-half years, NIOD presented its report on 10 April 2002. Some of the main results were:

- In general, *peacekeeping* forces had no chance at all in the Balkan whirlpool. There had been no opportunity for the Western world to intervene in the complex Balkan conflict; the war was an autonomous process, a deliberate act of political leaders in the region.
- For the Dutch government of the day, humanitarian motives paved the way to the Balkans—without foreseeing the impossibility of the mission. After the event, it remains questionable whether humanitarian motives can be a favourable companion for a peace-keeping mission to succeed.
- Dutchbat was ill-prepared for the job: communication with their Canadian and U.S. military predecessors failed, the mandate was not fully known, and blind faith in air support from the Allies was unjustified.
- The massacre of thousands was out of the sight of Dutchbat. However, they did witness the killing of hundreds of Muslims. Their reports, however, had no consequences, because communication failed. Moreover, the men and women of Dutchbat were struggling for their own survival (e.g., no fuel, no fresh food since May).

---

11 Blom, Romijn, et al., vol. I:16–17.

- After the fall of Srebrenica, Dutchbat evacuated civilians, in cooperation with Bosnian-Serbian forces, knowing that their destiny was uncertain. Dutch soldiers did not offer any resistance which might have prevented more bloodshed.
- The Royal Army command deliberately held back information from the Minister of Defence circumventing any difficult and unpleasant issues.

The Archival Issues

NIOD: "RECORDS MANAGEMENT IS A HINDRANCE."[12]

Most of the time, historians enjoy the advantages of well-arranged and described non-current records, deposited in the care of an archival institute. To investigate in the record creator's office, however, is a different task, far more complicated. The NIOD researchers considered their experience with current records as "chaotic": incomplete files, lack of finding aids, and even some material with no arrangement at all. It was difficult for them to find their way around those archives still in custody of the creator. According to NIOD, the (poor) quality of records management was more of a hindrance than a help and caused a serious delay in the course of the project. (It should be noted that, notwithstanding these hindrances, NIOD did accomplish its research successfully.)

Proper records management, which is legally required by the Public Records Act 1995, is often neglected, NIOD noticed.[13] Although troops in the middle of a battlefield may have a valid excuse for neglecting records management, other public agencies do not.[14] Concerning records management, NIOD concluded (and these were just some of its conclusions):

---

12 "Archieven," Blom, Romijn, et al., vol. III:3225–3260.
13 Blom, Romijn, et al., vol. I:15. At times, the NIOD report cannot distinguish between "archival records" and "collection of documents," the latter being archival records as well.
14 Blom, Romijn, et al., vol. I:15–16.

- The Ministry of Defence and its agencies lack records management standards; diversity reigns.[15]
- Rules and procedures on the records of military missions—for the army as well as for the air force—were not issued until after the fall of Srebrenica.[16]
- All the records of Dutchbat in the Srebrenica enclave were destroyed before the troops left, a non-procedural act that created a serious information gap.[17]
- The incompleteness of army records is worsened by a "rigorous" disposition policy.[18]

One can imagine how different professionals reacted to that. Information professionals (records managers and archivists) scrutinized these conclusions, historians knew all this already, and politicians could make their headlines—in the end everyone agreed: poorly organised records management is a curse to democracy; information gaps cannot be tolerated. NIOD scored this point. Indeed, there were reasons to be worried (though we have to keep in mind that, for example, destroying records is not in itself illegal). So the question is: was NIOD right about missing files and incomplete duplicate files, about files found by chance, surprising potpourris of records, rigorous disposition practices, and hidden personal papers? Before looking at these issues, I will consider some comments on the report by three public agencies with statutory responsibilities in archival procedures.

Reaction of Three Public Agencies

1.   THE COUNCIL OF CULTURE: RETENTION SCHEDULE REVISITED

The Council of Culture (COC) is the statutory advisory board to the Dutch government on issues of cultural policy. The COC (usually) presents recommendations following a request from the government, for example, on appraisal and disposition of archival records.

---

15 Blom, Romijn, et al., vol. III:3235.
16 Ibid.
17 Ibid.
18 Ibid.

The COC was shocked by NIOD's conclusions on records management at several defence agencies. On 26 April 2002, they asked the government to immediately stop the destruction of records of the Ministry of Defence and of all Defence agencies. This request did not imply any unauthorized destruction; that was, according to COC, not at issue. The main issue for COC was the growing awareness of the political relevance of several categories of records on military missions ("militaire operatiën"); to the COC, the NIOD report shed a new light on appraisal and disposition. COC wanted to revise and broaden Defence draft schedules under consideration.[19] Defence records schedules—some recently approved—were updated in 2003 and adjusted in conformity with the "new" perception.

2. NATIONAL ARCHIVES: "FREEZE"

The National Archives banned the disposition of all Defence records. The freeze lasted from 2 May to 19 June 2002 and burdened the organization with an estimated six tons of paper per week, not to mention the storage problems associated with electronic records.

3. THE STATE ARCHIVAL INSPECTORATE

The incompleteness, or supposed incompleteness, of Royal Army records drew the attention of the State Archival Inspectorate in particular.[20] An investigation into records management practice in several Army sections was requested.

Other Consequences

THE ROYAL ARMY ARCHIVES

In July 2002, the Royal Army asked consultants to investigate records management during the years 1992–1996, in order to confirm or refute

---

19 The retention schedule in use dated back to 1969 and was last revised in 1987.
20 Blom, Romijn, et al., vol. III: 3234–3242.

the NIOD allegations on Army sections' recordkeeping practices. In what ways did these practices conflict or conform with the 1995 Public Records Act?

CONSEQUENCES FOR THE ROYAL ARMY

The report by the consultants differentiated some of the NIOD conclusions, clarified some misunderstandings, and found out that specified records had not been destroyed unauthorized. In the eyes of NIOD, a "rigorous destruction policy," in fact, comprises routine disposition procedures, following retention schedules. Willful destruction had not been the case. However, in general—though in rather euphemistic terms—the recordkeeping failures in the sections investigated were confirmed. The failures related to both the macro-level and the micro-level: fragmentized and incomplete archives, weak procedures or scarcely any records management rules, and employees without the required level of qualification as a record professional.

CONSEQUENCES FOR THE MINISTRY OF DEFENCE

The Ministry of Defence also asked consultants to investigate the criticised records management practices. The consultants confirmed the inadequacy of records management at the Ministry of Defence, as noted by NIOD. The consequences of disfunctioning can be serious, they warned: efficiency, accountability, and cultural value are at risk. Records management is the responsibility of senior management, for whom, in general, it seems to lack priority even though it is part of the primary business process.

What next?

According to the Public Records Act, the Ministry of Defence had to produce new rules, and in September 2002, those were accepted. In order to improve records management, implementation of these rules is of growing concern. A task force called "Delta-plan"—named after the gigantic sea-defence construction in the Netherlands—is orchestrating the long march across agencies, from the basement to the top, aiming to change records management attitudes for the good. Part of the march is the introduction of a standard for records management, integrating paper and electronic records.

For all the projects coordinated by Delta-plan, 40 million Euro are available (2003–2007).

No Conclusions, Some Comments

This Dutch affair has not yet ended; it will be another 20 years or more before other information is available, and access to other records allowed. Therefore, I can only summarize and comment on some of the issues in the archival domain, the political domain, and the research domain.

Archival Domain

- Disposition schedules of military missions are being reconsidered from the perspective of (political) accountability. This expresses a changing perception on appraisal.
- In several army sections, commented the consultants, active records management does not fit in with corporate culture and context. This sounds to me rather laconic (ironic?), though it is a serious matter. As a matter of fact, there is a part of the regulated public sector that lacks enthusiasm for active records management. One has to keep in mind, however, that "neglectful records management"—that is, the power not to make records—or "agreed disorder" are ways to escape accountability.
- The Delta-plan for 2003–2007 is paved with good intentions. Can this project be successful in the context of budget cuts? In the next few years, around 10% of Defence Ministry employees, some 11,000 people, are going to be laid off.

POLITICAL DOMAIN

- How does a research project like NIOD affect the political debate? It is said that by commissioning NIOD, the government has bought time, time to prevent the explosive issue from becoming a political hot potato. In that way, the "independent" research helped put off the evil hour for the politicians in charge.

RESEARCH DOMAIN

- The act of commissioning an independent institute has, in itself, had more political impact than the research resulting from that act, concluded NIOD some months after publication of the report.[21] So maybe the question is whether independent historical research (history of the present) represents a substantial contribution to a public debate dominated by the media. Shades of meaning fade away against opinions, headlines, and the political agenda.

One final question: *What, in fact, is an accountable government in the heat of public debate?*

---

21 NIOD director Hans Blom, "De vraag of de historische beschrijvingen en analyses uit het rapport juist zijn, is nog maar nauwelijks besproken," *Academische Boekengids* (Amsterdam: Amsterdam University Press, December 2002), 5. "De politiek trekt zich toch niet veel van zo'n onderzoek aan" *Academische Boekengids* (Amsterdam: Amsterdam University Press, December 2002), 7.

Modelling the Future

19

THE RELEVANCE OF ARCHIVAL
PRACTICE WITHIN "E-DEMOCRACY"

Claire Johnson

It seems that "e-democracy," as identified by the current U.K. government, is at present a rather ill-defined initiative that raises some fundamental concerns for archivists and records managers alike. The digital world, with its demands and foibles, now encroaches upon us from practically every side. Whether we are entranced by the capabilities of the technology itself, concerned by the economics that dictate access to technology or the inherent usability of information that is delivered digitally, there is no escape from some part of current debates. What is the relevance of archival practice within the emergent arena of e-democracy? In particular, what is the contribution that records management[1] makes to ensure the delivery of high-quality information to individuals? Will the current reliance on web-based resources provide a valid medium to secure official accountability, and how will individuals use the information to hold government to account? These strands are inter-related and provide a sample area for archivists to consider how what they do at present might be relevant to

---

1   "A field of management responsible for the efficient and systematic control of the creation, maintenance, use and disposition of records." BS/ISO 15489-1:2001, Information and Documentation–Records Management, Part 1: General, 3.

the emergent digital age and to the requirements for building digital repositories for both current and non-current information.

Governments across Europe are already beginning to implement e-democracy initiatives, but they do not sit naturally with other initiatives that are modernising the administrative aspects of information creation and dissemination. There is no pre-existing call from parliamentary lobbyists or civil liberties groups to develop e-democracy initiatives and much scepticism about moves towards changes in the apparatus for voting. The complex issue of ensuring integrity and authenticity in the electoral process will remain whatever technology is deployed.

This study relates directly to the key issue of how well records can be used "as a tool of government." Linked with this issue is the need to establish how well the constraints, opportunities, and limitations of official information are understood in order to scrutinize government objectively—whether or not they are in the digital domain.

From the perspective of an interested citizen, I am firmly convinced that there are definite advantages to some aspects of recent civil liberties-inspired legislation and the e-government initiative. As a "data subject," the Data Protection Act 1998 offers to uphold my rights to privacy of personal data in all media in a comprehensive fashion. The Freedom of Information Act 2000 and Freedom of Information (Scotland) Act 2002 require public authorities to reveal their activities, but it is less obvious that the e-democracy agenda, as presented by the current government, will provide a citizen with any demonstrable or direct advantage.

Web-based resources are not unique in providing heavily mediated information. It is apparent, however, to even the most casual user that the tools for providing structure in the information and records they contain are not often used to best advantage. This reduces the level of effective interaction between humans and the information systems they are interrogating and relates to another important theme, that of accountability. Currently, the digital world has a wide and interchangeable terminology, which includes such mysterious things as digital images, digital objects, and digital surrogates. Within the Humanities Advanced Technology Information Institute (HATII),[2] we are discovering the extent to which this diverse lexicon belies a level of

---

2 See www.hatii.arts.gla.ac.uk. The HATII research community includes both academics and practitioners from Archives Services and Computing Service of the University of

theoretical uncertainty about the nature of the objects with which we (as information managers) have to deal. If all digital objects have visible and invisible links, and these vary depending on who is questioning and what those questions are, is it possible to arrive at a conclusion about what is the official record, irrespective of how and by whom it is mediated?

In a networked digital environment, the issues increase in complexity and volume. How do we establish the essential attributes of the digital record in terms of such things as context and metadata or relationship to a physical object? The way in which information is presented to you, on either screen or paper, is conditioned by the material itself and the machine setting, software in use, output device, style sheets, and so forth, so our experience of the digital object is variable. The work of the u.k. National Archives and others has begun to explore this area. It is difficult to see, however, that current government forays into e-democracy and e-government are taking full cognisance of the complexities that are part of managing a networked digital environment.

How are archivists to establish (and show evidence of) trust in digital records in this rapidly changing environment? Undoubtedly, we need to develop a more comprehensive theoretical underpinning of our professional methodologies and better define the terminology to understand how these entities behave (irrespective of their provenance) so that the concepts behind e-democracy can mature. Stephen Harries[3] wrote about the specific challenges for the government to deliver a qualitatively improved service through its "Modernising Government" agenda and the role that the e-records programme at the u.k. National Archives is playing in maintaining the continuity of the archival resource.

As a records manager, the key question to answer is how well we, archivists and records managers, understand the relative values of applying our professional methodologies to the records, information and technology that seek to deliver an improved and extended democ-

---

Glasgow. They seek to address a range of issues in the field of digital and digitalised resources and also extend the work of the Effective Records Management project which produced its final report "No going back?" in 2000. The report is available at http:// www.gla.ac.uk/ERM/InfoStrat/ERM/DOCS/ERM-Final.pdf (accessed 23 June 2005).

3   Stephen Harries, "The End of 'Print to Paper,'" *ASLIB Update* 1:3 (June 2002): 46–47.

racy. New dynamics have become apparent that challenge our function as custodian of textual artefacts which constitute the collective memory of our society. There are, for example, emergent areas of study that explore the culture and politics of archives[4] and the impact of postmodernism[5] on archival science (especially on appraisal). In addition, a new theoretical underpinning for records management is also emergent; a recent article by Zawiyah M.Yusof and Robert W. Chell[6] provides both a survey of its immediate origins and gives a perspective on where the future direction might lie.

Recent research in England, the Balancing Information Access and Privacy (BIAP) project,[7] has surveyed the new challenges for those engaged in recordkeeping in public authorities in English county and metropolitan local authorities (excluding Greater London) and their associated records offices. Its aim, in the three months of the study, was to

> survey the early response in local authorities to these core legislative changes [the Data Protection Act 1998 and Freedom of Information Act 2000] within their wider context, to assess what preparations were under way, and to gauge reactions to the need to balance providing access to protecting privacy.[8]

In this environment, the main role of records management is still to identify and manage records to maintain accountability. Thus establishing the clarity of legal interpretation and decision-making is ever more crucial in the online environment as the record creator acts as publisher, librarian, and archivist without the mediation or skills that these practitioners bring into play. From anecdotal evidence, the popular perception of archivists executing their professional role is one of passive curators who give access to a relatively unchanging resource. Practitioners may know that the situation can be very different, but those responsible for

---

4   For example, Sarah Tyacke, "Archives in a Wider World: The Culture and Politics of Archives," *Archivaria* 52 (Fall 2001): 1–25; or Verne Harris, "On (Archival) Odyssey(s)," *Archivaria* 51 (Spring 2001): 2–13.

5   Terry Cook, "Archival Science and Postmodernism: New Formulations for Old Concepts," *Archival Science* 1 (2001): 3–27; or Heather MacNeil, "Trusting Records in a Postmodern World," *Archivaria* 51 (Spring 2001): 36–47.

6   Zawiyah M. Yusof and Robert W. Chell, "Towards a Theoretical Construct for Records Management," *Records Management Journal* 12: 2 (2002): 55–64.

7   J. Whitman et al., "BIAP: Balancing Information Access and Privacy," *Journal of the Society of Archivists* 22:2 (2001).

8   Ibid., 253.

the production and dissemination of official information have yet to be convinced of the necessity for our involvement.

The assertions of the records continuum model[9] seek to give credence to the integration of the responsibilities of archivists and records managers within the digital domain, but this does not yet seem an obvious connection for those working to develop the e-government or e-democracy agenda. In Scotland, it is the emergent freedom of information legislation that is seen by many practitioners as the main tool for developing both archive and records management policies in the sphere of government activity, and within other public authorities. Unfortunately, it is not accompanied by the long- anticipated National Archives Act, championed by Donald Dewar, First Minister of the Scottish Parliament at its creation in May 1999, before his untimely death in October 2000.

Since the arrival of the Labour Westminster government in 1997, many statements and initiatives have been produced about the part that information, knowledge economy, and Information Communication Technologies (ICT) have to play in delivering democracy, so the issues surrounding access to technology and the usability of digital information have come to the forefront. It is self-evident that all levels of government need to organise their work more effectively to take advantage of the benefits of the digital environment, in both the back-office functions (which produce primarily transactional data and records) and their public interface—hence the e-government initiative. Government investment in information technology has a long tradition,[10] but only relatively recently has it been applied to improving the *dissemination* of information through the web. If the accountability and transparency of government, as required by the Freedom of Information Acts (FOIA), are viewed through the records and information that are proffered on the web, rather than from a wider range of media, the web pages need to meet elementary tests of authenticity, accuracy, and logical structure. It is too early to see whether the production of a publication scheme and the other apparatus that FOIA provides helps achieve this.

---

9 This is discussed in full by S.J.A. Flynn, "The Records Continuum Model in Context and Its Implications for Archival Practice," *Journal of the Society of Archivists* 22:1 (2001), 79–93.

10 This is discussed in K. Lenk, "Reform Opportunities Will Be Missed: Will the Innovative Potential of Information Systems in Public Administration Remain Dormant Forever?" *Information, Communication & Society* 1: 163–181.

Central government also needs to acknowledge that it has to evolve continually, particularly in its use of ICT and approach to information management[11] to make the most effective use of the crossover between greater openness and the web. One definition of e-government is to view it as the use of ICT infrastructure to provide direct access to public services, and to contextual information about those services.[12] This is manifest as online access to automated business processes through the medium of the Internet, which is used to provide information or references to other sources, communicate directly with government agencies and possibly accomplish transactions. The "Modernising Government" White Paper[13] has been accompanied by increased regulation within public networks, as more official information is managed through digital networked environments. As some commentators have already suggested, "regulation is [now] a much broader phenomenon than it is often conceived to be, and . . . recent developments in the political world are changing its nature further."[14]

It is a rather more complex process to define and subsequently accomplish defined aims of e-democracy. How are we to assess the healthiness of democracy? The difficulties in defining and understanding democracy are probably best left to political scientists to resolve, but archivists have some contribution to make to this assessment by ensuring that the sources of evidence (i.e., the records) are available, accessible, and preserved as archival resource. At present, the nature of organisations is changing at a fundamental level. The Internet is often glibly referred to as an innovation, enhanced by the technology of the World Wide Web, which provides an unfettered democratising force that will emancipate those traditionally disadvantaged through social, economic, or cultural position in society. It has been alleged that the "public service" agenda that was part of the founding principles of the web is in danger of being silenced by the way in which information is

11 C. Bellamy and J.A. Taylor, *Governing in the Information Age* (Buckingham: Open University Press, 1998).

12 See archived website of its office of the E-Envoy, http:www.e-envoy.gov.uk. E-government initiatives (in 2005) are managed through the e-government unit of the cabinet office, http://www.cabinetoffice.gov.uk/e-government. Related technical standards and policies are at http://www.govtalk.gov.uk.

13 Great Britain, Cabinet Office, *Modernising Government*, CM. 4310 (London: The Stationery Office, 1999).

14 L. MacGregor, T. Prosser, and C. Villiers, eds., *Regulation and Markets Beyond 2000* (Aldershot: Ashgate/Dartmouth, 2000), 1.

presented to the viewer. Choice is never objective, and the problem of locating authoritative, accurate and trustworthy information is created by many factors. A principle determinant of success in finding information is the choice of search engine. It is however not obvious, or even of interest, to most enquirers what criteria search engines use to index and ascribe relevancy to the web pages they retrieve. A recent article by Introna and Nissenbaum[15] characterizes this view, and it proposes that the inherent bias within the way certain sites were excluded and prominence given to others is a novel, and malevolent, force:

> Although the Internet and the Web offer exciting prospects for furthering the public good, the benefits are conditional, resting precariously on a number of political, economic and technical factors. . . . We are buoyed by clear instances where the Web and Internet have served broad political ends. But we also see irrefutable signs of gradual centralization and commercialisation of guiding forces. . . . The Web is preconfigured in subtle but politically important ways, resulting in the exclusion of significant voices.

It would seem, therefore, that the web is not different from any other source of information and should be treated as sceptically as any other. Democracy has always been affected by successive waves of subjective media comment—and its shortcomings are well understood. It is somewhat naïve for commentators to expect the web to be any different.

The result of recent u.k. government activity on the subject is a 2002 consultation document (Green Paper), "In the Service of Democracy."[16] It outlines ways in which the web could be used to improve political life in the u.k., which seems at odds with the underlying question of why citizens feel excluded from the democratic process and do not bother to vote. The paper is full of ideas and proposals, ranging from new ways to ensure that Members of Parliament are responsive to local interests and accountable to their electorate, through to commitments to put official information online. The goal is not to find ways to replace our representative democracy with something that lets us all vote online for the laws we want or to alter the

---

15 L.D. Introna and H. Nissenbaum, "Shaping the Web: Why the Politics of Search Engines Matters," *The Information Society* 16: 169–185 (2000), 170.

16 U.K. Office of the Deputy Prime Minister website for E-democracy at http://www.edemocracy.gov.uk/knowledgepool/default.htm?mode=1&pk.document=196 (accessed 25 June 2005).

existing constitutional settlement in any way. Instead, the government is looking for ways in which new technologies—specifically the web but including mobile phones and digital television—can make democracy more relevant in everyday life.

For the government, the two strands that make up e-democracy are ways to enhance participation (e-participation) and electronic voting (e-voting). Recent media comment has suggested that e-voting could replace the traditional ballot box by 2006. Under the plan, online polling, accompanied by postal votes and voting by telephone, would replace ballot papers and ballot boxes. All of the proposed ways allow the opportunity for coercion and pressure on the voter which is not true in a polling booth.

The Green Paper also indicates an awareness of the need for action to encourage more people to vote amid fears of political apathy. While it admits that the use of technology alone cannot re-ignite participation in the democratic process, it does not offer any suggestions as to how this might be achieved or how to change the way that politics is run to re-engage those who feel apathetic at present.[17] Does the fact that e-voting can be done in one's pajamas over breakfast actually help motivate the apathetic voter? Where is the strategy to improve Information Technology (IT) literacy for those who do not encounter IT via the National Curriculum in schools? In an international context various pilot projects to test systems architecture have emerged but there is little debate about core issues of exclusion or voter apathy. The citizen is still primarily seen as a consumer of e-services from an essentially faceless bureaucracy which follows a supply-driven model of information provision rather than being consumer led.

The archivist needs to engage with these realities in both the e-government and e-democracy initiatives at a fundamental level. The processes of democracy are many and varied but include all aspects of public debate (canvassing, campaigning, and live debates), and no matter how these are delivered, they are all dependent on being embraced by the electorate.

The experience of devolved democracy on a national level is still a fresh experience for Scotland. Its architects may have imagined it as

17 For a fuller treatment see Dan Remenyi, "E-Democracy—An Application Too Far?" *Proceedings of the 3rd European Conference on E-Government,* Dublin, July 2003 (Reading, U.K.: Management Centre International Ltd., 2003), 369–380.

principally a digitally mediated experience, and we have yet to see this emerge. If it does, will a new type of professional ideology for the archivist emerge? Does the nature of the power relationship between the records creators (the elected representatives of the people) and the records users (principally the electorate) hold the key?[18] There are power relationships to acknowledge in many aspects of the democratic process. Introna and Nissenbaum try to assess the implications of technical developments as well as human participation:

> We would predict that information seekers on the Web, whose experiences are mediated through search engines, are most likely to find popular, large sites whose designers have enough technical savvy to succeed in the ranking game, and especially those sites whose proprietors are able to pay for various means of improving their site's positioning.[19]

One particular innovation scrutinised in the Scottish context is the role of the Scottish Civic Forum as a means of widening participation in democracy. The ethos of the civic forum has been defined in the first review published in 2001:

> The vision of a "civic forum" flows from the belief held by the people of Scotland that whatever constitutional arrangements emerged in Scotland—devolution or independence—there should be a "new politics" characterised by participation and sharing of power.[20]

The Civic Forum was established in accordance with the principles set out by the Consultative Steering Group (CSG):

- The Scottish Civic Forum is complementary to the role of the Scottish Parliament and the Executive but is separate and independent from it. The Scottish Civic Forum is led by its members.

- The Scottish Civic Forum works to enable the participation of civic interests in civic dialogue and in work with the Scottish Parliament and the Executive. It facilitates discussion and acts as a gateway, not a gatekeeper. It adopts policies to seek active participation from otherwise excluded groups and unheard voices.

---

18 For a wider treatment of this issue see T. Cook and Joan M. Schwartz, "Archives, Records and Power: from (Postmodern) Theory to (Archival) Performance," *Archival Science* (2:3-4) 2002, 171–85.

19 Introna and Nissenbaum, "Shaping the Web," 175.

20 Scottish Civic Forum, *Building Participation in the New Scotland, the first review of the Scottish Civic Forum,* 2001. Available at www.civicforum.org.uk/aboutus/building-participationalbum/First_Review_2001.pdf (accessed 23 June 2005).

- The Scottish Civic Forum seeks membership from a very broad range of civic society. Although statutory bodies are not able to join, the Forum works closely with government agencies and local authorities to influence the policies and operation of these bodies by its work.

- The Scottish Civic Forum establishes governance and management arrangements which place the highest emphasis on transparency and openness and which allow for organic, adaptable structures, which evolve with the active consent of its membership.[21]

One of its current projects is the "Audit of Democratic Participation," which will provide a systematic evaluation of the ways in which it is possible for members of the public to take part in the processes of governing. The Audit scrutinises the arrangements that have been made to allow people to take part in the processes of government, and seeks to assess how well are they working. It is an ongoing project that intends to chart the development of a more participatory democratic culture in Scotland. In 2000, the Joseph Rowntree Charitable Trust agreed to provide funding for the project, and a reference group was formed from civic forum members to receive information about the work, guide the research and monitor the researcher. It made its first interim report available in September 2002,[22] and among its findings it indicated that the Parliament still relies too much on people coming to it, rather than bringing its work to local communities around Scotland.

Less than 3% of the Parliament's committee meetings have been outside Edinburgh, and some of the committees appear to be drawing back from the direct links that community groups had set up with them. The report recommended that the Parliament make its information available in more accessible formats and advertise more widely the ways in which it is possible to participate in its work. In addition, the usability of their information (in terms of navigation, structure, and so forth) and the levels of accessibility to ICT at low or no cost need to be improved.

In Scotland only 58.08% of the electorate voted in the 2000 general election, whereas in the other devolved administrations (which are

---

21 http://www.civicforum.org.uk.

22 http://www.civicforum.org.uk/projects/auditproject/audit_report_top.htm (accessed 23 June 2005).

Assemblies and not full Parliaments), the figures for participation were markedly healthier. In Northern Ireland, for example, the figure was 68.04% and in Wales it was 61.38%.[23]

This assessment is set against the backdrop of the British General Election in 2000, which was significant for the fact that the turnout was only 59.4%[24] of the electorate, which was the lowest level of participation for over 80 years. This is in direct contrast to the increased amount of information that has been made available following devolution into the constituent assemblies for Wales and Northern Ireland and, for Scotland, its own Parliament. Web-based information promoting the democratic process, whether from official government sources, political party sites, lobby groups, or media sources, now abounds in a way that was only hinted at in the 1997 general election.

The measure proposed by the government to tackle the problem of establishing a verified, unique, and persistent identification of individuals in order to interact digitally with government is the "citizenship entitlement card."[25] The proposed entitlement card scheme would establish, for official purposes, a personal identity which can be used in communication and transactions, between the citizen and government departments, and which, it is believed, would help prevent identity fraud—a necessary prerequisite for any digital voting activity. The satisfactory verification of identity, whether personal or corporate, is a fundamental issue in any sphere of information exchange. (Even from our own limited arena in the University of Glasgow, it is no small task. On an academic level, it is an issue that underpins much of the discussion held in HATII research meetings.)

A piece of research by the Hansard Society, known as the "The Digital Jury," conducted between November 2001 and April 2002,[26] provides a useful insight into the level of media literacy of one group in the electorate and their ability to access, analyse and evaluate official information. Its objective was to conduct a programme that would examine how the 16–24 age group made use of the media to inform themselves as citizens. It assessed their use of technology, understanding of process,

---

23 http://www.parliament.uk/commons/lib/research/rp2003/rp03-046.pdf.

24 http://www.parliament.uk/parliament/guide/coelec.htm.

25 http://www.homeoffice.gov.uk/dob/ecu.htm.

26 S. Coleman with B. Griffiths and E. Simmons, *Digital Jury: The Final Verdict* (London: Hansard Society for Parliamentary Government, 2002).

media literacy, and involvement with, or sense of being a disenfranchised sector of, the electorate. It collected data on the methods they used to find information online, considered the barriers to effective online navigation and quality control, and looked at how the group evaluated civic information. There was a definite gap between information-gathering and subsequent knowledge-production, and this applied especially to information from the U.K. Parliament site, as they were unclear about the purpose and procedural structure of Parliament. The report concludes by stating:

> The digital jurors belong to a fortunate generation. They have access to more information resources than at any time before; they can interact, communicate and even produce their own web sites at low cost. However the internet, often depicted as an almost magical medium, is in reality an underdeveloped and disorganised information source. If it is to mature into a reliable, accessible, navigable and relevant medium, it is to the needs of the jurors' generation that it must now attend.[27]

The quality of current examples of online government resources is variable, and once they have passed from current use to semi-current state, they begin to disappear beneath layers of more current information (for example, try looking for the online papers from the Scott Inquiry, the *Report of the Inquiry into the Export of Defence Equipment and Dual-Use Goods to Iraq and Related Prosecutions*, without the aid of Google or a government search engine). Since 1997, the government has invested much funding in producing such tools as the e-Government Interoperability Framework (e-GIF) to deliver the strategy for providing web-enabled government through the Internet. The e-Government Metadata Standard (e-GMS)[28] delivers the standards for the form and content of elements, and refinements that will be used by the public sector to create metadata for information resources. It also gives guidance on the purpose and use of each element. What it has failed to do, as the *Digital Jury* research exposed, is to deal sufficiently with the more complex issue of ensuring that the whole electorate is able to engage in informed and objective debate about where these investments and any further measures might lead us.

---

27 Ibid., 35.
28 http://www.govtalk.gov.uk/. "Setting standards for seamless electronic government."

The facets of the e-democracy initiative have resonance in a more general debate about the digital domain, as information practitioners should work with recordkeeping as a holistic process and in cooperation with other information professionals to provide an integrated and consistent resource. While this may also be true in the paper-based world, in practice any oversights and errors may be more easily rectified there, essentially because the medium is more familiar. The effective use of digital objects depends on many issues. These are, to a great extent, already familiar to the archivist, as they relate to the establishment of trust between the creator and user—in the authenticity of the content and the transparency of the practice and procedure governing the creation of information and verifiable process. Some established skills are directly transferable to the digital domain while others need to be learned from other disciplines and are specific only to digital objects—especially when they relate to a particular feature of the creating technology.

Being an archivist in the early twenty-first century means that, more than ever before, we are part of a multi-skilled and multi-stranded profession. As Sarah Tyacke indicated:

> [T]he skills needed for the selection of the archives of the future—describing, preserving and making them accessible—continue to be at the core of the archivist's work, but they now come in e-guises.[29]

Archival science research is concerned with an impressive range of issues to establish the long-term value of the digital record. The current challenge for archivists is, therefore, to assess all research resources in terms of navigation, quality, and selection (indexing and relevancy/role of search engines, etc.) and quantify the integrity of both record series and unstructured information sources, whether they appear on paper or digitally. The security and authenticity of the information produced by the processes of e-democracy remain at present largely untested.

Digital information systems present new challenges to prove integrity, security, and authenticity that are distinct from, but not independent of, the intellectual attributes of the record. Though these

29 Tyacke, "Archives in a Wider World," 22.

issues may not be of immediate or conscious concern to the average citizen, they are of fundamental concern to the archivist. Any discussion about the development of archival practice and the theoretical underpinning and practical understanding of systems as well as technologies requires new types of interaction with records creators.

20

"BRAVE NEW WORLD"? ELECTRONIC RECORDS MANAGEMENT: WHO WILL BE IN A POSITION TO INFLUENCE THE ARCHIVAL RECORD IN THE FUTURE?

Malcolm Todd

State archives in the main come from records management[1] systems. In the future, there may not be any, unless steps are taken to manage electronic records from their inception, possibly even from the design of the system before they are born.[2] Electronic records management, though, is as much about organisational behaviour as system capability, hardware, or software. The focus here is on a series of refinements of the subtitle question, *Who will be in a position to influence the [electronic[3]] archival record in the future?* The first of these refinements is an

---

1 The United Kingdom is unusual in treating the professional disciplines and missions as partially separate. The situation is even more divergent in the United States. The author has maintained this distinction for the purposes of the arguments put forward in this paper as it has some use, though his personal view is that the separation, however partial, is unfortunate and unsustainable.

2 *Management, Appraisal, and Preservation of Electronic Records,* 2nd ed., 2 vols. (London: Public Record Office, 1999).

3 "Electronic" here means principally the born-digital object, not the digital surrogate of archives from other environments.

overarching one; perhaps it would be better asked as, *At what points is the electronic archive vulnerable to mutation and how far could this be a deliberate act?*

Record Capture and Fixity

Examine any of the many standards for electronic records management in the public sector and a number of important high-level concerns are usually present: capturing the record, preventing it from being changed wittingly or otherwise, providing it with a safe environment for some period of time, and perhaps passing it on to some other environment for the next phase of its life.[4]

Records are not created for the purposes of research; they occur in the course of business.[5] To develop our premise, the tighter the integration of the record capture process into the conduct of the business itself, the more likely a good record will result. In the paper environment, this might well have been a by-product that was difficult to avoid and hard to conceal without a wilful act of destruction. In the electronic world, it is easy to conduct transactions without an explicit record resulting, easy to delete an e-mail or other communication used to convey or support a decision. The trick is to arrive at a "system"[6] that makes these scenarios difficult.

This is best achieved through automation: If users are only aware that they are conducting the transaction of government, the machine does the rest with minimum intervention and therefore maximum objectivity. This is the tightest possible integration with business process.

---

4   Examples are the U.S. Department of Defense Standard 5015.2, the European Union MoREQ standard, the Norwegian NOARK standard, and the U.K. National Archives requirements of 1999 and 2002.
5   Otherwise, they are not "records" as understood by ISO15489; see footnote 14.
6   The word "system" does not mean just software and hardware; it also means what is done with them.

Vulnerabilities

So what are the weak points? The answer is in the stress laid in those standards documents on unstructured or semi-structured digital objects arising in the course of business.[7] The main threat to the capture of a proper record and its maintenance in a form that is reliable and authentic lies in the desktop computer technologies that we all implemented enthusiastically in the early 1990s and previously. Many of these technologies are ill-suited to conducting public business, especially e-mail.

We have been through a difficult period. Records managers have been engaged in enforcing "print to paper" policies while the software industry has been busy finding ways of creating file formats that cannot be represented by a printout: video, audio, dynamic websites, and databases. To be fair, some of these have been around a long time and many have been extremely useful to organizations, so much so that records managers have been fighting a battle they cannot win without changing the rules. Thus, even where there is rigorous enforcement, the weak point is the time lag that can occur before the print button is pressed. Printed documents created electronically suffer from this murky provenance.

Fortunately, the solution can often come from the same source as the problem—persuading the software industry that we need records management software for the office document environment as much as we need audit trails in structured data systems. This has transpired after over a decade of the attempted "hard sell" of document management systems—mostly unsuccessful attempts. There are artificial technology and expert system technologies around in the twenty-first century that can comprehend content in some way and process it accordingly on that basis, but these are not the run-of-the-mill technologies afforded to front-line public servants.

Standard office software—word processors, spreadsheets, small databases, presentation packages and, most pertinent of all, e-mail—is used for a variety of communication purposes. "Communication," not

---

7   The most common examples are documents created on personal computers using standard office software suites such as Microsoft® Office.

record capture. To achieve the latter, someone has to make a conscious decision such as, this e-mail is not me asking my partner to put dinner in the oven and feed the dog but my authorising a member of the staff to make a payment to the benefit claimant. This requires a business decision. They—and/or I—might duck this process and not capture the record. If this risk is to be avoided consistently, it needs to be the normal organisational behaviour in the workplace, reinforced by personnel and disciplinary as well as "recordkeeping" policy and guidance. Records management is a corporate governance imperative. If in doubt, just think of the fallout for the Arthur Andersen firm in the wake of the Enron scandal.

So where is this leading? If the last paragraph seems a little bleak, it need not be. There are technologies that can deliver structured text to the citizen/client as well as to the official record without the stilted prose of the dreaded computer-driven letter from the bank manager or utility company. More granularity to the "script" and more developed systems, albeit still falling short of artificial intelligence, can deliver this, and already does. You have probably "consumed" some recently without realizing it. You will certainly consume a lot more in the near future with the advent of XML and the semantic web. So, documents will probably become more structured—and if we can train our staff correctly, there is a realistic hope that government will capture a proper record of its business.

"Originals" and "Copies"

The concept of an "original" is meaningless in this environment. Every time a document is accessed in a networked computer environment, a "copy" is what is presented to the user's PC screen. This can emanate from the local network server, the remote one, the hard disk of that very PC, or a combination of these and/or other intermediary devices. The most we can do to achieve the same outcome as we demanded in the paper world is to establish the degree to which the evidence shows that the viewed record is what it purports to be.

Organising, Keeping and Sustaining Records

Assuming that a reliable record has been captured, how is it to be kept inviolate? Contrary to popular belief, this is not a case of absolutes, but of relatives—and always has been. "Manual" records—paper, vellum, papyrus, and even clay and stone tablets—can be manipulated as well as counterfeited, albeit with more difficulty and physical effort. For "inviolate" as well as "original," then, substitute words like "reliable" or "authentic."[8]

Not all public records[9] can be kept indefinitely, in the electronic as well as in the paper environment. We must select the minority to preserve anything of our heritage. The problem of the cost of storage is superseded by potentially far costlier problems of software and hardware obsolescence and media degradation.[10] How is this to be achieved?

Objectivity in Appraisal and Archival Selection

How we maintain objectivity in appraisal and archival selection is the subject of lively debate. Many of the leading archivists of Australia and Canada take the functional approach to the classification of business records, carrying this forward into the archival domain in our terminology—or seeing the whole as a continuum of use and repurposing in theirs.[11] It is difficult to do justice to this approach in a passing reference. The debate in the pages of the Canadian professional journal *Archivaria* has continued for an extended period with many distinguished contributions, including mapping forward from business requirements for the retention of records to the archival domain

---

8 Both the subject of task forces within the auspices of the InterPARES project and their respective reports are available from http://www.interpares.org.

9 This term is used loosely in this paper to refer to the records of public bodies, whether municipal or state.

10 Lack of space precludes amplification of these points, but there are many excellent Internet resources on digital preservation, such as Cedars, http://www.leeds.ac.uk/cedars/, TNA [UK], http://www.nationalarchives.gov.uk/preservation/digital.htm (accessed 21 June 2005), National Archives of Australia, http://www.naa.gov.au/recordkeeping/er/summary.html (accessed 21 June 2005).

11 As articulated in the various resources hosted by the University of Monash and linked from http://rcrg.dstc.edu.au/. A useful summary of the appraisal issues is provided by the report of the InterPARES appraisal taskforce, http://www.interpares.org.

and—effectively—seeing archival preservation as a business function in its own right.[12]

Record organisation is based on an analysis of the functions of the organisation and not on either subject content or organisational provenance (including the structure of the organisation).[13] This takes place without looking at any actual records and involves examining what records *should* be arising as well as those that are. More objective appraisal and archival selection decisions can then perhaps be made on the same criteria: Do we wish to preserve all the records of x function or those of y?

Misgivings

There is a weakness here as well as a refreshing robustness: Is our functional analysis right, are our appraisal decisions on whole archival fonds sound? Most national archival institutions, for example, have been loath to take repetitive case material in bulk into their collections. In the paper environment, this was because of the storage of such bulky collections. Selection by reviewing—reading and assessing—the content is both time-consuming and likely to result in a distorted picture: the "interesting" content is by its nature misrepresentative.

Random (mathematical) sampling techniques have been devised to select along another criterion from such collections. The most extreme approach to the functional model outlaws the case file itself as a type of subject file—the "subject" being you or me or my brother-in-law's company. It might prove to be difficult to explain to the harassed benefit claimant that there is no such thing as "their file" because the government keeps a routine claim for a year, their national insurance identity until they reach 72, and fraud suspicions for five. How do we earn and keep public trust in our new "objectivity"?

There is further misgiving associated with functional analysis being no more infallible than the techniques it is designed to supersede. For example, if we wind the clock back to the 1980s, how would

---

12 Honourable mention probably belongs (though not exclusively) to the writings of Frank Upward, Terry Cook, and Heather MacNeil. MacNeil in particular relates the discussion to political thought.

13 The last is still a requirement of archival description as articulated in ISAD(G), the International Standard on Archival Description.

the function of the U.K. government concerned with the licensing of certain enumerated exports be analysed and appraised had the Board of Trade used that methodology?

Further, the model applied in U.K. central government meant that those reviewing records—to establish which should be taken into archival custody—typically required a 25-year time lapse since their creation, which effectively ruled out involvement by the protagonists of the recorded activity. It also gave the process the magical ingredient of hindsight. This last luxury is not available to us in the electronic environment for reasons that can only be hinted at here; the costs of organising electronic information and preserving it across technical platforms, media, and software migrations are prohibitive, and while disk space continues to get cheaper, there are issues with meaningful retrieval from large repositories.

Earning the Trust of Stakeholders

Where does this leave the research community? The methodology we choose for archival selection is important, as it requires consultation, understanding, and trust. How do we set about building these with the esoteric-sounding methodologies that have only been touched upon here? Further, the ordinary citizen as well as the academic professional has a stake in this process.

Technical Preservation: A Few Aspects

Preserving electronic material through generations of hardware and software is highly demanding even when sound archival selection decisions have been made. The academic and archival communities have been well-exercised on this issue since software companies have reduced their product development, making their product obsolescence cycles ever shorter. We can build emulators and try to keep the old hardware and software maintained, or we can migrate the content to another platform—but each approach involves compromise and risk to the reliability, authenticity and trust in the results.

Standards for records management in the electronic environment reduce the chances of isolated documents or e-mails having no context. The International Standard[14] states:

> As well as the content, the record should contain, or be persistently linked to, or associated with, the metadata necessary to document a transaction, as follows:
>
> a. the structure of a record, that is, its format and the relationships between the elements comprising the record, should remain intact;
> b. the business content in which the record was created, received and used should be apparent in the record (including the business process of which the transaction was part, the date and time of the transaction and the participants in the transaction);
> c. the links between documents, held separately but combining to make up a record, should be present.

This statement does not explain what a record is. The definition appears a little earlier in the section and is argued firmly from the context of creation in the conduct of business:

> A record should correctly reflect what was communicated or decided or what action was taken. It should be able to support the needs of the business to which it relates and be used for accountability purposes.

Records professionals use and reinterpret these generic definitions on a daily basis and find them very useful tools, but they give us a problem: How do we communicate this specialist information and its consequences to our citizens?

The 'M' Word

If you are a dedicated archive researcher, you will hear more and more about something called "metadata." Metadata is contextual information captured along with the content of a record about its origins, when it came under the control of a records management system, and what other processes it has been subjected to—"data about data" to

---

14 This and the following quotation are taken from paragraph 7.2 of ISO (International Organization for Standardization), ISO 15489, *Information and Documentation—Records Management*, 2001.

confirm (hopefully) that it is an accurate representation of what it purports to be representing.

This is not just a question of providing search terms. It also involves capturing information enabling the internal structuring of the records and the attributes of the electronic components underlying the records. This is for the "recordness" to have a chance of surviving after the obsolescence of the hardware and software that produced the records and possibly even facilitating their reconstruction if a similar enough environment does not exist in the future to "replay" them with the original "look and feel."[15]

The Balance of Power

There are government and commercial organisations that do not (yet) subscribe to these standards. The software industry is responding with software products, but a great deal of power resides now in IT managers who may or may not be working with information professionals with a sufficient awareness of robust records management. Do these people have the means to affect the archival record and if so, how? My instinct is to say, "Yes they do, but mainly by default": non-survival, non-migration, non-preservation. The potential for the record being distorted by these negatives could be significant but it is unlikely to amount to political pressure. It is more an issue of mismanagement, a failure to identify the objects forming records and to move them from one technical platform to another—hence, the vital importance of the initial organisation of the records in the first place.

In addition, many public bodies acquire information technology (IT) services from the private sector under partnership contracts. These—and the specifications of the services that are provided through them—could remove the archival record still further from the custody of those who might have a stake in tampering with it. It would take substantial collusion between a number of different people to render the archival record vulnerable to deliberate tampering: systems administrators, contractors, records managers, users, and organisation managers.[16]

---

15 There are also a host of other issues about preserving the underlying electronic objects that make up records of public business activities.

16 The revision of *Functional Requirements for Electronic Records Management* by the National Archives in 2002 deliberately separated out the functional access rights to run a disposal

The main point to make in summary is that whatever threat is posed to the accountability of government springs more probably from a lack of good practice than from corruption, political ideology, or repression.

Freedom of Information and Accountability

There are many dramatic and disturbing tales to tell about secrecy and repression. Even in a stable, liberal parliamentary system such as the one existing in the United Kingdom, it should not be assumed that there are no political threats. Some political scientists may even conclude that in a parliamentary representative system rather than a strictly democratic one, these could be seen as insidious. Rather than join that political debate, a few observations are offered, backed up by some material from authoritative official sources already in the public domain.[17]

There have been Cassandra-like voices in the media and elsewhere deploring what they see as the increasing politicisation of the u.k. Government Information Service. It is ironic that the latest is contained in a book written by the chief press secretary from a previous administration.[18] The main criticism has been the relationship with the media and the frequent accusation of attempted manipulation or "spin."

One of the most celebrated instances was the departure of a ministerial special adviser from the former Department of Transport, Local Government and the Regions after the leaking of an e-mail describing 11 September 2001 as a "good day to bury bad news" about the performance of the u.k. railway industry. Like the Oliver North/ John Poindexter case (where $30 million, obtained by the illegal sale of arms to Iran, was provided, illegally, to the right-wing Contra guerillas in Nicaragua), perhaps we should be reassured that even an e-mail

routine from the rights to apply a disposal schedule to groups of records. This was largely in response to the new offences in Section 76 of the Freedom of Information Act 2000: to distinguish legitimate records management activity from willful unauthorised destruction of records.

17 The best single analytic reference is probably A. Macdonald and G. Terrill, eds., *Open Government* (London: Macmillan, 1998), not least for its coverage of other jurisdictions and further references.

18 B. Ingham, *The Wages of Spin* [sic.] (London: John Murray, 2003), and possibly the author's only apologist œuvre.

without the sort of context demanded by our standards can have so devastating an effect.

The following is a brief quotation from the outgoing Head of the Civil Service on records management issues, extracted from the proceedings of the Public Administration Committee of the House of Commons as it examined him in 2001. When asked about the capture of e-mails, Sir Richard Wilson said:

> [W]hen I joined the [Civil] Service, which was before photocopiers, files were kept in good order. You could see what has happened on them and quite a lot of resource and effort went into keeping them. I think we are now a long way from that. A number of things have happened. One of them is photocopying where the volume of paper has increased massively and everybody has a way of scribbling on their own copy of a photocopy. To have a file which has all the relevant documents on it is more challenging although we have not greatly increased resources for it. Secondly, technology has meant that emails are now very important. As everyone knows, emails are a very different way of doing business from either an oral conversation or a properly written document. People use language differently. I have a real worry that fairly important decisions get taken in emails which are actually a fairly ephemeral medium. I have quite a worry about public records in that area.[19]

"Open Government" and the Archival Record

It may not have escaped your notice that the same grilling of the most senior U.K. official involved issues of access to recent records as well as records capture.[20] Some ideas need to be "floated" about changes in our democracy that have profound implications for our archives and the writing of our political science and history. Archives have a very impor-

---

19 "Examination of Witnesses, Questions 260–279, Sir Richard Wilson GCB AND Mr. John Gieve CB" by the House of Commons Public Administration Committee on 11 July 2002, http://www.publications.parliament.uk.

20 Most memorably, Cabinet Office civil servants under the administration responsible for enacting the Freedom of Information Act 2000 refusing to grant access to papers requested by the Parliamentary Commissioner for Administration and arguing that they were exempt from the preceding administration's Code of Practice on Access to Official Information (2nd ed., 1998): contained in the same extract as the preceding reference to Sir Richard Wilson's evidence.

tant role to play in public accountability of governments, and most of us are motivated by a desire for free access to information unless there is an overriding legitimate reason why not.[21] With public information policy about to make recent information—records, archives of the future or not—available far sooner than the 30-year point, and with fewer exceptions than before, what are the implications?

This goes to the heart of the archival mission and the relationship we have with both political science and history. When there is a general right of access to recent material—and not just the "official record"—how will our history be written? Will there simply be too much information, making it difficult to interpret? Will interpretation become a journalistic task—opinion and commentary rather than the mature reflection and analysis of qualitative and quantitative data? Reflect also on the issues about identifying the "official record" in the first place and subsequently the "official archival record." What locus do we have as archivists and records managers to do this, rather than letting the citizen do that for him or herself?[22] What of information that is accessed and used as the subject of research but subsequently (and perhaps justifiably) disposed of and lost to our successors? Reflection on these things needs to inform consideration of some of the points already made.

The Insidious Danger?

Returning to the idea of records or archives capture as a key corporate governance issue for public bodies, there is a danger that we shall succumb to a "creeping problem" rather than a conspiracy from a repressive or malevolent regime. Broadly, this scenario boils down to an anodyne "official" or "public" record being captured, while the real one—the one reflecting our business activities—remains for awhile in e-mail boxes, and so on, for administrative use but is lost to the archives. Whereas serendipity seems to have been a part of the capture of tradi-

---

21 Archivists' personal political convictions have not been considered here: the point is about the collective behaviour and ethics of the profession, about which more is said below.

22 Some of the benefits of the methods of appraisal discussed earlier are designed to counter this objection.

tional paper records and archives, we cannot sleepwalk our way into the electronic future.

It does not take a large leap of logic to see how a bureaucracy with an instinct towards discretion might respond to a freedom of information regime—especially one that is implemented rapidly—in this way. That serves also to illustrate a further point: this might more plausibly be the response of a bureaucratic machine rather than a (party) political act, although a politically damaging one at that. There are moves afoot that have the potential to ensure these threats cannot be realised: there is a growing realisation that corporate governance and audit have a lot of commonality with modern records management. There have been calls for a civil service act[23] from the Committee on Standards in Public Life.[24] We probably need something explicit in such a measure as a stated duty to capture an accurate record of activity in the official record system of government.

Professional Codes of Conduct

Government archivists and records managers perhaps need ethical codes too. They would be subject to the provisions of a civil service act along with everyone else, but they—we—have a greater responsibility to ensure that the activities of the state are faithfully recorded. Without vigilance and energy from that quarter, this is unlikely to happen. Our influence on the archival record will depend less on our custody of ageing documents and more on our influence within our organisations and in government more broadly—and on how far we and the records we seek to have captured and preserved are trusted by the citizen.[25]

Much of the sort of evidence that we can gather around electronic resources to establish its evidential weight will be highly circumstantial, so this aspect of trust remains important. Under the 1958 Public

---

23 The formal constitution of the civil service normally depends on statutory provisions giving ministers power to do things and perhaps to appoint officials to carry it out.

24 The records management agenda is perhaps not the main driving force, but is increasingly acknowledged as an important lever in these areas.

25 Recent initiatives by the Parliamentary Public Administration Committee in publishing a consultation draft of a *Civil Service Bill* would leave the detail of such things to secondary legislation, though whether that Committee's interest in public records matters would be carried through by the Cabinet Office into a revitalised Civil Service Code remains to be seen.

Records Act, the certification powers of the Keeper of Public Records are limited to attesting that a record is an extracted one from the public records, not that it is—evidentially speaking—authentic.[26] This rests on the trust placed in the National Archives as an institution by the legislature. With new archives legislation possibly in view, we have to renew the compact with our stakeholders. Our custody of electronic archives is harder to establish and document. The possibilities and also the difficulties of applying the science of archival diplomatics in the electronic environment have been analysed extensively by the InterPARES project.[27]

Wider Changes in "The Information Society"

Although some of the 1990s' euphoria about the "dot.com" boom is only a distant memory, a major problem lies in certain changes in popular perception arising from the developing technical environment. We have seen the IT industry's "death of records" predictions. However, we cannot reverse changes in how we—all of us—read electronic materials compared with their traditional predecessors.

Put at its simplest, we live in a more visual—or multimedia—environment. Consider the phenomenon of the World Wide Web from the origins of the Internet. Far from being a network consisting exclusively of erudite discourse (and military secrets), it is democratised and verging on the chaotic. Most web pages are best "consumed" according to the following sequence: scan, get the general gist, and move on through hyperlinks or the back arrow (possibly missing the point of the actual content, if indeed there was one). Following this process, "meaning" is sometimes picked up as much from links—structures such as, "what follows what in the sequence?"—as from the content.

---

26 There is a public policy intent to have enabling legislation that would make electronic communications with some sort of digital signature admissible for certain purposes in citizens' or organisations' interactions with government to the same degree as manual communications, perhaps to the degree of making a communication so signed "non-repudiable." This is not however likely to prompt a general change to the laws of evidence which the legal profession can be expected to defend: determination of admissibility is in general a matter for the courts.

27 Authenticity task force report, accessible from http://www.interpares.org/book/index.cfm (accessed 21 June 2005).

We are—so they hope—even more prey than before to the subliminal messages of the marketing departments.

Willing Accomplices?

The flippancy of the previous paragraph's indulgence in amateur information science has a serious point for our discussions: do we (literally) "believe what we want to believe"? If we adhere to the traditional view of history as an essentially literary (i.e., content-based) discipline, where does that leave us in this new world as citizens, researchers, and archivists? The archival mission has managed—often deftly and even quite artistically—to smudge this definition into the separate definitions of archaeology and museums. Provided interpretational keys are available, the information content even of corrupt sources is sometimes valuable.

Are we now becoming more naive about information as we become more cynical about political process? In our determination to hold our political representatives accountable in the short term, are we losing something more precious: the ability to judge them with due reflection? Ultimately, do human beings create their "reality" by what they believe—essentially what we, collectively, wish it to? Having created our myths, do we have the maturity to revise them in the light of further revealed or discovered evidence?

Conclusions

How far do these reflections and discussions address the five important themes below?

1. The use of records as a tool of government
2. Destruction of records as a political act
3. The effects of corruption or ideology on the record
4. Secrecy and accountability
5. The nature and use of records resulting from repressive policies

Although the last theme was left almost entirely for others to consider, I hope the resulting picture from the discussion has convinced you that we are not complacent about the challenge we are facing at this turning point in records and archives management in U.K. government.

The focus has been, *force majeure*, about public administration and "politics" rather than "Politics." This means that in majoring on the first and fourth of these themes, and excluding the last, the intervening ones have been adjusted slightly to allow them to be considered from this viewpoint. Thus, appraisal and disposal are approached from the administrative and archival perspective, with consequences for the political picture whose relevance has, hopefully, been established.

The most overarching need, however, seems to be a reinterpretation of the third theme—to read something like: "the possible effects of mismanagement and complacency on the record." Even the environment of a stable liberal parliamentary democracy such as ours is not without its threats to the archival record, especially in a time of fundamental technological change. Naturally, we should also be very concerned at the possibility of a decline in professional standards in this area having an adverse effect on the political systems that we serve.

EDITORS & CONTRIBUTORS

Masahito Ando has been a professor at the University of Tokyo since 1988 and has worked with the Department of Historical Documents at Tokyo's National Institute of Japanese Literature since 1977. He holds a BA and MA in Japanese History from the University of Tokyo, and an MA in Overseas Archive Studies from the University of London. He contributed a chapter, "Recovering Memory, Sharing Memory: Archives Lost and Displaced in the Asian-Pacific War and the Responsibility of Japanese Archivists," to the book *Essays in Honour of Michael Cook* (2003).

Richard Barry is an international information and records management consultant and author (*www.mybestdocs.com*). Formerly chief of World Bank information services, including archives/records management, he is a cofounder of the Open Reader Consortium (*www.openreader.org*) aimed at developing an XML-based, open-source, e-Book/e-Document reader that will embrace PDF-A and other long-term access standards.

Photo by Justin A. Knight.

Jeannette A. Bastian is associate professor and director of the archives management concentration in the Simmons College Graduate School of Library and Information Science in Boston, Massachusetts. She is a former director of the libraries and archives of the United States Virgin Islands. Her research interests focus on archives in colonial/post-colonial contexts, relationships between archives, communities and collective memory, and archives education. Her publications include *Owning Memory: How a Caribbean Community Lost Its Archives and Found Its History* (2003). She is currently book reviews editor of the *American Archivist*.

Michael Cook is a senior practitioner in archives and records management, with experience both in Britain and in two African countries, and as an academic in British and African universities. He has also served as a consultant in different parts of the world, participated in international research and development activities, and has conducted research teams developing technical standards for archives management. The author of several textbooks and technical studies in archive and records management practice, Cook is currently a senior fellow at the Liverpool University Centre for Archive Studies (LUCAS) in the U.K.

Thomas James Connors has been curator of the National Public Broadcasting Archives at the University of Maryland since 1993. He is also an adjunct professor in the university's College of Information Studies, teaching a course in audiovisual archives. He served on the governing council of the Society of American Archivists from 2000–2003, and is a founder of SAA's International Archival Affairs Roundtable. He also serves as coordinator of the North American Archival Network of the International Council on Archives. He holds a master's degree in American civilization from Brown University.

Dwayne Cox currently heads the Special Collections and Archives Department at Auburn University. Formerly, he served as associate archivist at the University of Louisville. Cox holds a PhD in United States history from the University of Kentucky.

Astrid M. Eckert is assistant professor of modern German history at Emory University in Atlanta. She received her doctorate from the Free University Berlin in 2003. Her doctoral thesis, *Kampf um die Akten. Die Westalliierten und die Rueckgabe von deutschem Archivgut nach dem Zweiten Weltkrieg* ["Battle for the Files. The Western Allies and the Return of Captured German Records after World War II"] (Stuttgart, 2004), was awarded the 2004 Friedrich Meinecke Dissertation Prize of Free University's history department, and the biennial Hedwig Hintze Dissertation Award of the German Historical Association. Her research interests include German-American relations, Germany post-1945, archival and library history, issues of looting and destruction of cultural property during wartime, and transnational historiography.

Clive Emsley is a professor of history and co-director of the International Centre for Comparative Criminological Research at the Open University in the U.K. His publications include *The English Police: A Political and Social History* (2nd ed., 1996) and *Hard Men: Violence in England Since 1750* (2005).

Jackie R. Esposito is a university archivist and associate librarian at Penn State University Archives in University Park, Pennsylvania. She joined the faculty of the University Libraries in July 1991 as an assistant university archivist for records management. She was tenured and promoted to associate librarian in 1998. Her appointment to the faculty followed five years of service with the university archives in a variety of grant-funded positions. She is pursuing a EdD in higher education.

Verne Harris is project manager for the Centre of Memory at the Nelson Mandela Foundation. He is also an honorary research associate and part-time lecturer in archives for the University of the Witwatersrand's postgraduate programme in heritage studies. From 2001 to 2004 he was director of the South African History Archive, and before that he was a deputy director with South Africa's National Archives.

Chris Hurley has worked for 35 years in government and the private sector in Australia and New Zealand. He headed the Public Record Office of Victoria from 1981 to 1990 and was acting chief archivist of New Zealand for two and a half years from 1997 to 2000. He has served on the boards and committees of professional bodies and authored many articles and conference papers on documentation, legislation, and accountability.

Claire Johnson joined the University of Glasgow in 1997 and currently serves as Senior Records Manager and Freedom of Information Officer. Her research interests include the development of records management for an age of digital governance and the usability of digitally disseminated information. She teaches several courses and is a member of the editorial board of the *Journal of E-Government*.

Agnes E.M. Jonker joined the Archiefschool, the Netherlands Institute for Archival Education and Research, in 1999. She is currently a lecturer in the Bachelor and the Master of Archival Studies Programme of the Universiteit van Amsterdam and in the postgraduate programme on Archivistics. Educated as a social scientist and social historian, she has worked as a university research fellow in the field of the history of education. Since graduating as an archivist in 1995, she has been involved in the National Archives PIVOT-project at the Ministry of Education and Science. As a co-researcher of InterPARES(1), she has been a member of the Appraisal Task Force. She served as co-editor of the 2004 Yearbook for Dutch Archivists, *Waardering, selectie en acquisitie van archieven* (Appraisal, selection, and acquisition), in which she wrote on both appraisal in the Netherlands and the international debate, and electronic records and appraisal.

Friedrich Kahlenberg was born in 1935 in Mainz, Germany. He studied history, German literature and philosophy, and received his PhD in 1962. He joined the staff of the Bundesarchiv—the Federal Archives of Germany—as an archivist in 1964, and was appointed director from 1989 to 1999. Since 1973 he has been honorary professor for public administration and for the history of mass media.

Godfried Kwanten has a doctorate in history from Katholieke Universiteit Leuven (Belgium). Since 1987, he has been head of the university's archive division of KADOC, the Centre for Religion, Culture and Society. He is a long-time member of the board of management of the Association of Flemish Archivists and also serves on in the editorial board of the association's newsletter.

Rachel Lilburn is a lecturer in the School of Information Management, Victoria University, Wellington, New Zealand. Prior to joining the school in 1992, she was head appraisal archivist, Wellington Head Office, National Archives (now Archives New Zealand). She was also the first National Archives Advisory Archivist in the Auckland region from 1984–1987, consulting for many local authorities and private companies. Lilburn holds an MA in history (archives and records management) from Western Washington University in Bellingham, Washington.

George MacKenzie is head of the National Archives of Scotland. As deputy secretary general of the International Council on Archives, 1995–1996, he carried out missions to Bosnia and Herzegovina, advising on the protection of archives. He has also carried out archives consultancy work for UNESCO and the World Bank.

Trudy Huskamp Peterson is an archival consultant. She spent 24 years with the U.S. National Archives, including more than two years as Acting Archivist of the United States. After retiring from the U.S. government, she was the founding executive director of the Open Society Archives in Budapest, Hungary, and then the director of Archives and Records Management for the United Nations High Commissioner for Refugees. She is a past president of the International Conference of the Round Table on Archives (1993–1995) and the Society of American Archivists (1990–1991) and has lectured on archives throughout the world. *Final Acts: A Guide to Preserving the Records of Truth Commissions* (2005) is her study of the records of 20 truth commissions.

Margaret Procter is a faculty member of the Liverpool University Centre for Archive Studies (LUCAS) in the U.K. and previously held both archives and records management posts in local government and university repositories. She has published in a wide range of areas including freedom of information and the future of archival education in the U.K. and co-edited *Essays in Honour of Michael Cook* (2003). She is a long-standing member of the editorial boards of the International Council on Archives' journals *Comma* and its predecessor *Janus*.

Maureen Spencer is a principal lecturer in law at Middlesex University Business School, London. She teaches "Evidence and Public Law" and is currently writing a history of public interest immunity in the U.K. and U.S.A. Her research into the wartime case of *Duncan v. Cammell Laird* was first published in the *Northern Ireland Legal Quarterly* (Autumn 2004).

Malcolm Todd is a digital records specialist from a government records management practice background and is currently head of standards at the U.K. National Archives. He collaborates on leading research initiatives in Canada and Australia and is particularly interested in metadata and aspects of information policy.

Photo by Justin A. Knight.

Tywanna Whorley is an assistant professor at the Simmons College Graduate School of Library and Information Science in Boston, Massachusetts, where she teaches in the Archives Management Program. Whorley holds masters' degrees in U.S. history from the University of Virginia and in social history from Carnegie Mellon University. Her areas of interest include access issues as they relate to privacy, collective memory, and governmental accountability. She is a PhD candidate in the School of Information Science at the University of Pittsburgh.

Caroline Williams is director of the Liverpool University Centre for Archives Studies (LUCAS) and chair of the Forum for Archives and Records Management Education and Research (FARMER), the collective voice of U.K. educators. She is a member of the U.K. National Council on Archives (NCA) and the International Council on Archives Section on Archival Education.

Chris A. Williams is a lecturer in the history department of the Open University in the U.K. His research has focused on British policing, and he has published articles on the history of police surveillance and the (ab)uses of criminal statistics. He is editor of *Giving the Past a Future: Preserving the Heritage of the U.K.'s Criminal Justice System* (2004).

INDEX

Boldface indicates figures and tables.